© **Copyright 2022** - Jasmine T Williams. All rights reserved.

The content contained within this book may not be reproduced, duplicated or transmitted without direct written permission from the author or the publisher.
Under no circumstances will any blame or legal responsibility be held against the publisher, or author, for any damages, reparation, or monetary loss due to the information contained within this book. Either directly or indirectly.

### Legal notice:

This book is copyright protected. This book is only for personal use. You cannot amend, distribute, sell, use, quote or paraphrase any part, or the content within this book, without the consent of the author or publisher.

### Disclaimer Notice:

Please note the information contained within this document is for educational and entertainment purposes only. All effort has been executed to present accurate, up-to-date, and reliable, complete information, No warranties of any kind are declared or implied. Readers acknowledge that the author is not engaging in the rendering of legal, financial, medical, or professional advice. The content within this book has been derived from various sources. Please consult a licensed professional before attempting any techniques outlined in this book.

By reading this document, the reader agrees that under no circumstances is the author responsible for any loss, direct or indirect, which are incurred as a result of the use of the information contained within this document, including, but not limited to, errors, omissions, or inaccuracies.

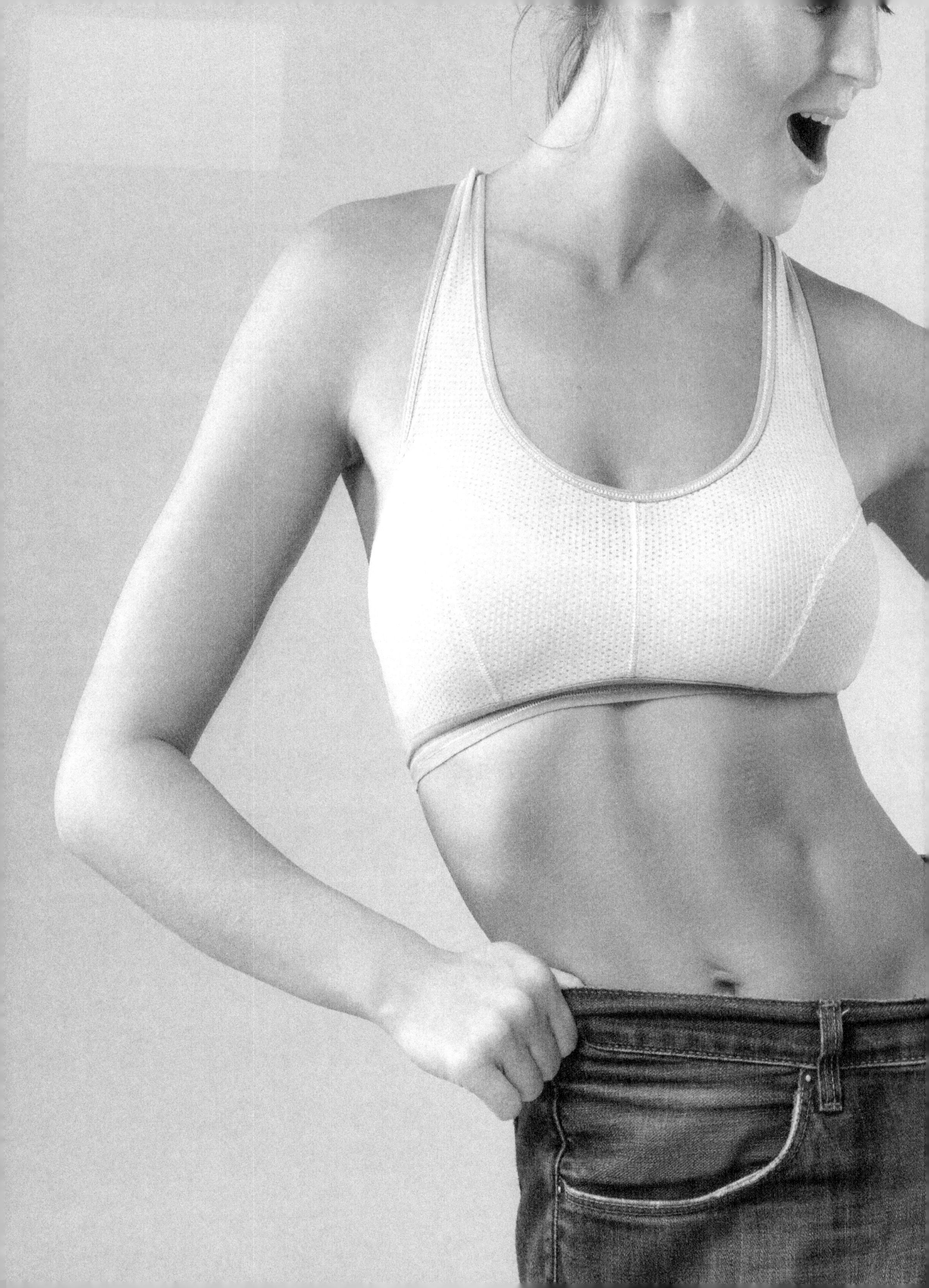

# CONTENTS

| | |
|---|---|
| **Introduction** | 4 |
| **What is Gastric Sleeve Surgery** | 5 |
| **Food Lifestyle Before and After Surgery** | 5 |
| Diet prior to Surgery | |
| Diet following Surgery | |
| **Recipes** | 9 |
| **Clear Liquid Diet** | 10 |
| **Full Liquid Diet** | 27 |
| **Puree Diet** | 42 |
| **Soft Food Diet** | 63 |
| **Maintenance Diet** | 93 |
| • Breakfast | 94 |
| • Lunch | 113 |
| • Dinner | 121 |
| • Dessert | 150 |
| **Meal Plans** | 156 |
| **Appendix 1: Recipe Index** | 162 |
| **Appendix 2: Measurement Conversion Chart** | 168 |
| **Conclusion** | 169 |
| **BONUS: 12 Months Weight Loss Journal** | 170 |

# Introduction

Congratulations on the decision to have Gastric sleeve surgery for losing weight. This is an exciting new start, a chance to start over with your body, mind, and way of life. Your choice probably took a lot of thought and planning. Even if you know a lot about the surgery, procedure, and the changes you have to make to your life can be overwhelming. Some of your friends and family may have doubted your decision or recommended other, more conventional ways to lose weight and enhance your health. But surgery seemed like a necessary step toward taking better care of your health.

We all want to get healthy and lose weight so we can look smart and good-looking. Gastric Sleeve Bariatric surgery is a procedure that reduces the size of the stomach so that the person can lose weight.

Most of the time, getting surgery is a scary choice, but these days, surgeries are very common. Gastric Bariatric Sleeve Surgery is performed to make your stomach smaller, so you can eat much less and start losing weight quickly. This surgery is very common around the world, especially in the United States, where the number of obese people is very high. Many people have this surgery to help them lose weight and get rid of their obesity. The problems start after the surgery, and many people don't feel ready to deal with the problems that come up after the surgery. After surgery, it's very important to eat right and stay healthy so that your body can work well.

In this book, you'll find lots of great recipes that are easy to make on your own and will help you deal with all the problems your body is having after gastric sleeve surgery. This book is a great resource for people who have already had surgery or are planning to have surgery. This book will help you get over your worries and give you the tools you need to start living your new life.

## What Is Gastric Sleeve Surgery?

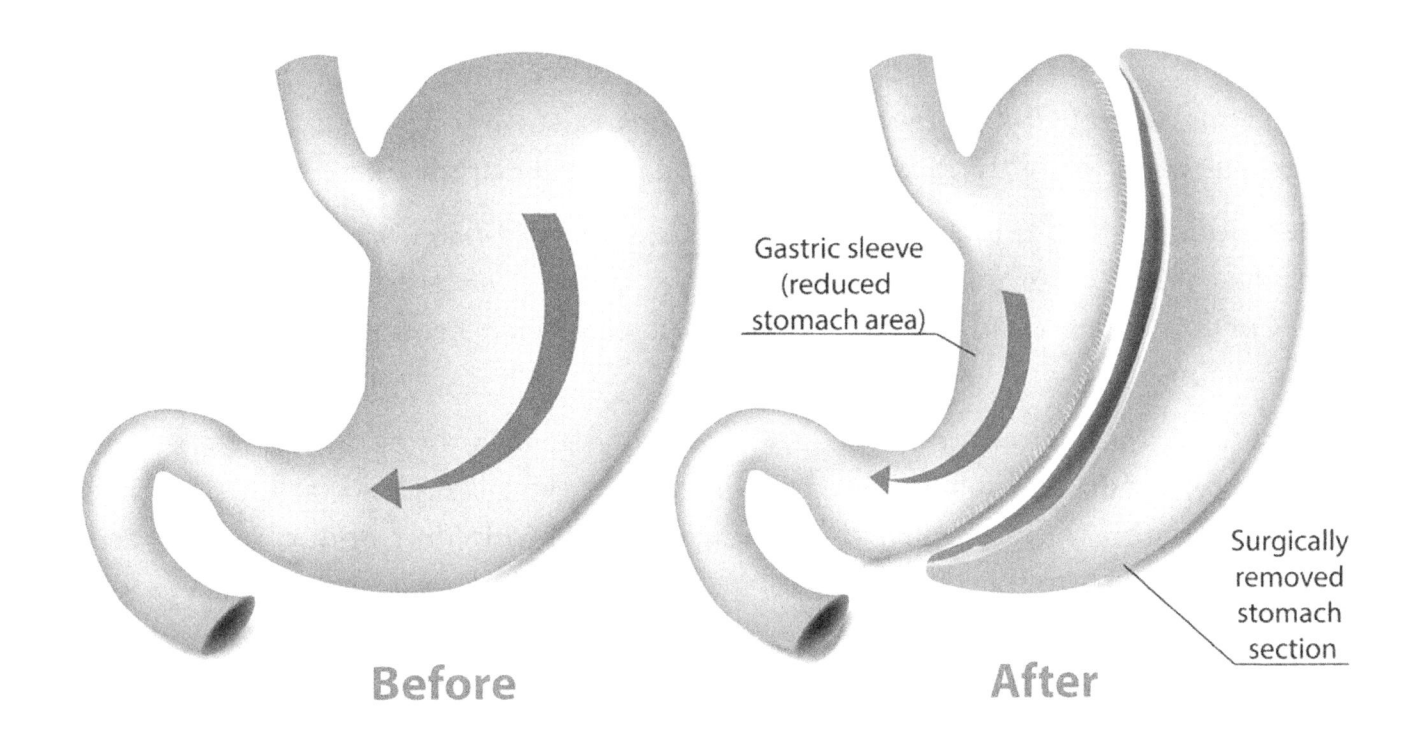

Weight loss surgery, often known as gastric sleeve surgery is a restrictive procedure that reduces stomach size to help you feel full faster and consume fewer calories. Through this operation, more than half of your stomach will be taken out. During surgery, surgeons cut away tissue from the patient's stomach along its bigger curved area. All that will be left of you after surgery is a thin, slender tube roughly the size of a banana. Those seeking drastic measures to reduce their weight often turn to this surgery.

Because the patient will need to eat healthily and exercise after surgery, this procedure should be viewed as a tool for weight loss rather than a fast fix. To aid with weight loss, surgeons can remove a significant portion of the stomach using a straightforward surgical operation known as gastric sleeve. It will not only lower the size of your stomach and the amount of food you physically consume, but it will also alter the hormonal signals that go between your stomach, brain, and liver. In layman's terms, this means less hunger and less need to eat. In this case, liposuction is not considered aesthetic surgery. The stomach is just partially cut off.

## Food Lifestyle Before And After Surgery

Surgery is just one step on your way to losing weight and getting healthy. Your new way of life will take practice, time, and commitment, just like a new hobby or sport. In this chapter, you'll learn what to eat before and after surgery.

**A) Diet Prior to Surgery**

The two-week diet we're going to describe here might not be the one your doctor advises, but it should serve as the standard for all diets before weight reduction surgery, if you would call it that. Start by eating leaner meats and boosting your protein intake while reducing your carbohydrate intake. Avoiding grains, pasta, and bread is necessary. Finally, you must stop eating anything sweet. You name it: candy, drink, juice, and cake.

Consider ingesting additional protein smoothies, such as those from a supplement store, for breakfast. Making sure there are no sweets in these shakes is the main thing to look out for. Concentrate on consuming more veggies and lean proteins for both lunch and dinner.

Snacks can be had throughout the day, but only healthy ones for example, berries, vegetables, almonds, and salads are all low in carbohydrates. Additionally, it's crucial that you keep hydrated throughout the day, which makes drinking enough water crucial. Drinking water will also help you to regulate your appetite. Additionally, it is well known that water is healthy for you.

You will need to follow a strict liquid diet for the three days before surgery and refrain from consuming any fizzy or caffeine-containing beverages. Infused water, popsicles (as long as they're sugar-free), broth and Jell-O are some examples of clear liquids you can consume.

Overall, if you can follow this sort of tight surgical protocol, your chance of developing any potential issues during surgery as well as the size of your liver in the weeks leading up to surgery should both be significantly reduced.

**B) Diet Following Surgery**

You must stick to clear drinks solely for the first week. The time you previously spent consuming only clear liquids for two to three days will now need to be extended by an additional seven days. Fortunately, by this time, the ghrelin hormone will have almost completely disappeared, and with it, your urge to consume large quantities of 'regular meals' Water, non-carbonated beverages, broth, coffee and decaf tea are all acceptable foods to ingest at this period because they are all sugar-free. You should refrain from eating certain items, such as sweets, carbonated beverages, sugary beverages, and non-decaf coffee.

You'll still need to follow a liquid diet for the second week following surgery, but with fewer restrictions than the clear liquid diet. You should include additional proteins in the mix for this week. You can consume things like liquidized protein powders, oatmeal, sugar-free ice cream, sugar-free liquids, creamy soups, smoothies, protein shakes, non-fat yogurts, sugar-free pudding and soupy noodles at this period. Even though this diet has fewer restrictions than the previous one did, you shouldn't become overconfident at this stage and eat things you shouldn't be.

Positive news! You'll be allowed to include some actual meals in your diet during the third week following surgery as opposed to just liquids. Nevertheless, you should limit, if not fully prevent, your consumption of fats and sweets. This week, concentrate on eating smaller pieces more slowly, limiting yourself to one new food per meal (you shouldn't eat two or more types of food at the same meal), and continuing to consume a lot of protein. Because your body has already gone well over a month without the meals it is accustomed to ingesting and digesting, you must allow it the time it needs to respond to these "new" foods. It will require additional time to properly adapt. You can consume a few of the new items, but you should still stay away from a few others. Protein shakes with yogurt or nonfat milk, mashed fruit, canned tuna or salmon, low-fat cheese, steamed fish, mayonnaise, scrambled eggs, soup, ground beef, ground chicken, soft vegetables, soft cereals, almond milk, soft cheese, and coconut milk are a few new foods you can include. All of these foods shouldn't be crunchy, and remember to chew each one thoroughly. In the third week, you still shouldn't eat any sweets, pasta, bread, rice, fibrous vegetables, or smoothies with a lot of sugar.

You can keep introducing more actual meals that you're used to for the fourth week. Keep in mind that, you're still not at the stage where you can eat anything you like and your stomach is still quite sensitive. You must continue to eat carefully, try to just introduce one new thing every meal, and always choose soft foods. Protein shakes are one of your finest sources of protein during this diet process, therefore you should keep drinking them during this period. More fish, softened vegetables, fruits, poultry, and meat can be added. All of these items should be eaten completely after being as softened as possible. You may include cereal and potatoes back into your diet, whether baked, mashed, or sweetened. You can add caffeine-containing goods back into your diet, but not so much that they become a regular part of it. When introducing caffeine to your diet, exercise extreme caution. You should concentrate on eating three modest meals throughout the day and drinking a lot of water throughout the fourth week. You should, however, be permitted to include snacks in your diet at this stage as long as your surgeon gives the go-ahead. Fresh fruit, tiny servings of sweetened or baked potatoes, small servings of oats, one egg, a small serving of baby carrots, or a small serving of crackers can all be included as snacks. You will need to keep avoiding these meals. The fourth week of your diet will need you to continue abstaining from the majority of drinks, fried foods, fibrous vegetables, sweets and sugar, pasta, desserts, whole milk, pizzas, dairy products in general, and nuts.

Your body will be able to accept more meals during the fifth week, but you could sometimes have stomach distress. Continue to have three small meals throughout the day, and drink plenty of water. Continue taking your prescription medications and supplements, and pay special attention to consuming adequate protein (sixty grams at the least). Once more, protein shakes are a great approach to ensure that you get an adequate amount of protein. Now that you're exercising more, your body should start to shed weight more quickly. Continue following a rigorous eating plan, and when you do have snacks, limit yourself to minimal servings.

RECIPES

# CLEAR LIQUID DIET

## PEPPERMINT TEA

**Prep time: 1 mins**

**Cooking time: 5 mins**

**Total time: 6 mins**

**Servings: 2**

**INGREDIENTS:**

- 4 cups hot water
- ½ cup peppermint leaf, dried

**DIRECTIONS:**

1. Put the water on to boil. Add the peppermint leaves when it starts to boil, then turn off the heat.
2. Cover the pot and let it sit for a few minutes to cool down.
3. When it has cooled, pour the mixture through a strainer and serve.

**NUTRITIONAL VALUE:**

Calories: 34 /kcal; Carbs: 9 g; Protein: 0.1 g; Fat: 0 g.

## ALMOND TEA

**Prep time: 1 mins**

**Cooking time: 5 mins**

**Total time: 6 mins**

**Servings: 2**

**INGREDIENTS:**

- 1 cup water
- 5 tbsp. almond powder
- 1 tsp. cinnamon

**DIRECTIONS:**

1. Bring out a pan and turn up the heat. Add all the ingredients in the pan.
2. Bring it to a boil, and then turn off the heat when it's boiling.
3. Serve hot, and have fun.

**NUTRITIONAL VALUE PER SERVING:**

Calories: 40 /kcal; Carbs: 1.4 g; Protein: 1.5 g; Fat: 3 g.

## ORANGE VANILLA TEA

**Prep time: 2 mins**

**Cooking time: 8 mins**

**Total time: 10 mins**

**Servings: 2**

**INGREDIENTS:**

- ¼ tsp. vanilla
- 2 cups water
- 2 oranges, sliced

**DIRECTIONS:**
1. Get a pan and put it on the stove over high heat. After you add the ingredients, let this boil.
2. Put the pan away from the heat and let it sit for a few minutes.
3. When the mixture has cooled, pour it through a strainer and serve.

**NUTRITIONAL VALUE PER SERVING:**
Calories: 60 /kcal; Carbs: 14 g; Protein: 2 g; Fat: 1 g.

## APRICOT AND ORANGE JUICE

*Prep time:* 10 mins

*Cooking time:* 0 mins

*Total time:* 10 mins

*Servings: 3*

**INGREDIENTS:**
- 1 inch peeled ginger slice
- 1 cup green grapes
- 1 lemon, Peeled
- 2 apricots, pitted and sliced
- 1 cup pomegranate seeds
- 2 oranges, peeled and sliced

**DIRECTIONS:**
1. Ginger, pomegranate, lemon, oranges and apricots should be put into a juicer.
2. Process until all of the juice comes out. Allow it to chill for a few minutes before serving.

**NUTRITIONAL VALUE PER SERVING:**
Calories: 196 /kcal; Carbs: 48 g; Protein: 4 g; Fat: 0.8 g.

## CHICKEN BONE BROTH

*Prep time:* 5 mins

*Cooking time:* 2 hours

*Total time:* 2 hours 5 mins

*Servings: 6*

**INGREDIENTS:**
- 1 oz. chicken bones, cleaned
- 1 onion, sliced
- 2 tbsp. apple cider vinegar
- 1 tbsp. cooking oil
- 5-6 garlic cloves
- ½ tsp. white pepper
- ½ tsp. salt
- 6 cups water
- 1-inch ginger slice

**DIRECTIONS:**
1. Add chicken bones, water, garlic, onion, oil, ginger, vinegar, salt, and pepper to a large skillet and stir. Put a lid on it.
2. Let it cook for 2 hours on low heat.
3. Strain the broth and throw away the residue.
4. Enjoy it while it's hot.

**NUTRITIONAL VALUE PER SERVING:**
Calories: 147 /kcal; Carbs: 9 g; Protein: 10 g; Fat: 5 g.

## LEMON, MINT AND CUCUMBER INFUSED WATER

*Prep time:* 5 mins

*Cooking time:* 0 mins

*Total time:* 5 mins

*Servings: 6*

**INGREDIENTS:**
- ½ cup cucumber slices
- 6 cups water
- 1 orange, sliced
- 1 grapefruit, sliced

**DIRECTIONS:**
1. Mix everything together in a pitcher.
2. Put in the fridge for two hours or overnight.
3. You can drink it in the morning or drink it all day.

**NUTRITIONAL VALUE PER SERVING:**
Calories: 1.3 /kcal; Carbs: 0.4 g; Protein: 0 g; Fat: 0 g.

## CITRUS AND MINT INFUSED WATER

*Prep time:* 5 mins

*Cooking time:* 0 mins

*Total time:* 5 mins

*Servings: 3*

**INGREDIENTS:**
- ½ red grapefruit, segmented
- ½ lemon, sliced
- 1 cucumber, sliced
- 2 mint leaves
- ½ gallon spring water
- ½ lime sliced

**DIRECTIONS:**
1. Mix everything together in a pitcher.
2. Put in the fridge for 2 hours and serve.

**NUTRITIONAL VALUE PER SERVING:**
Calories: 2 /kcal; Carbs: 0.4 g; Protein: 0 g; Fat: 0 g.

## MANGO AND PINEAPPLE WATER

Prep time: 5 mins

Cooking time: 0 mins

Total time: 5 mins

Servings: 10

**INGREDIENTS:**

- 1 cup pineapple slices
- 10 cups water
- 1 cup ripe mango, chunks
- 1-inch ginger sliced, peeled
- ½ tsp. protein powder

**DIRECTIONS:**

1. Put all of the ingredients in a pitcher and put it in refrigerator for at least an hour.
2. Pour into glasses to serve.

**NUTRITIONAL VALUE PER SERVING:**
Calories: 10 /kcal; Carbs: 12 g; Protein: 0 g; Fat: 0 g.

## HONEYDEW AND KIWI INFUSED WATER

Prep time: 5 mins

Cooking time: 0 mins

Total time: 5 mins

Servings: 10

**INGREDIENTS:**

- 2 cups honeydew melon, chopped
- 1 kiwi, peeled and sliced
- 10 cups Water

**DIRECTIONS:**

1. Mix the fruits together in a pitcher.
2. Fill with water up to the top.
3. Refrigerate it for 1 hour and serve.

**NUTRITIONAL VALUE PER SERVING:**
Calories: 12 /kcal; Carbs: 4.4 g; Protein: 0 g; Fat: 0 g.

## MINT MOJITO

Prep time: 20 mins

Cooking time: 5 mins

Total time: 25 mins

Servings: 1

**INGREDIENTS:**

- ½ cup natural sweetener
- 2 cups water
- 1 oz. lime juice
- ½ cup fresh mint leaves

**DIRECTIONS:**

1. Boil the water and natural sweetener for about 5 minutes, or until the mixture thickens into a syrup.
2. Put mint leaves in a mason jar. Pour syrup over the mint leaves and let them sit for at least 20 minutes.
3. Put some ice in the glass. Pour 1/2 cup of cold water and 1 tbsp. of mint syrup. Add 1 oz. lime juice into the Mason jar.
4. Mix, and then serve.

**NUTRITIONAL VALUE PER SERVING:**
Calories: 32 /kcal; Carbs: 3 g; Protein: 0 g; Fat: 0 g.

## INFUSED CHICKEN BROTH

Prep time: 5 mins

Cooking time: 20 mins

Total time: 25 mins

Servings: 2

**INGREDIENTS:**

- 1/2 cup chopped onion
- 2 cups chicken broth, store bought
- 1/2 cup chopped celery
- 1/2 cup chopped carrots

**DIRECTIONS:**

1. Put all of the ingredients in a sauce pot and turn the heat up to high.
2. Once it's boiling, turn down the heat to low and let it cook for 20 minutes.
3. Take off the heat. Put a strainer over a bowl and pour the broth through it to get rid of the vegetables. Sip the broth and enjoy it.

**NUTRITIONAL VALUE PER SERVING:**
Calories: 10 /kcal; Carbs: 1 g; Protein: 1 g; Fat: 1 g.

## SWEET AND SOUR LYCHEE INFUSED WATER

Prep time: 5 mins

Cooking time: 0 mins

Total time: 5 mins

Servings: 10

**INGREDIENTS:**

- 1 cup lychees, peeled, seeded
- 10 cups water
- 1 tbsp. ginger powder
- 3 tbsp. lemon juice

**DIRECTIONS:**

1. Mix the fruits together in a pitcher.
2. Fill with water up to the top.
3. Refrigerate it for 1 hour and serve.

**NUTRITIONAL VALUE PER SERVING:**
Calories: 31 /kcal; Carbs: 2 g; Protein: 0 g; Fat: 0 g.

## KIWI AND KALE DETOX WATER

**Prep time:** 5 mins

**Cooking time:** 0 mins

**Total time:** 5 mins

**Servings:** 10

**INGREDIENTS:**
- 5 kale leaves
- 4 kiwis, sliced
- 10 cups cold water

**DIRECTIONS:**
1. Put all of the ingredients in a pitcher and put it in refrigerator for at least an hour.
2. Pour into glasses to serve.

**NUTRITIONAL VALUE PER SERVING:**
Calories: 1.7 /kcal; Carbs: 8 g; Protein: 0 g; Fat: 0 g.

## WATERMELON AND LEMON WATER

**Prep time:** 5 mins

**Cooking time:** 0 mins

**Total time:** 5 mins

**Servings:** 10

**INGREDIENTS:**
- 3 cups watermelon, chunks, seeded
- 2-3 mint leaves
- 3 tbsp. lemon juice
- 10 cups water
- 1 pinch salt

**DIRECTIONS:**
1. Mix the watermelon, mint leaves and lemon juice together in a pitcher.
2. Fill with water up to the top.
3. Refrigerate it for 1 hour and serve.

**NUTRITIONAL VALUE PER SERVING:**
Calories: 105 /kcal; Carbs: 24 g; Protein: 2 g; Fat: 1 g.

## MANGO AND GINGER INFUSED WATER

**Prep time:** 5 mins

**Cooking time:** 0 mins

**Total time:** 5 mins

**Servings:** 4

**INGREDIENTS:**
- 1 cup diced mango
- 2 cups ice
- 1-inch ginger
- Water, to top off

**DIRECTIONS:**
1. Peel the ginger and cut it into 3–4 slices about the size of coins.
2. Ginger should be put in a pitcher with the mango.
3. Add 2 cups of ice on top and fill with water.
4. Put in the fridge for 3 hours, and then serve.

**NUTRITIONAL VALUE PER SERVING:**
Calories: 1.3 /kcal; Carbs: 0.4 g; Protein: 0 g; Fat: 0 g.

## LAVENDER AND BLUEBERRY INFUSED WATER

**Prep time:** 5 mins

**Cooking time:** 0 mins

**Total time:** 5 mins

**Servings:** 8

**INGREDIENTS:**
- 8 cups water
- 1 tbsp. lavender flowers
- 1-pint fresh blueberries

**DIRECTIONS:**
1. Mix everything together in a big pitcher.
2. Stir gently, and then put in the fridge for an hour.
3. Strain and serve.

**NUTRITIONAL VALUE PER SERVING:**
Calories: 1.3 /kcal; Carbs: 0.4 g; Protein: 0 g; Fat: 0 g.

## PINA COLADA INFUSED WATER

**Prep time:** 5 mins

**Cooking time:** 0 mins

**Total time:** 5 mins

**Servings:** 6

**INGREDIENTS:**
- 2 cups ice
- 1 cup pineapple, peeled and thinly sliced
- 6 cups coconut water

**DIRECTIONS:**
1. Add the pineapple slices into a large pitcher.
2. Add ice on top.
3. Fill it up with coconut water and put a lid on it.
4. Put in the fridge for an hour and serve.

**NUTRITIONAL VALUE PER SERVING:**

Calories: 1.3 /kcal; Carbs: 0.4 g; Protein: 0 g; Fat: 0 g.

## STRAWBERRY, ORANGE AND MINT INFUSED WATER

Prep time: 5 mins

Cooking time: 0 mins

Total time: 5 mins

Servings: 6

**INGREDIENTS:**

- 6 cups water
- 2 oranges, cut into wedges
- 4 leaves mint
- ½ cup strawberries

**DIRECTIONS:**

1. Mix everything together in a pitcher.
2. Cover and put in the fridge for at least 2 hours or overnight.

**NUTRITIONAL VALUE PER SERVING:**

Calories: 1.3 /kcal; Carbs: 0.4 g; Protein: 0 g; Fat: 0 g.

## WATERMELON JUICE

Prep time: 5 mins

Cooking time: 0 mins

Total time: 5 mins

Servings: 2

**INGREDIENTS:**

- 1 watermelon, peeled, deseeded, cubed
- ½ of key lime, juiced, zest
- 1 tbsp. date sugar
- 2 cups coconut water

**DIRECTIONS:**

1. Put watermelon cubes in a high-speed blender or food processor, add lime zest and juice, date sugar, and pulse until smooth.
2. Take two tall glasses and fill them halfway with the watermelon mixture. Then, pour coconut water into the glasses.
3. Mix everything together, and then serve.

**NUTRITIONAL VALUE PER SERVING:**

Calories: 55 /kcal; Carbs: 7 g; Protein: 10 g; Fat: 1 g.

## GINGER TEA

Prep time: 5 mins

Cooking time: 5 mins

Total time: 10 mins

Servings: 3

**INGREDIENTS:**

- 3 cups water
- 3 tsp. grated ginger root

**DIRECTIONS:**

1. Bring out a pan and turn up the heat. Add water and grated ginger root in the pan.
2. Bring it to a boil, and then turn off the heat when it's boiling.
3. Serve hot, and have fun.

**NUTRITIONAL VALUE PER SERVING:**

Calories: 13 /kcal; Carbs: 0.4 g; Protein: 0 g; Fat: 0 g.

## ORANGE JUICE

Prep time: 10 mins

Cooking time: 0 mins

Total time: 10 mins

Servings: 2

**INGREDIENTS:**

- 6 medium oranges; peeled and sliced

**DIRECTIONS:**

1. Put orange pieces in a juicer and follow the manufacturer's instructions to get the juice out.
2. Put the freshly made juice into two glasses and serve it right away.

**NUTRITIONAL VALUE PER SERVING:**

Calories: 259 /kcal; Carbs: 64 g; Protein: 5 g; Fat: 0.1 g.

## KEY LIME TEA

Prep time: 5 mins

Cooking time: 5 mins

Total time: 10 mins

Servings: 2

**INGREDIENTS:**

- 2 cups spring water
- 1 sprig of dill weed
- 1 tbsp. key lime juice
- 1/8 tsp. cayenne pepper

**DIRECTIONS:**
1. Put some water in a medium saucepan, put it on medium-high heat, and bring it to a boil.
2. Boil the tea for 5 minutes, and then pour it through a strainer into a bowl.
3. Mix in the lime juice, and then stir in the cayenne pepper.
4. Then, pour the tea into two mugs and serve.

**NUTRITIONAL VALUE PER SERVING:**
Calories: 24 /kcal; Carbs: 0 g; Protein: 0.5 g; Fat: 0 g.

## STRAWBERRY JUICE

Prep time: 10 mins

Cooking time: 0 mins

Total time: 10 mins

Servings: 2

**INGREDIENTS:**
- 1 tsp. fresh key lime juice
- 2 cups fresh strawberries, hulled
- 2 cups chilled spring water

**DIRECTIONS:**
1. Put all of the ingredients into a blender with a lot of power and pulse them well.
2. Put the juice through a strainer and pour it into 2 glasses.
3. Serve right away.

**NUTRITIONAL VALUE PER SERVING:**
Calories: 46 /kcal; Carbs: 11 g; Protein: 1 g; Fat: 0 g.

## GRAPE JUICE

Prep time: 5 mins

Cooking time: 0 mins

Total time: 5 mins

Servings: 2

**INGREDIENTS:**
- ½ lime
- 2 cups seedless red grapes
- 2 cups spring water

**DIRECTIONS:**
1. Put all of the ingredients into a blender and pulse them well.
2. Put the juice through a strainer and pour it into 2 glasses.
3. Serve right away.

**NUTRITIONAL VALUE PER SERVING:**
Calories: 63 /kcal; Carbs: 16 g; Protein: 0.6 g; Fat: 0.1 g.

## MANGO JUICE

Prep time: 10 mins

Cooking time: 0 mins

Total time: 10 mins

Servings: 4

**INGREDIENTS:**
- 2 cups spring water
- 4 cups mangoes; peeled, pitted, and chopped

**DIRECTIONS:**
1. Put all of the ingredients into a blender and pulse them well.
2. Put the juice through a strainer and pour it into 4 glasses.
3. Serve right away.

**NUTRITIONAL VALUE PER SERVING:**
Calories: 99 /kcal; Carbs: 24 g; Protein: 1.4 g; Fat: 0.2 g.

## APPLE AND KALE JUICE

Prep time: 10 mins

Cooking time: 0 mins

Total time: 10 mins

Servings: 2

**INGREDIENTS:**
- 2 large green apples, cored and sliced
- ¼ cup fresh parsley leaves
- 4 cups fresh kale leaves
- 1 key lime, peeled and seeded
- 1 tbsp. fresh ginger, peeled
- 1 cup chilled spring water

**DIRECTIONS:**
1. Put all of the ingredients into a blender and pulse them well.
2. Put the juice through a strainer and pour it into 2 glasses.
3. Serve right away.

**NUTRITIONAL VALUE PER SERVING:**
Calories: 196 /kcal; Carbs: 48 g; Protein: 5 g; Fat: 0.1 g.

## CLEAR VEGETABLE STOCK

Prep time: 10 mins

Cooking time: 40 mins

Total time: 50 mins

Servings: 4

### INGREDIENTS:

- 1 tbsp. olive oil
- 1 stalk of celery
- 1 onion
- 1 bunch chopped green onions
- 1 carrot
- 2 sprigs parsley, fresh
- 2 cloves garlic, minced
- 2 bay leaves
- 2 sprigs thyme, fresh
- 2 quarts water
- 1 tsp. salt

### DIRECTIONS:

1. Cut vegetables that have been washed into 1-inch pieces.
2. In a soup pot, heat the oil. Put in the garlic, celery, onion, green onions, carrot, thyme, bay leaves, and parsley. Cook for 5–10 minutes on high heat, stirring often.
3. Add salt and water, and then bring to a boil. Cook on low for 30 minutes.

### NUTRITIONAL VALUE PER SERVING:
Calories: 80 /kcal; Carbs: 2 g; Protein: 5 g; Fat: 3 g.

## WATERMELON SORBET

Prep time: 5 mins

Cooking time: 0 mins

Total time: 5 mins

Servings: 6

### INGREDIENTS:

- 4½ cups crushed ice cubes,
- 1 tbsp. orange zest, grated
- ½ lb. cubed melon

### DIRECTIONS:

1. Put all of the ingredients into a blender and pulse them well.
2. Serve right away.

### NUTRITIONAL VALUE PER SERVING:
Calories: 231 /kcal; Carbs: 59 g; Protein: 0.6 g; Fat: 0.2 g.

## LEMON BALM TEA

Prep time: 5 mins

Cooking time: 10 mins

Total time: 20 mins

Servings: 5

### INGREDIENTS:

- 5 cups water
- 1 cup lemon balm
- 1 tbsp. lemon zest

### DIRECTIONS:

1. Bring the water to a boil. Once the water is boiling, add the lemon balm and lemon zest and turn off the heat.
2. Pour, serve, and enjoy.

### NUTRITIONAL VALUE PER SERVING:
Calories: 13 /kcal; Carbs: 3 g; Protein: 0 g; Fat: 0 g.

## ORANGE CARROT TEA

Prep time: 5 mins

Cooking time: 10 mins

Total time: 15 mins

Servings: 4

### INGREDIENTS:

- 12 oz. diced carrots
- 4 halved oranges
- 4 cups water

### DIRECTIONS:

1. Put all of the ingredients into a pot and let them boil.
2. Turn off the heat and let it cool.
3. Pour, serve, and enjoy!

### NUTRITIONAL VALUE PER SERVING:

Calories: 93 /kcal; Carbs: 22 g; Protein: 2.2 g; Fat: 0.4 g.

## RED APPLE AND CARROT TEA

Prep time: 5 mins

Cooking time: 10 mins

Total time: 15 mins

Servings: 2

### INGREDIENTS:

- 1 cup red apples, peeled, chunks
- ½ cup seeded lychee
- 2 sliced carrots
- 2 cups water

### DIRECTIONS:

1. Blend apples, lychees, carrots, and water in a blender.
2. Put all of the above ingredients into a saucepan and bring to a boil.
3. Take it off the heat and let it sit for 5 minutes.
4. Pour, serve, and enjoy.

### NUTRITIONAL VALUE PER SERVING:

Calories: 184 /kcal; Carbs: 44 g; Protein: 1 g; Fat: 0 g.

## PORK BONE BROTH

Prep time: 10 mins

Cooking time: 2 hours

Total time: 2 hours 10 mins

Servings: 5

### INGREDIENTS:

- 1 oz. pork bones
- 1 sliced onion
- 6 garlic cloves
- 2 tbsp. apple cider vinegar
- ½ tsp. salt
- ½ tsp. white pepper
- 1 tbsp. cooking oil
- 10 cups Water
- 1-inch ginger slice

### DIRECTIONS:

1. Add the bones, water, garlic, onion, oil, ginger, vinegar, salt, and pepper to a large skillet and stir. Put a lid on it.
2. Cook on low for 2 hours.
3. Strain the broth and serve hot, and enjoy.

### NUTRITIONAL VALUE PER SERVING:

Calories: 37 /kcal; Carbs: 8 g; Protein: 1 g; Fat: 0.2 g.

## PEANUT TEA

Prep time: 5 mins

Cooking time: 5 mins

Total time: 10 mins

Servings: 2

### INGREDIENTS:

1. 1 tsp. cinnamon
2. 5 tbsp. peanuts, ground
3. 2 cups water

### DIRECTIONS:

1. Heat the water in a saucepan, then stir in the rest of the ingredients.
2. Serve hot.

### NUTRITIONAL VALUE PER SERVING:

Calories: 40 /kcal; Carbs: 1 g; Protein: 2 g; Fat: 4 g.

## SAVORY BEEF BROTH

Prep time: 5 mins

Cooking time: 5 hours

Total time: 5 hours 5 mins

Servings: 8

### INGREDIENTS:

- Nonstick cooking spray
- 1 cup diced celery
- 1 onion, chopped
- 3 lb. beef bones
- 1 cup peeled, diced carrot
- 12 cups water
- 1 lb. stew beef
- 2 bay leaves
- 1 tbsp. minced garlic
- 1 tsp. salt

### DIRECTIONS:

1. Get the oven ready at 400°F.-200°C.
2. Spray cooking spray on a shallow roasting pan and set it aside.
3. Put an even layer of onion, carrot and celery in the roasting pan. On top of the vegetables, put the beef bones and stew meat in the pan. For 40 minutes, roast the bones, vegetables and meat, flipping the bones and meat halfway through.
4. Take the pan out of the oven and put the meat, bones, and vegetables in a big stock pot. Add the water, bay leaves, salt, and garlic, and bring to a boil.
5. Turn the heat down to medium-low and let the

6. food cook for at least 4 hours. Remove the meat, bones, and vegetables from the pot with a strainer spoon. Enjoy the warm broth.

**NUTRITIONAL VALUE PER SERVING:**
Calories: 70 /kcal; Carbs: 1 g; Protein: 7 g; Fat: 4 g.

## VEGETABLE CHICKEN BROTH

**Prep time:** 5 mins

**Cooking time:** 5 hours

**Total time:** 5 hour 5 mins

**Servings:** 8

**INGREDIENTS:**
- Nonstick cooking spray
- 1 onion, sliced
- 4 large carrots, peeled and chopped
- 2 cups diced celery
- 2 bay leaves
- 12 to 16 cups water
- 7 lb. whole chicken
- 1 tsp. salt

**DIRECTIONS:**
1. Get the oven ready at 400°F.-200°C.
2. Spray cooking spray on a shallow baking pan.
3. Put the carrots, celery, and onion in the roasting pan. Put the raw chicken in the pan and roast for 90 minutes.
4. Take the pan out of the oven and pull the meat off the bones. Set the meat aside to use in other recipes.
5. Put the carcass and the vegetables in a big pot. Put enough water in the pot to completely cover the carcass and vegetables. Put the salt and bay leaves in the pot and bring to a boil.
6. Simmer for at least 4 hours over medium heat, or longer if you want more flavor.
7. To get the bones and vegetables out of the pot, use a strainer spoon.
8. Enjoy the warm broth.

**NUTRITIONAL VALUE PER SERVING:**
Calories: 70 /kcal; Carbs: 0.5 g; Protein: 8 g; Fat: 1 g.

## SOUTHWEST STYLE CHICKEN BROTH

**Prep time:** 5 mins

**Cooking time:** 5 hours

**Total time:** 5 hour 5 mins

**Servings:** 8

**INGREDIENTS:**
- Nonstick cooking spray
- 1 large tomato, quartered
- 4 large carrots, peeled and chopped
- 1 red bell pepper, sliced
- 1 red onion, quartered
- 1 whole chicken
- 1 tsp. salt
- 12 to 16 cups water
- 1 tsp. dried cilantro
- 1 tsp. ground cumin
- 2 bay leaves

**DIRECTIONS:**
1. Get the oven ready at 400°F.-200°C.
2. Spray a shallow broiler pan with cooking spray that won't stick.
3. Put an even layer of onion, carrot, bell pepper and tomato in the pan. Put the chicken in the pan and bake it for an hour and a half.
4. Take the pan out of the oven and pull the meat off the bones. Set the meat aside to use in other recipes.
5. Put the body and the vegetables in a big pot. Put enough water in the pot to completely cover the carcass and vegetables. Put the salt, cumin, cilantro, and bay leaves in the pot and bring to a rolling boil.
6. Turn the heat down to medium and let it simmer for 4 hours.
7. To get the bones, vegetables and meat out of the pot, use a strainer spoon.
8. Serve and enjoy the delicious broth.

**NUTRITIONAL VALUE PER SERVING:**
Calories: 70 /kcal; Carbs: 0.5 g; Protein: 8 g; Fat: 1 g.

## LEMON AND CUCUMBER WATER

**Prep time:** 5 mins + chilling time

**Cooking time:** 0 mins

**Total time:** 5 mins + chilling time

**Servings:** 8

**INGREDIENTS:**
- 8 cups water
- ½ cucumber, sliced
- 1 lime, sliced
- 1 lemon, sliced
- 2 fresh mint sprigs

**DIRECTIONS:**
- Mix the water, lime, lemon, mint and cucumber in a 2¼ -quart pitcher.
- Chill and serve.

**NUTRITIONAL VALUE PER SERVING:**
Calories: 8 /kcal; Carbs: 3 g; Protein: 0 g; Fat: 0 g.

## STRAWBERRY LEMONADE WATER

Prep time: 5 mins + chilling time

Cooking time: 0 mins

Total time: 5 mins + chilling time

Servings: 2

### INGREDIENTS:

1. 1 bunch of mint, washed
2. 1/2 lemon washed and sliced
3. 2 liters water
4. 6 strawberries washed and sliced

### DIRECTIONS:

1. Put all herbs and fruits in a pitcher.
2. Use a muddler to gently crush the herbs and fruits to release their flavors.
3. Add the water, stir, and let it sit in the fridge for two hours before serving.

### NUTRITIONAL VALUE PER SERVING:

Calories: 7 /kcal; Carbs: 2 g; Protein: 0.1 g; Fat: 0.1 g.

## APPLE CINNAMON WATER

Prep time: 5 mins + chilling time

Cooking time: 0 mins

Total time: 5 mins + chilling time

Servings: 1

### INGREDIENTS:

- 1 cinnamon stick
- 1 apple, thinly sliced
- 1 liter water

### DIRECTIONS:

1. Put the ingredients at the bottom of a pitcher.
2. Put water on top.
3. Put in the refrigerator for one hour before serving.

### NUTRITIONAL VALUE PER SERVING:

Calories: 1 /kcal; Carbs: 0 g; Protein: 0 g; Fat: 0 g.

## BLUEBERRY AND ORANGE WATER

Prep time: 5 mins + chilling time

Cooking time: 0 mins

Total time: 5 mins + chilling time

Servings: 2

### INGREDIENTS:

- 2 mandarin oranges, cut into wedges
- 1 liter water
- handful of blueberries

### DIRECTIONS:

1. Put the ingredients at the bottom of a pitcher.
2. Put water on top.
3. Put in the refrigerator for one hour before serving.

### NUTRITIONAL VALUE PER SERVING:

Calories: 1 /kcal; Carbs: 0 g; Protein: 0 g; Fat: 0 g.

## WATERMELON AND STRAWBERRY MINT WATER

Prep time: 5 mins + chilling time

Cooking time: 0 mins

Total time: 5 mins + chilling time

Servings: 2

### INGREDIENTS:

- 4 cups watermelon, 2 inch cubes
- 6 sprigs mint, lightly crushed
- 5 cups water
- ½ pint strawberries, sliced in half

### DIRECTIONS:

1. Put the strawberry, mint and watermelon at the bottom of a pitcher.
2. Put water on top.
3. Put in the refrigerator for one hour before serving.

### NUTRITIONAL VALUE PER SERVING:

Calories: 7 /kcal; Carbs: 1.7 g; Protein: 0.1 g; Fat: 0 g.

## MANGO GINGER WATER

**Prep time:** 5 mins + chilling time

**Cooking time:** 0 mins

**Total time:** 5 mins + chilling time

**Servings:** 2

### INGREDIENTS:

- 1 inch ginger root peeled and sliced
- 1 liter water
- 1 cup fresh or frozen mango

### DIRECTIONS:

1. Put the mango chunks and ginger at the bottom of a pitcher.
2. Put water on top.
3. Put in the refrigerator for one hour before serving.

### NUTRITIONAL VALUE PER SERVING:

Calories: 2 /kcal; Carbs: 0 g; Protein: 0 g; Fat: 0 g.

## RASPBERRY ORANGE WATER

**Prep time:** 5 mins + chilling time

**Cooking time:** 0 mins

**Total time:** 5 mins + chilling time

**Servings:** 2

### INGREDIENTS:

- 1 thinly sliced orange
- 1 liter water
- 1 pint raspberries, lightly crushed

### DIRECTIONS:

1. Put the oranges and raspberries at the bottom of a pitcher.
2. Put water on top.
3. Put in the refrigerator for one hour before serving.

### NUTRITIONAL VALUE PER SERVING:

Calories: 1/kcal; Carbs: 0.1 g; Protein: 0.1 g; Fat: 0 g.

## CLASSIC CUCUMBER WATER

**Prep time:** 5 mins + chilling time

**Cooking time:** 0 mins

**Total time:** 5 mins + chilling time

**Servings:** 1

### INGREDIENTS:

- 1 medium cucumber, sliced
- 1 liter water

### DIRECTIONS:

1. Put the cucumber at the bottom of a pitcher.
2. Put water on top.
3. Put in the refrigerator for one hour before serving.

### NUTRITIONAL VALUE PER SERVING:

Calories: 1 /kcal; Carbs: 0 g; Protein: 0 g; Fat: 0 g.

## LEMON BERRY WATER

**Prep time:** 5 mins + chilling time

**Cooking time:** 0 mins

**Total time:** 5 mins + chilling time

**Servings:** 1

### INGREDIENTS:

- 1/2 cup blueberries fresh or frozen
- 1 liter water
- 1 lemon sliced
- 1/2 cup raspberries fresh or frozen

### DIRECTIONS:

1. Put the blueberries, lemon slices and raspberries at the bottom of a pitcher.
2. Put water on top.
3. Put in the refrigerator for one hour before serving.

### NUTRITIONAL VALUE PER SERVING:

Calories: 2/kcal; Carbs: 0 g; Protein: 0.1 g; Fat: 0 g.

## STRAWBERRY, MINT, AND LEMON DRINK

**Prep time:** 5 mins + chilling time

**Cooking time:** 0 mins

**Total time:** 5 mins + chilling time

**Servings:** 2

### INGREDIENTS:

1. 1 lemon, thinly sliced
2. 5 mint leaves
3. 15 strawberries quartered
4. 2 liter water

### DIRECTIONS:

1. Put the strawberries, lemon slices and mint leaves at the bottom of a pitcher.
2. Put water on top.
3. Put in the refrigerator for one hour before serving.

### NUTRITIONAL VALUE PER SERVING:

Calories: 2 /kcal; Carbs: 0 g; Protein: 0.1 g; Fat: 0 g.

## BLUEBERRY LAVENDER WATER

**Prep time:** 5 mins + chilling time

**Cooking time:** 0 mins

**Total time:** 5 mins + chilling time

**Servings:** 2

### INGREDIENTS:

- 1 cup frozen blueberries
- 2 liter water
- 1 tbsp. dried culinary lavender

### DIRECTIONS:

1. Put the blueberries and lavender at the bottom of a pitcher.
2. Put water on top.
3. Put in the refrigerator for one hour before serving.

**NUTRITIONAL VALUE PER SERVING:**
Calories: 1 /kcal; Carbs: 0 g; Protein: 0.1 g; Fat: 0 g.

## LEMON LIME WATER

**Prep time:** 5 mins + chilling time

**Cooking time:** 0 mins

**Total time:** 5 mins + chilling time

**Servings:** 1

### INGREDIENTS:

- 1 lemon, sliced
- 1 liter water
- 3 limes, sliced

### DIRECTIONS:

1. Put the lime and lemon at the bottom of a pitcher.
2. Put water on top.
3. Put in the refrigerator for one hour before serving.

**NUTRITIONAL VALUE PER SERVING:**
Calories: 1 /kcal; Carbs: 0 g; Protein: 0 g; Fat: 0 g.

## PINEAPPLE AND ORANGE WATER

**Prep time:** 5 mins + chilling time

**Cooking time:** 0 mins

**Total time:** 5 mins + chilling time

**Servings:** 1

### INGREDIENTS:

- 1 orange, peeled and sliced
- 1 liter water
- 1/2 cup pineapple, thinly sliced

### DIRECTIONS:

1. Put the orange and pineapple slices at the bottom of a pitcher.
2. Put water on top.
3. Put in the refrigerator for one hour before serving.

**NUTRITIONAL VALUE PER SERVING:**
Calories: 4 /kcal; Carbs: 0 g; Protein: 0 g; Fat: 0 g.

## LIME CUCUMBER MINT WATER

**Prep time:** 5 mins + chilling time

**Cooking time:** 0 mins

**Total time:** 5 mins + chilling time

**Servings:** 2

### INGREDIENTS:

- 5 mint leaves
- 1 liter water
- 1 lime, thinly sliced
- 1 cucumber, sliced into rings

### DIRECTIONS:

1. Put the mint leaves, lime and cucumber slices at the bottom of a pitcher.
2. Put water on top.
3. Put in the refrigerator for one hour before serving.

**NUTRITIONAL VALUE PER SERVING:**
Calories: 1 /kcal; Carbs: 0 g; Protein: 0 g; Fat: 0 g.

## CITRUS CUCUMBER WATER

**Prep time:** 5 mins + chilling time

**Cooking time:** 0 mins

**Total time:** 5 mins + chilling time

**Servings:** 2

**INGREDIENTS:**

- 2 large oranges sliced
- 1 lemon, sliced
- 2 liter water
- ½ large cucumber, sliced
- 10 fresh mint leaves

**DIRECTIONS:**

1. Put the mint leaves, orange, lemon and cucumber slices at the bottom of a pitcher.
2. Put water on top.
3. Put in the fridge for one hour before serving.

**NUTRITIONAL VALUE PER SERVING:**

Calories: 2 /kcal; Carbs: 0 g; Protein: 0.1 g; Fat: 0 g.

## PEACH MINT WATER

**Prep time:** 5 mins + chilling time

**Cooking time:** 0 mins

**Total time:** 5 mins + chilling time

**Servings:** 1

**INGREDIENTS:**

- 1 handful mint leaves
- 1 liter water
- 10 frozen Peach Slices

**DIRECTIONS:**

1. Put the mint leaves and peach slices at the bottom of a pitcher.
2. Put water on top.
3. Put in the refrigerator for one hour before serving.

**NUTRITIONAL VALUE PER SERVING:**

Calories: 2 /kcal; Carbs: 0 g; Protein: 0.1 g; Fat: 0 g.

## BEEF AND SEAWEED STOCK

**Prep time:** 10 mins

**Cooking time:** 25 mins

**Total time:** 35 mins

**Servings:** 8

**INGREDIENTS:**

- 8 oz. lean ground beef
- 5 cups water
- 1 oz. dried seaweed
- 2 cloves garlic
- cooking spray
- Salt, to taste

**DIRECTIONS:**

1. Seaweed needs to soak for 10 minutes. After soaking chop them and set it aside.
2. Spray cooking spray on a large pot. Cook the garlic in a pan over medium heat. Put the ground beef in and cook it.
3. Add water and bring to a boil after the meat has been browned. Cover it, turn down the heat, and let it cook for 15 minutes. Skim off the fat that will rise to the top.
4. Now add seaweed cook further for 10 more minutes.
5. Strain to get rid of all the solids and keep just the broth.
6. Keep stock in the fridge overnight. Take off the layer of fat before using.

**NUTRITIONAL VALUE PER SERVING:**

Calories: 80 /kcal; Carbs: 2 g; Protein: 8 g; Fat: 0 g.

## PORK RIB AND BEAN STOCK

**Prep time:** 10 mins

**Cooking time:** 45 mins

**Total time:** 55 mins

**Servings:** 4

**INGREDIENTS:**

- 12 oz. lean pork spareribs
- Salt, to taste
- 6 oz. bean sprouts
- 3 cups water
- 2 cloves garlic, minced
- 2 slices fresh ginger
- 1 green onion, chopped
- Cooking spray
- 6 cups water

**DIRECTIONS:**

1. Put 3 cups of water in a large pot to a boil. For 5 minutes, boil the pork. Throw away the water.
2. Put 3 cups of clean water, ginger, pork, onion, and garlic in the pot and bring to a boil. Turn the heat to low and cover and simmer for 30 minutes. Skim off the fat that will rise to the top.
3. Put the bean sprouts in the pot and let them cook for 10 minutes.
4. Strain to get rid of all the solids and keep just the broth.
5. Keep stock in the fridge overnight. Take off the layer of fat before using.

**NUTRITIONAL VALUE PER SERVING:**

Calories: 90 /kcal; Carbs: 5 g; Protein: 10 g; Fat: 4 g.

## VEGETABLE FISH STOCK

**Prep time:** 10 mins

**Cooking time:** 55 mins

**Total time:** 1 hour 5 mins

**Servings:** 12

**INGREDIENTS:**

- 1 lb. fish bones
- 1 onion, chopped
- 7 cups water
- 4 stalks celery, chopped
- 3 slices ginger root
- 2 tbsp. fresh parsley, chopped
- 2 tbsp. black peppercorns
- 1 bay leaf
- 2 tbsp. fresh thyme, chopped
- Salt

**DIRECTIONS:**

1. Put water in a big pot and bring it to a boil. Boil the water with the fish bones and ginger for 10 minutes.
2. Add onion and celery. Take 5 minutes to cook. Add thyme, parsley, peppercorns, bay leaf, and salt.
3. Turn the heat down to low and cover. Simmer for 40 minutes.
4. Strain to get rid of all the solids and keep just the broth.
5. Keep stock in the fridge overnight. Take off the layer of fat before using.

**NUTRITIONAL VALUE PER SERVING:**

Calories: 111 /kcal; Carbs: 8 g; Protein: 18 g; Fat: 1 g.

## BOK CHOY STOCK

**Prep time:** 5 mins

**Cooking time:** 50 mins

**Total time:** 55 mins

**Servings:** 4

**INGREDIENTS:**

- 12 oz. bone-in chicken
- 1 green onion, chopped
- 3 cups water
- ½ lb. bok choy
- Salt, to taste

**DIRECTIONS:**

1. Put chicken and water in a large pot and bring to a boil.
2. Turn the heat down to low, cover, and let it cook for 40 minutes. Remove the layer of fat that will rise to the top.
3. Put in some bok choy and green onions. Keep cooking for 10 more minutes.
4. Strain to get rid of all the solids and keep just the broth.
5. Keep stock in the fridge overnight. Take off the layer of fat before using.

**NUTRITIONAL VALUE PER SERVING:**

Calories: 89 /kcal; Carbs: 3 g; Protein: 9 g; Fat: 1 g.

## VEGETABLE BEEF STOCK

**Prep time:** 10 mins

**Cooking time:** 55 mins

**Total time:** 1 hour 5 mins

**Servings:** 12

**INGREDIENTS:**

- 1 pound lean beef shank, dice
- 2 slices fresh ginger
- 7 cups water
- ½ radish, chopped
- 2 carrots, chopped
- Salt, to taste

**DIRECTIONS:**

1. In a big pot, cook the onion until it is translucent. Bring the beef and water to a boil.
2. Turn the heat down to low, cover, and let it cook for 40 minutes. Remove the layer of fat that will rise to the top.
3. Add salt, carrots, and radishes. Keep cooking for 10 more minutes.
4. Strain to get rid of all the solids and keep just the broth.
5. Keep stock in the fridge overnight. Take off the layer of fat before using.

**NUTRITIONAL VALUE PER SERVING:**

Calories: 87 /kcal; Carbs: 5 g; Protein: 12 g; Fat: 3 g.

## FISHY TOMATO BROTH

**Prep time:** 15 mins

**Cooking time:** 50 mins

**Total time:** 1 hour 5 mins

**Servings:** 12

**INGREDIENTS:**

- 1 lb. fish bones
- 1 block silken tofu, cubed
- 7 cups water
- 2 cups tomatoes, finely chopped
- Salt, to taste
- 4 slices ginger root

**DIRECTIONS:**

1. Put water in a big pot and bring it to a boil. Boil the water with the fish bones and ginger for 10 minutes.
2. Put in the tomatoes and tofu. Turn the heat down to low and cover. Simmer for 40 minutes.
3. Strain to get rid of all the solids and keep just the broth.
4. Refrigerate stock overnight. Take off the layer of fat before using.

**NUTRITIONAL VALUE PER SERVING:**

Calories: 99 /kcal; Carbs: 8 g; Protein: 18 g; Fat: 6 g.

## PORK AND FUZZY GOURD BROTH

Prep time: 10 mins

Cooking time: 1 hour 5 mins

Total time: 1 hour 15 mins

Servings: 12

### INGREDIENTS:

- 1 lb. pork bones
- ½ cups peanuts
- ½ cup black eyed peas
- 8 cups water
- 3 medium fuzzy gourd, cubed
- Salt, to taste

### DIRECTIONS:

1. Give the peanuts and peas 15 minutes to soak in water.
2. Bring a lot of water to a boil in a large pot. For 5 minutes, boil the pork bones. Throw away the water.
3. Put in the pot 8 cups of clean water, peanuts, pork bones and peas. Bring to a boil, then turn heat down.
4. Cover and cook for 30 minutes on low heat. Skim off the fat that will rise to the top.
5. Put gourd sprouts in the pot and let them cook for 30 minutes on low heat.
6. Strain to get rid of all the solids and keep just the broth.
7. Refrigerate stock overnight. Take off the layer of fat before using.

### NUTRITIONAL VALUE PER SERVING:

Calories: 111 /kcal; Carbs: 6 g; Protein: 12 g; Fat: 5 g.

## ROSEMARY GRAPEFRUIT INFUSED WATER

Prep time: 5 mins + chilling time

Cooking time: 0 mins

Total time: 5 mins + chilling time

Servings: 4

### INGREDIENTS:

- ½ grapefruit, peeled and sliced
- 4 cups water
- 1 sprig fresh rosemary
- Liquid stevia, to taste

### DIRECTIONS:

1. Put water, grapefruit and rosemary in a jar that can be sealed.
2. Wrap it up and put it in the fridge for at least 8 hours.
3. Take out everything solid from the jar.
4. Before serving, add liquid stevia to the taste you want and enjoy.

### NUTRITIONAL VALUE PER SERVING:

Calories: 5 /kcal; Carbs: 0 g; Protein: 0 g; Fat: 0 g.

## CITRUS INFUSED GREEN TEA

Prep time: 5 mins + chilling time

Cooking time: 0 mins

Total time: 5 mins + chilling time

Servings: 8

### INGREDIENTS:

- 2 green tea bags
- ½ grapefruit, peeled and sliced
- 1 lemon, sliced
- Liquid stevia, to taste
- 4 cups water

### DIRECTIONS:

1. Put water, lemon, tea bags and grapefruit in a jar that can be sealed.
2. Cover and put in the fridge for four hours. Take out the tea bags and chill for another 4 hours.
3. Take out everything solid from the jar.
4. Before serving, add liquid stevia to the taste you want and enjoy.

### NUTRITIONAL VALUE PER SERVING:

Calories: 3 /kcal; Carbs: 0 g; Protein: 0 g; Fat: 0 g.

## SPICY INFUSED CUCUMBER WATER

Prep time: 5 mins + chilling time

Cooking time: 0 mins

Total time: 5 mins + chilling time

Servings: 8

### INGREDIENTS:

- 4 cups water
- ½ jalapeno, deseeded
- 1 sprig mint leaves
- 1 cucumber, sliced

### DIRECTIONS:

1. Put water, jalapeno, cucumber and mint in a jar that can be sealed.
2. Cover and put in the fridge for eight hours.
3. Take out everything solid from the jar and serve.

### NUTRITIONAL VALUE PER SERVING:

Calories: 4 /kcal; Carbs: 0 g; Protein: 0 g; Fat: 0 g.

## STRAWBERRY LEMON AND BASIL WATER

Prep time: 5 mins + chilling time

Cooking time: 0 mins

Total time: 5 mins + chilling time

Servings: 1

### INGREDIENTS:

- 8 strawberries
- 5 cups water
- 4 sprigs fresh basil
- 1 lemon

### DIRECTIONS:

Rinse and slice the ingredients.
1. To extract the extra flavor from herbs muddle them in the pitcher.
2. Add herbs and fruits in a bottle infuser or pitcher and add water in it. Put it in the fridge for at least 8 hours.
3. Take out everything solid from the jar.
4. Serve and enjoy.

### NUTRITIONAL VALUE PER SERVING:

Calories: 11/kcal; Carbs: 0 g; Protein: 0 g; Fat: 0 g.

## WATERMELON, JALAPENO AND MINT WATER

Prep time: 5 mins + chilling time

Cooking time: 0 mins

Total time: 5 mins + chilling time

Servings: 1

### INGREDIENTS:

- 2 cups watermelon
- 4 sprigs mint
- 1 jalapeno
- 5 cups water

### DIRECTIONS:

1. Rinse and slice the ingredients.
2. To extract the extra flavor from herbs muddle them in the pitcher.
3. Add herbs and fruits in a bottle infuser or pitcher and add water in it. Put it in the fridge for at least 8 hours.
4. Take out everything solid from the jar.
5. Serve and enjoy.

### NUTRITIONAL VALUE PER SERVING:

Calories: 11/kcal; Carbs: 0 g; Protein: 0 g; Fat: 0 g.

## MANGO COCONUT AND LIME WATER

Prep time: 5 mins + chilling time

Cooking time: 0 mins

Total time: 5 mins + chilling time

Servings: 1

### INGREDIENTS:

- 1 cup coconut chunks
- 1 lemon
- 1 cup mango cubes
- 5 cups water

### DIRECTIONS:

1. Rinse and slice the ingredients.
2. To extract the extra flavor from herbs muddle them in the pitcher.
3. Add herbs and fruits in a bottle infuser or pitcher and add water in it. Put it in the fridge for at least 8 hours.
4. Take out everything solid from the jar.
5. Serve and enjoy.

### NUTRITIONAL VALUE PER SERVING:

Calories: 11/kcal; Carbs: 0 g; Protein: 0 g; Fat: 0 g.

## ORANGE GRAPE AND ROSEMARY WATER

Prep time: 5 mins + chilling time

Cooking time: 0 mins

Total time: 5 mins + chilling time

Servings: 1

### INGREDIENTS:

- 1 orange
- 4 sprigs rosemary
- 1 cup grapes
- 5 cups water

### DIRECTIONS:

1. Rinse and slice the ingredients.
2. To extract the extra flavor from herbs muddle them in the pitcher.
3. Add herbs and fruits in a bottle infuser or pitcher and add water in it. Put it in the fridge for at least 8 hours.
4. Take out everything solid from the jar.
5. Serve and enjoy.

### NUTRITIONAL VALUE PER SERVING:

Calories: 11/kcal; Carbs: 0 g; Protein: 0 g; Fat: 0 g.

## KIWI PASSION FRUIT AND MINT WATER

**Prep time:** 5 mins + chilling time

**Cooking time:** 0 mins

**Total time:** 5 mins + chilling time

**Servings:** 1

### INGREDIENTS:

- 2 kiwi
- 4 sprigs mint
- 1 passion fruit
- 5 cups water

### DIRECTIONS:

1. Rinse and slice the ingredients.
2. To extract the extra flavor from herbs muddle them in the pitcher.
3. Add herbs and fruits in a bottle infuser or pitcher and add water in it. Put it in the fridge for at least 8 hours.
4. Take out everything solid from the jar.
5. Serve and enjoy.

### NUTRITIONAL VALUE PER SERVING:
Calories: 11/kcal; Carbs: 0 g; Protein: 0 g; Fat: 0 g.

## CUCUMBER LIME AND THYME WATER

**Prep time:** 5 mins + chilling time

**Cooking time:** 0 mins

**Total time:** 5 mins + chilling time

**Servings:** 1

### INGREDIENTS:

1. 1 lime
2. 1 cucumber
3. 5 cups water
4. 4 sprigs fresh thyme

### DIRECTIONS:

1. Rinse and slice the ingredients.
2. To extract the extra flavor from herbs muddle them in the pitcher.
3. Add herbs and fruits in a bottle infuser or pitcher and add water in it. Put it in the fridge for at least 8 hours.
4. Take out everything solid from the jar.
5. Serve and enjoy.

### NUTRITIONAL VALUE PER SERVING:
Calories: 11/kcal; Carbs: 0 g; Protein: 0 g; Fat: 0 g.

## APPLE GINGER AND CINNAMON WATER

**Prep time:** 5 mins + chilling time

**Cooking time:** 0 mins

**Total time:** 5 mins + chilling time

**Servings:** 1

### INGREDIENTS:

- 1 apple
- 1 inch ginger root
- 3 cinnamon sticks
- 5 cups water

### DIRECTIONS:

1. Rinse and slice the ingredients.
2. To extract the extra flavor from herbs muddle them in the pitcher.
3. Add herbs and fruits in a bottle infuser or pitcher and add water in it. Put it in the fridge for at least 8 hours.
4. Take out everything solid from the jar.
5. Serve and enjoy.

### NUTRITIONAL VALUE PER SERVING:
Calories: 11/kcal; Carbs: 0 g; Protein: 0 g; Fat: 0 g.

## STRAWBERRY LIME AND ROSEMARY WATER

**Prep time:** 5 mins + chilling time

**Cooking time:** 0 mins

**Total time:** 5 mins + chilling time

**Servings:** 1

### INGREDIENTS:

- 1 strawberry
- 1 lime
- 4 sprigs fresh rosemary
- 5 cups water

### DIRECTIONS:

1. Rinse and slice the ingredients.
2. To extract the extra flavor from herbs muddle them in the pitcher.
3. Add herbs and fruits in a bottle infuser or pitcher and add water in it. Put it in the fridge for at least 8 hours.
4. Take out everything solid from the jar.
5. Serve and enjoy.

### NUTRITIONAL VALUE PER SERVING:
Calories: 11/kcal; Carbs: 0 g; Protein: 0 g; Fat: 0 g.

FULL LIQUID DIET

## BANANA AND CHOCOLATE SMOOTHIE

**Prep time:** 5 mins

**Cooking time:** 0 mins

**Total time:** 5 mins

**Servings:** 1

### INGREDIENTS:
- ½ cup frozen banana chunks
- 1 cup low-fat milk
- ½ cup frozen chocolate chunks

### DIRECTIONS:
1. Put all the ingredients in a blender and mix them well for five minutes.
2. Pour it into a tall glass and enjoy.

**NUTRITIONAL VALUE PER SERVING:**
Calories: 99 /kcal; Carbs: 7 g; Protein: 3 g; Fat: 1 g.

## SUPERFOOD SMOOTHIE

**Prep time:** 5 mins

**Cooking time:** 0 mins

**Total time:** 5 mins

**Servings:** 1

### INGREDIENTS:
- ½ cup frozen kiwi chunks
- 1/ cup cucumber chunks
- ½ cup fresh spinach
- 1 cup low-fat almond milk
- 1 tsp. chia seeds
- ½ cup vanilla protein powder

### DIRECTIONS:
1. Put all the ingredients in a blender and blend them well for five minutes.
2. Pour it into a tall glass and enjoy.

**NUTRITIONAL VALUE PER SERVING:**
Calories: 112 /kcal; Carbs: 12 g; Protein: 10 g; Fat: 1 g.

## STRAWBERRY AND BANANA SMOOTHIE

**Prep time:** 5 mins

**Cooking time:** 0 mins

**Total time:** 5 mins

**Servings:** 1

### INGREDIENTS:
- 1 cup low fat almond milk
- ½ cup frozen strawberry chunks
- 1 scoop peanut butter ice cream
- ½ cup frozen banana chunks
- ½ cup vanilla protein powder

### DIRECTIONS:
1. Put all the ingredients in a blender and blend on high speed for about three to four minutes.
2. Pour it into a glass and drink it.
3. You can save this smoothie by putting it in the freezer.
4. You can blend the smoothie again before you use it later.

**NUTRITIONAL VALUE PER SERVING:**
Calories: 121 /kcal; Carbs: 5 g; Protein: 12 g; Fat: 3 g.

## GREEK YOGURT AND BERRY SMOOTHIE

**Prep time:** 5 mins

**Cooking time:** 0 mins

**Total time:** 5 mins

**Servings:** 1

### INGREDIENTS:
- ½ cup frozen Greek yogurt
- ½ cup frozen berries chunks
- ½ cup vanilla protein powder
- 1 cup low fat almond milk

### DIRECTIONS:
1. Put all the ingredients in a blender and blend on high speed for about five minutes.
2. Pour it into a glass and drink it.

**NUTRITIONAL VALUE PER SERVING:**
Calories: 123 /kcal; Carbs: 5 g; Protein: 12 g; Fat: 2 g.

## CARAMEL ALMOND PROTEIN SHAKE

**Prep time:** 5 mins

**Cooking time:** 0 mins

**Total time:** 5 mins

*Servings: 1*

**INGREDIENTS:**

- 1/4 cup low-fat cottage cheese
- 1/2 tsp. caramel extract
- 1 scoop vanilla protein powder
- 1 cup water
- 1/2 tsp. almond extract
- 6 ice cubes

**DIRECTIONS:**

1. Mix all of the ingredients in a blender on high until they are smooth.

**NUTRITIONAL VALUE PER SERVING:**

Calories: 145 /kcal; Carbs: 6 g; Protein: 29 g; Fat: 1 g.

## PEANUT BUTTER CUP SMOOTHIE

*Prep time: 10 mins*

*Cooking time: 0 mins*

*Total time: 10 mins*

*Servings: 2*

**INGREDIENTS:**

- 1/2 cup skim milk
- 2 tbsp. creamy natural peanut butter
- 1/2 cup plain Greek yogurt
- 8 to 10 ice cubes
- 2 tbsp. unsweetened cocoa powder

**DIRECTIONS:**

1. Put all of the ingredients in a blender and pulse it until everything is well mixed and smooth.
2. Pour the mixture into two big glasses to serve. Enjoy!

**NUTRITIONAL VALUE PER SERVING:**

Calories: 175 /kcal; Carbs: 15 g; Protein: 11 g; Fat: 9 g.

## PUMPKIN SPICE SMOOTHIE

*Prep time: 5 mins*

*Cooking time: 0 mins*

*Total time: 5 mins*

*Servings: 1*

**INGREDIENTS:**

- 1 cup low fat milk, one cup
- ¼ tsp. ground ginger powder
- ¼ tsp. cinnamon powder
- ¾ cup decaffeinated coffee
- ½ cup frozen pumpkin puree
- ¼ tsp. ground cloves powder
- ¼ cup vanilla protein powder

**DIRECTIONS:**

1. Put all the ingredients in a blender and blend on high speed for about three to four minutes.
2. Pour it into a glass and drink it.
3. You can save this smoothie by putting it in the freezer.
4. You can blend the smoothie again before you use it later.

**NUTRITIONAL VALUE PER SERVING:**

Calories: 89 /kcal; Carbs: 7 g; Protein: 12 g; Fat: 2 g.

## DOUBLE CHOCOLATE SMOOTHIE

*Prep time: 5 mins*

*Cooking time: 0 mins*

*Total time: 5 mins*

*Servings: 1*

**INGREDIENTS:**

- ½ cup frozen Greek yogurt
- ½ banana chunks
- ¼ tsp. unsweetened cocoa powder
- 1 cup low fat milk
- ¼ cup chocolate protein powder

**DIRECTIONS:**

1. Put all the ingredients in a blender and blend on high speed for about five minutes.
2. Pour it into a glass and drink it.

**NUTRITIONAL VALUE PER SERVING:**

Calories: 167 /kcal; Carbs: 11 g; Protein: 14 g; Fat: 3 g.

## MANGO AND PINEAPPLE SMOOTHIE

*Prep time: 5 mins*

*Cooking time: 0 mins*

*Total time: 5 mins*

*Servings: 1*

**INGREDIENTS:**

- ½ cup frozen Pineapple chunks
- ½ cup frozen mango chunks
- 1 cup low fat milk

**DIRECTIONS:**

1. Put all the ingredients in a blender and mix them well for three to four minutes.
2. Pour it into a cup and drink it.

**NUTRITIONAL VALUE PER SERVING:**

Calories: 100 /kcal; Carbs: 10 g; Protein: 6 g; Fat: 2 g.

## PINA COLADA SMOOTHIE

**Prep time:** 5 mins

**Cooking time:** 0 mins

**Total time:** 5 mins

**Servings:** 2

### INGREDIENTS:

- ½ cup pineapple chunks
- ½ cup nonfat plain Greek yogurt
- ½ tsp. coconut extract
- 4 oz. unsweetened coconut milk

### DIRECTIONS:

1. Put the pineapple, yogurt, coconut milk and coconut extract into a blender and mix.
2. Blend until smooth or until you get the texture you want. Pour into tall glasses and enjoy your smoothie.

### NUTRITIONAL VALUE PER SERVING:

Calories: 148 /kcal; Carbs: 19 g; Protein: 13 g; Fat: 3 g.

## AVOCADO SMOOTHIE

**Prep time:** 5 mins

**Cooking time:** 0 mins

**Total time:** 5 mins

**Servings:** 2

### INGREDIENTS:

- 3 ripe bananas
- 1/2 avocado, mashed
- 2 cups coconut water
- 12 ice cubes
- 2 tbsp. honey
- 1 tsp. vanilla extract
- Dash of salt
- 1 tsp. ground cinnamon

### DIRECTIONS:

1. Bananas and coconut water should be mixed in a blender. Blend until it's smooth.
2. Add the remaining ingredients and keep blending until the mixture is smooth.

### NUTRITIONAL VALUE PER SERVING:

Calories: 85 /kcal; Carbs: 4 g; Protein: 11 g; Fat: 2 g.

## GREEN MANGO SMOOTHIE

**Prep time:** 5 mins

**Cooking time:** 0 mins

**Total time:** 5 mins

**Servings:** 2

### INGREDIENTS:

- 1/3 avocado, peeled and pitted
- ½ cup canned mango chunks, drained
- 1/3 cup fresh spinach
- ½ cup nonfat milk
- ½ cup nonfat plain Greek yogurt
- 1 tsp. honey

### DIRECTIONS:

1. Put the spinach, avocado, yogurt, mango chunks, milk, and honey in a blender and blend until smooth.
2. Blend until smooth or until you get the texture you want. Pour into tall glasses and have a drink.

### NUTRITIONAL VALUE PER SERVING:

Calories: 261 /kcal; Carbs: 30 g; Protein: 21 g; Fat: 8 g.

## BANANA CREAM PROTEIN SHAKE

**Prep time:** 5 mins

**Cooking time:** 0 mins

**Total time:** 5 mins

**Servings:** 1

### INGREDIENTS:

- 1 scoop vanilla protein powder
- 1/4 tsp. vanilla extract
- 1/2 tsp. banana extract
- 8 oz. water

### DIRECTIONS:

1. Put all the ingredients in a shaker cup and shake them well.
2. Add ice and pour in a glass and serve.

### NUTRITIONAL VALUE PER SERVING:

Calories: 143 /kcal; Carbs: 4 g; Protein: 21 g; Fat: 5 g.

## GUAVA SMOOTHIE

**Prep time:** 5 mins

**Cooking time:** 0 mins

**Total time:** 5 mins

FULL LIQUID DIET

*Servings: 2*

**INGREDIENTS:**

- 1 cup chopped guava, seeds removed
- 1 banana, peeled and sliced
- 1 tsp. fresh ginger, grated
- 1 cup baby spinach, finely chopped
- 2 cups water
- ½ medium-sized mango, peeled and chopped

**DIRECTIONS:**

1. Using a blender, combine guava, banana, baby spinach, mango and ginger until everything is well blended. Gradually pour in the water and blend until everything is smooth.
2. Place in serving glasses and put in the fridge for 20 minutes.
3. Enjoy.

**NUTRITIONAL VALUE PER SERVING:**

Calories: 166 /kcal; Carbs: 39 g; Protein: 2 g; Fat: 1 g.

## WATERMELON, CANTALOUPE AND MANGO SMOOTHIE

**Prep time:** 5 mins

**Cooking time:** 0 mins

**Total time:** 5 mins

*Servings: 2*

**INGREDIENTS:**

- 1 cup coconut water
- ½ of a large mango, peeled
- ½ cup cantaloupe, peeled
- ½ of burro banana, peeled
- ½ cup watermelon chunks
- ½ cup amaranth greens

**DIRECTIONS:**

1. Put all the ingredients in the jar of a high-speed blender or food processor and plug it in.
2. Pulse it for 60 seconds until smooth.
3. The drink should be divided into two glasses and served.

**NUTRITIONAL VALUE PER SERVING:**

Calories: 132 /kcal; Carbs: 3 g; Protein: 30 g; Fat: 1 g.

## BLACKBERRY AND BANANA SMOOTHIE

**Prep time:** 5 mins

**Cooking time:** 0 mins

**Total time:** 5 mins

*Servings: 2*

**INGREDIENTS:**

- 1 burro banana, peeled
- 2 dates, pitted
- ½ cup blackberries
- ¼ cup walnut milk, unsweetened
- 1 cup mango chunks
- ¾ cup of coconut water

**DIRECTIONS:**

1. Put all the ingredients in the jar of a high-speed blender or food processor and plug it in.
2. Pulse it for 60 seconds until smooth.
3. The drink should be divided into two glasses and served.

**NUTRITIONAL VALUE PER SERVING:**

Calories: 147 /kcal; Carbs: 4 g; Protein: 34 g; Fat: 5 g.

## GREEN SMOOTHIE WITH RASPBERRIES

**Prep time:** 5 mins

**Cooking time:** 0 mins

**Total time:** 5 mins

*Servings: 2*

**INGREDIENTS:**

- 1 cup coconut milk
- 1 cup raspberries
- 1 tbsp. sea moss
- 1 cup kale leaves
- 2 tbsp. key lime juice

**DIRECTIONS:**

1. Put all the ingredients in the jar of a high-speed blender or food processor and plug it in.
2. Pulse it for 60 seconds until smooth.
3. The drink should be divided into two glasses and served.

**NUTRITIONAL VALUE PER SERVING:**

Calories: 151 /kcal; Carbs: 8 g; Protein: 37 g; Fat: 3 g.

## CHOCOLATE CHERRY SHAKE

**Prep time:** 5 mins

**Cooking time:** 0 mins

**Total time:** 5 mins

*Servings: 1*

**INGREDIENTS:**

- 2 tbsp. Unsweetened cherry juice
- 1 Packet Chocolate Shake Mix
- 1 cup Cold water

**DIRECTIONS:**

1. Mix the contents of the chocolate shake packet, the cherry juice, and the water in a measuring cup. Stir until all the lumps are gone.
2. Pour into a glass and serve.

**NUTRITIONAL VALUE PER SERVING:**
Calories: 108 /kcal; Carbs: 10 g; Protein: 15 g; Fat: 1 g.

## VEGGIE-FULL SMOOTHIE

Prep time: 5 mins

Cooking time: 0 mins

Total time: 5 mins

Servings: 2

**INGREDIENTS:**
- ½ cup spring water
- 1 pear, cored, deseeded
- ¼ of avocado, peeled
- ½ cup watercress
- ½ of cucumber, peeled, deseeded
- ½ cup Romaine lettuce

**DIRECTIONS:**
1. Put all the ingredients in the jar of a high-speed blender or food processor and plug it in.
2. Pulse it for 60 seconds until smooth.
3. The drink should be divided into two glasses and served.

**NUTRITIONAL VALUE PER SERVING:**
Calories: 145 /kcal; Carbs: 6 g; Protein: 25 g; Fat: 1 g.

## MANGO PEACH PINEAPPLE SMOOTHIE

Prep time: 5 mins

Cooking time: 0 mins

Total time: 5 mins

Servings: 2

**INGREDIENTS:**
- ¼ cup unsweetened pineapple juice
- ½ cup frozen diced mango
- ¼ cup unsweetened almond milk
- ½ cup frozen peach slices

**DIRECTIONS:**
1. Blend the pineapple juice, almond milk, peaches and mango on medium speed for about 60 seconds, until the mixture is smooth
2. Pour into two glasses and have a drink.

**NUTRITIONAL VALUE PER SERVING:**
Calories: 60 /kcal; Carbs: 10 g; Protein: 0.86 g; Fat: 0.5 g.

## GREEN KIWI SPINACH SMOOTHIE

Prep time: 5 mins

Cooking time: 0 mins

Total time: 5 mins

Servings: 1

**INGREDIENTS:**
- 1 cup frozen chopped spinach
- ½ cup water
- 1 cup peeled and chopped kiwi

**DIRECTIONS:**
1. Put the spinach, water, and kiwi in a blender and blend on low speed until smooth, about 15 to 30 seconds.
2. Pour into a glass and enjoy.

**NUTRITIONAL VALUE PER SERVING:**
Calories: 75 /kcal; Carbs: 16 g; Protein: 4 g; Fat: 1 g.

## SIMPLE CANTALOUPE SMOOTHIE

Prep time: 5 mins

Cooking time: 0 mins

Total time: 5 mins

Servings: 2

**INGREDIENTS:**
- ½ cup plain nonfat Greek yogurt
- 1 tsp. alcohol-free vanilla extract
- 1 cup ice
- 1¾ cups diced cantaloupe

**DIRECTIONS:**
1. Blend the cantaloupe, yogurt, vanilla, and ice in a blender on low speed for about 30 seconds, until the mixture is smooth.
2. Pour into two glasses and have a drink.

**NUTRITIONAL VALUE PER SERVING:**
Calories: 90 /kcal; Carbs: 13 g; Protein: 8 g; Fat: 0.4 g.

## CHERRY BERRY LIME SMOOTHIE

Prep time: 5 mins

Cooking time: 0 mins

Total time: 5 mins

Servings: 1

**INGREDIENTS:**
- ½ cup frozen strawberries
- ¼ cup water
- ½ cup frozen pitted cherries
- 1½ tsp. stevia
- 1 tsp. lime juice

**DIRECTIONS:**
1. Put the cherries, strawberries, water, lime juice, and stevia in a blender. Blend on high speed for about 45 seconds, or until the mixture is smooth.

2. Pour into a glass and have a drink.

**NUTRITIONAL VALUE PER SERVING:**

Calories: 43 /kcal; Carbs: 10 g; Protein: 0.5 g; Fat: 0.1 g.

## STRAWBERRY BANANA AND ORANGE SMOOTHIE

**Prep time:** 5 mins

**Cooking time:** 0 mins

**Total time:** 5 mins

**Servings:** 2

**INGREDIENTS:**

- ½ cup unsweetened almond milk
- 2 tbsp. freshly squeezed orange juice
- ¼ tsp. orange zest
- ½ cup sliced bananas
- 1 cup frozen strawberries

**DIRECTIONS:**

1. Put the orange zest, almond milk, strawberries, orange juice, and bananas in a blender. Blend on medium speed for about 60 seconds, or until the mixture is smooth.
2. Pour into two glasses and have a drink.

**NUTRITIONAL VALUE PER SERVING:**

Calories: 75 /kcal; Carbs: 17 g; Protein: 1 g; Fat: 1 g.

## 3.25 Banana Mixed Berry Smoothie

**Prep time:** 5 mins

**Cooking time:** 0 mins

**Total time:** 5 mins

**Servings:** 2

**INGREDIENTS:**

- ½ cup unsweetened almond milk
- ½ cup sliced banana
- ½ cup plain nonfat Greek yogurt
- ½ cup frozen raspberries
- ½ cup ice
- ½ cup frozen blackberries
- 1 tsp. stevia

**DIRECTIONS:**

1. Blend the almond milk, blackberries, banana, ice, raspberries, and stevia on medium speed for about 60 seconds, or until the mixture is smooth.
2. Pour into two glasses and have a drink.

**NUTRITIONAL VALUE PER SERVING:**

Calories: 79 /kcal; Carbs: 14 g; Protein: 5 g; Fat: 1 g.

## RASPBERRY PLUM SMOOTHIE

**Prep time:** 5 mins

**Cooking time:** 0 mins

**Total time:** 5 mins

**Servings:** 2

**INGREDIENTS:**

- ½ cup almond milk, unsweetened
- 1 cup chopped plums
- ½ cup frozen raspberries
- ½ cup ice

**DIRECTIONS:**

1. Blend the raspberries, almond milk, ice and plums on medium speed for about 30 seconds, until the mixture is smooth.
2. Pour into two glasses and have a drink.

**NUTRITIONAL VALUE PER SERVING:**

Calories: 65 /kcal; Carbs: 14 g; Protein: 1 g; Fat: 1 g.

## BANANA APPLE FLAX SMOOTHIE

**Prep time:** 5 mins

**Cooking time:** 0 mins

**Total time:** 5 mins

**Servings:** 2

**INGREDIENTS:**

- ½ cup almond milk, unsweetened
- ½ cup peeled and chopped apple
- ½ cup sliced banana
- ¼ tsp. ground cinnamon
- 1 tbsp. ground flaxseed

**DIRECTIONS:**

1. Blend the almond milk, apple, banana, cinnamon and flaxseed on low speed for about 30 seconds, until the mixture is smooth.
2. Pour into two glasses and have a drink.

**NUTRITIONAL VALUE PER SERVING:**

Calories: 76 /kcal; Carbs: 14 g; Protein: 1.4 g; Fat: 2.2 g.

## POWER C SMOOTHIE

**Prep time:** 5 mins

**Cooking time:** 0 mins

**Total time:** 5 mins

**Servings:** 2

### INGREDIENTS:

- 2 tbsp. grapefruit juice, no-sugar-added
- 1 tbsp. lemon juice
- 2 tbsp. orange juice, no-sugar-added
- 2 tsp. pure maple syrup
- 1 tbsp. lime juice
- ½ cup water
- 1 cup ice
- ½ cup water

### DIRECTIONS:

1. Mix the orange juice, grapefruit juice, lime juice, lemon juice, water, maple syrup, and ice in a blender and blend on medium speed for about 30 seconds, or until the mixture is smooth.
2. Pour into two glasses and have a drink.

### NUTRITIONAL VALUE PER SERVING:
Calories: 34 /kcal; Carbs: 9 g; Protein: 0.27 g; Fat: 0.06 g.

## BLACKBERRY PEACH SMOOTHIE

**Prep time:** 5 mins

**Cooking time:** 0 mins

**Total time:** 5 mins

**Servings:** 2

### INGREDIENTS:

- ½ tsp. vanilla extract
- 1 cup almond milk, unsweetened
- ½ cup frozen blackberries
- 1 cup frozen sliced peaches

### DIRECTIONS:

1. Blend the peaches, almond milk, blackberries, and vanilla on medium speed for about 90 seconds, until the mixture is smooth.
2. Pour into two glasses and have a drink.

### NUTRITIONAL VALUE PER SERVING:
Calories: 63 /kcal; Carbs: 13 g; Protein: 1 g; Fat: 1 g.

## STRAWBERRY PINEAPPLE SMOOTHIE

**Prep time:** 5 mins

**Cooking time:** 0 mins

**Total time:** 5 mins

**Servings:** 2

### INGREDIENTS:

- ½ cup plain nonfat Greek yogurt
- 1 cup diced pineapple, frozen
- ½ cup water
- ½ cup strawberries, frozen

### DIRECTIONS:

1. Blend the yogurt, pineapple, water, and strawberries on medium speed for about 60 seconds, until the mixture is smooth.
2. Pour into two glasses and have a drink.

### NUTRITIONAL VALUE PER SERVING:
Calories: 88 /kcal; Carbs: 15 g; Protein: 7 g; Fat: 0.35 g.

## BERRY SPINACH SMOOTHIE

**Prep time:** 5 mins

**Cooking time:** 0 mins

**Total time:** 5 mins

**Servings:** 2

### INGREDIENTS:

- ½ cup soy milk
- 1 cup strawberries, frozen
- ½ cup plain nonfat Greek yogurt
- 1 tsp. lemon juice
- 1 cup baby spinach leaves

### DIRECTIONS:

1. Blend the soy milk, strawberries, yogurt, spinach, and lemon juice in a blender on medium speed for about 60 seconds, or until the mixture is smooth.
2. Pour into two glasses and have a drink.

### NUTRITIONAL VALUE PER SERVING:
Calories: 95 /kcal; Carbs: 13 g; Protein: 8 g; Fat: 1 g.

## ULTIMATE BERRY BLEND SMOOTHIE

**Prep time:** 5 mins

**Cooking time:** 0 mins

**Total time:** 5 mins

**Servings:** 4

### INGREDIENTS:

- ½ cup water
- ½ cup frozen strawberries
- ¾ cup unsweetened coconut yogurt
- ½ cup frozen blueberries
- ½ cup frozen raspberries
- 2 tsp. honey
- ½ cup frozen blackberries

**DIRECTIONS:**

1. Put the water, strawberries, yogurt, raspberries, blackberries, blueberries, and honey into a blender. Blend on high speed for about 60 seconds, or until the mixture is smooth.

**NUTRITIONAL VALUE PER SERVING:**

Calories: 36 /kcal; Carbs: 14 g; Protein: 1 g; Fat: 2 g.

## GREEN KIWI SPINACH SMOOTHIE

**Prep time: 5 mins**

**Cooking time: 0 mins**

**Total time: 5 mins**

**Servings: 2**

**INGREDIENTS:**

- 1 cup chopped spinach, frozen
- ½ cup water
- 1 cup peeled and chopped kiwi

**DIRECTIONS:**

1. Put the spinach, water, and kiwi in a blender and blend on low speed until smooth, about 15 to 30 seconds.
2. Pour into two glasses and have a drink.

**NUTRITIONAL VALUE PER SERVING:**

Calories: 75 /kcal; Carbs: 16 g; Protein: 4 g; Fat: 1 g.

## COCONUT LIME AND MINT COOLER

**Prep time: 5 mins**

**Cooking time: 0 mins**

**Total time: 5 mins**

**Servings: 1**

**INGREDIENTS:**

- ½ cup almond milk
- ½ tsp. alcohol-free vanilla extract
- 5 tbsp. unsweetened coconut milk
- 6 fresh mint leaves
- 2 tbsp. lime juice
- 1 cup ice
- 2 tsp. pure maple syrup

**DIRECTIONS:**

1. Blend the coconut milk, vanilla, almond milk, lime juice, mint leaves, maple syrup, and ice in a blender on medium speed for about 60 seconds, or until the mixture is smooth.
2. Pour into a glass and have a drink.

**NUTRITIONAL VALUE PER SERVING:**

Calories: 100 /kcal; Carbs: 11 g; Protein: 3 g; Fat: 2 g.

## PINEAPPLE COCONUT COOLER

**Prep time: 5 mins**

**Cooking time: 0 mins**

**Total time: 5 mins**

**Servings: 1**

**INGREDIENTS:**

- ½ cup coconut milk, unsweetened
- 1 tsp. vanilla extract
- ½ cup pineapple juice, unsweetened

½ cup ice

**DIRECTIONS:**

1. Blend the pineapple juice, coconut milk, vanilla, and ice on low speed for 15 to 30 seconds, until the mixture is smooth.
2. Pour into a glass and have a drink.

**NUTRITIONAL VALUE PER SERVING:**

Calories: 240 /kcal; Carbs: 15 g; Protein: 1 g; Fat: 19 g.

## BLUEBERRY VANILLA SMOOTHIE

**Prep time: 5 mins**

**Cooking time: 0 mins**

**Total time: 5 mins**

**Servings: 1**

**INGREDIENTS:**

- 1 tbsp. unsweetened vanilla protein powder
- ¾ cup nonfat plain Greek yogurt
- ¼ tsp. stevia
- ½ cup fresh or frozen blueberries

**DIRECTIONS:**

1. In a blender, combine the yogurt, protein powder, blueberries, and stevia.
2. Mix on low for about 2 minutes, or until everything is well mixed. Enjoy immediately.

**NUTRITIONAL VALUE PER SERVING:**

Calories: 185 /kcal; Carbs: 18 g; Protein: 29 g; Fat: 0 g.

## PEACHES AND CREAMY COCONUT SMOOTHIE

**Prep time:** 5 mins

**Cooking time:** 0 mins

**Total time:** 5 mins

**Servings:** 1

### INGREDIENTS:
- 2 tbsp. unsweetened vanilla protein powder
- ¾ cup nonfat plain Greek yogurt
- ¼ cup coconut cream
- ¾ cup frozen peaches
- ¼ tsp. stevia

### DIRECTIONS:
1. In a blender, combine the peaches, yogurt, protein powder, coconut cream, and stevia.
2. Mix on low for about 2 minutes, or until everything is well mixed. Enjoy immediately.

### NUTRITIONAL VALUE PER SERVING:
Calories: 162 /kcal; Carbs: 13 g; Protein: 19 g; Fat: 4 g.

## STRAWBERRY KIWI COOLER

**Prep time:** 5 mins

**Cooking time:** 0 mins

**Total time:** 5 mins

**Servings:** 2

### INGREDIENTS:
- ¾ cup almond milk
- 1 cup frozen strawberries
- ½ cup chopped kiwi, peeled
- 1 cup ice
- 1½ tsp. stevia

### DIRECTIONS:
- Blend the strawberries, almond milk, stevia, kiwi, and ice in a blender on medium speed for about 90 seconds or until the mixture is smooth.
- Pour into two glasses and have a drink.

### NUTRITIONAL VALUE PER SERVING:
Calories: 80 /kcal; Carbs: 17 g; Protein: 1 g; Fat: 1 g.

## PEANUT BUTTER AND BANANA POWER SMOOTHIE

**Prep time:** 5 mins

**Cooking time:** 0 mins

**Total time:** 5 mins

**Servings:** 1

### INGREDIENTS:
- 1 cup nonfat plain Greek yogurt
- ½ cup ice
- 1 small banana
- 1 tbsp. unsweetened vanilla protein powder
- ¼ cup dry peanut butter powder, unsweetened
- ¼ tsp. stevia

### DIRECTIONS:
1. In a blender, combine the banana, yogurt, peanut butter powder, ice, protein powder, and stevia.
2. Mix on low for about 2 minutes, or until everything is well mixed. Enjoy immediately.

### NUTRITIONAL VALUE PER SERVING:
Calories: 178 /kcal; Carbs: 20 g; Protein: 24 g; Fat: 2 g.

## LEMON MERINGUE PIE SMOOTHIE

**Prep time:** 5 mins

**Cooking time:** 0 mins

**Total time:** 5 mins

**Servings:** 1

### INGREDIENTS:
- ¾ cup nonfat plain Greek yogurt
- 3 tbsp. lemon juice
- ½ cup unsweetened almond milk
- 1 tsp. vanilla extract
- 1 tbsp. unsweetened vanilla protein powder
- ¼ tsp. stevia

### DIRECTIONS:
1. In a blender, combine the yogurt, lemon juice, almond milk, vanilla extract, protein powder and stevia.
2. Mix on low for about a minute, or until everything is well mixed. Enjoy immediately.

### NUTRITIONAL VALUE PER SERVING:
Calories: 126 /kcal; Carbs: 3 g; Protein: 11 g; Fat: 2 g.

## REFRESHING STRAWBERRY SMOOTHIE

**Prep time:** 5 mins

**Cooking time:** 0 mins

**Total time:** 5 mins

**Servings:** 1

### INGREDIENTS:
- 1 cup frozen strawberries
- 1 cup nonfat plain Greek yogurt
- ¼ tsp. stevia

### DIRECTIONS:

1. Add the strawberries, yogurt, and stevia in a blender.
2. Mix on low for about 2 minutes, or until everything is well mixed.
3. Serve and enjoy immediately

#### NUTRITIONAL VALUE PER SERVING:

Calories: 170 /kcal; Carbs: 20 g; Protein: 24 g; Fat: 0 g.

## CREAMY PUMPKIN PIE SMOOTHIE

Prep time: 5 mins

Cooking time: 0 mins

Total time: 5 mins

Servings: 1

### INGREDIENTS:

- 1 cup nonfat plain Greek yogurt
- 1 tbsp. unsweetened vanilla protein powder
- 2/3 cup unsweetened canned pumpkin
- ½ tsp. stevia
- 1¼ tsp. ground cinnamon

### DIRECTIONS:

1. In a blender, combine the pumpkin, yogurt, cinnamon, protein powder, and stevia.
2. Mix on low for about 2 minutes, or until everything is well mixed. Enjoy immediately.

#### NUTRITIONAL VALUE PER SERVING:

Calories: 242 /kcal; Carbs: 25 g; Protein: 36 g; Fat: 1 g.

## BLUE RASPBERRY COOLER

Prep time: 5 mins

Cooking time: 0 mins

Total time: 5 mins

Servings: 2

### INGREDIENTS:

- ¾ cup water
- ½ cup fresh raspberries
- 1 cup frozen blueberries
- 1 cup ice
- 2 tsp. pure maple syrup

### DIRECTIONS:

1. Blend the water, maple syrup, blueberries, raspberries, and ice in a blender on medium speed for 60 to 90 seconds, until the mixture is smooth.
2. Pour into two glasses and have a drink.

#### NUTRITIONAL VALUE PER SERVING:

Calories: 73 /kcal; Carbs: 17 g; Protein: 2 g; Fat: 0 g.

## NEAPOLITAN SMOOTHIE

Prep time: 5 mins

Cooking time: 0 mins

Total time: 5 mins

Servings: 1

### INGREDIENTS:

- 1 cup nonfat plain Greek yogurt
- ¼ cup unsweetened almond milk
- ½ cup frozen strawberries
- 1 tsp. vanilla extract
- ½ tbsp. unsweetened cocoa powder
- ¼ tsp. stevia

### DIRECTIONS:

1. Put the strawberries, yogurt, cocoa powder, almond milk, vanilla extract, and stevia, in a blender.
2. Mix on low for about 2 minutes, or until everything is well mixed. Enjoy immediately.

#### NUTRITIONAL VALUE PER SERVING:

Calories: 189 /kcal; Carbs: 20 g; Protein: 24 g; Fat: 2 g.

## HIGH PROTEIN MILK

Prep time: 5 mins

Cooking time: 0 mins

Total time: 5 mins

Servings: 4

### INGREDIENTS:

- 1 1/3 cups instant nonfat dry milk powder
- 4 cups low-fat milk

### DIRECTIONS:

1. Mix the milk powder and milk well in a large pitcher.
2. Serve and enjoy.

### NUTRITIONAL VALUE PER SERVING:

Calories: 127 /kcal; Carbs: 15 g; Protein: 11 g; Fat: 3 g.

## COOL CUCUMBER-LIME SMOOTHIE

Prep time: 5 mins

Cooking time: 0 mins

Total time: 5 mins

Servings: 1

### INGREDIENTS:

- 1 small cucumber, peeled
- ½ to ¾ cup water
- 10 frozen green grapes
- 1 tbsp. fresh lime juice
- ½ cup ice cubes
- 6 oz. plain fat-free Greek yogurt

### DIRECTIONS:

1. Blend or process the grapes, lime juice, cucumber, yogurt, and ice in a food processor or blender until smooth.
2. Add the water and process until smooth.

### NUTRITIONAL VALUE PER SERVING:

Calories: 220 /kcal; Carbs: 11 g; Protein: 22 g; Fat: 6 g.

## RASPBERRY REFRESHER

Prep time: 5 mins

Cooking time: 0 mins

Total time: 5 mins

Servings: 3

### INGREDIENTS:

- 1 cup almond milk, unsweetened
- 1 tbsp. + 1 tsp. pure maple syrup
- 2 tsp. alcohol-free vanilla extract
- 1 cup ice
- 1 cup fresh raspberries

### DIRECTIONS:

1. Blend the vanilla, almond milk, maple syrup, raspberries, and ice in a blender on medium speed for 60 to 90 seconds, until the mixture is smooth.
2. Pour into glasses and have a sip.

### NUTRITIONAL VALUE PER SERVING:

Calories: 65 /kcal; Carbs: 12 g; Protein: 1 g; Fat: 1 g.

## VANILLA BEAN PROTEIN SHAKE

Prep time: 5 mins

Cooking time: 0 mins

Total time: 5 mins

Servings: 2

### INGREDIENTS:

- 4 ice cubes
- 1 cup low-fat milk
- 1 tsp. vanilla extract
- ½ cup low-fat, vanilla Greek yogurt
- ¼ cup vanilla protein powder

### DIRECTIONS:

1. Mix the milk, vanilla, yogurt, protein powder, and ice together in a blender. Blend on high until the protein powder is mixed and the mixture is smooth.
2. Pour the shake into two glasses and serve.

### NUTRITIONAL VALUE PER SERVING:

Calories: 153 /kcal; Carbs: 14 g; Protein: 16 g; Fat: 2 g.

## BANANA CREAM PROTEIN SHAKE

Prep time: 5 mins

Cooking time: 0 mins

Total time: 5 mins

Servings: 2

### INGREDIENTS:

- 1½ cups low-fat milk
- 1 small banana
- ¼ cup low-fat, plain Greek yogurt
- ¼ cup vanilla protein powder
- 1 tsp. vanilla extract
- 1 tbsp. instant banana pudding mix, sugar-free

### DIRECTIONS:

1. Mix the milk, banana, yogurt, pudding mix and vanilla, protein powder all together in a blender. Blend on high until the powder is mixed and the mixture is smooth.
2. Pour the shake into two glasses and serve.

FULL LIQUID DIET

**NUTRITIONAL VALUE PER SERVING:**
Calories: 226 /kcal; Carbs: 30 g; Protein: 17 g; Fat: 4 g.

## LEMON PIE PROTEIN SHAKE

*Prep time:* 5 mins

*Cooking time:* 0 mins

*Total time:* 5 mins

*Servings:* 2

**INGREDIENTS:**

- 1 cup low-fat milk
- ½ medium banana
- ¼ cup vanilla protein powder
- ½ cup low-fat, plain Greek yogurt
- 2 tsp. freshly squeezed lemon juice
- 1 tsp. lemon zest
- ¼ tsp. vanilla extract
- ⅛ tsp. lemon extract
- 2 to 4 ice cubes

**DIRECTIONS:**

1. Put the milk, banana, yogurt, lemon juice, lemon zest, vanilla, lemon extract, protein powder, and ice in a blender and blend until smooth.
2. Pour the shake into two glasses and serve.

**NUTRITIONAL VALUE PER SERVING:**
Calories: 189 /kcal; Carbs: 21 g; Protein: 18 g; Fat: 4 g.

## ABC SMOOTHIE

*Prep time:* 5 mins

*Cooking time:* 0 mins

*Total time:* 5 mins

*Servings:* 2

**INGREDIENTS:**

- 1 red beet, chunks
- 1 apple, chunks
- 1 cup cold water
- 3 carrots, chunks
- 1 orange, juiced
- 1 2-inch piece fresh ginger, peeled

**DIRECTIONS:**

1. Put all of the ingredients in a powerful blender and blend for about 1-2 minutes, or until the mixture is smooth.
2. Pour the smoothie into tall glasses and drink it right away.

**NUTRITIONAL VALUE PER SERVING:**
Calories: 130/kcal; Carbs: 2 g; Protein: 7 g; Fat: 1 g.

## CAFÉ MOCHA PROTEIN BLEND

*Prep time:* 5 mins

*Cooking time:* 0 mins

*Total time:* 5 mins

*Servings:* 2

**INGREDIENTS:**

- ½ cup low-fat milk
- ¼ cup vanilla protein powder
- 1 cup decaffeinated coffee, brewed and chilled
- ½ tsp. vanilla extract
- 1 tsp. unsweetened cocoa powder
- 4 ice cubes

**DIRECTIONS:**

1. Put the milk, protein powder, coffee, vanilla, cocoa powder, and ice into a blender. On high, blend until smooth.
2. Pour the shake into two glasses and serve.

**NUTRITIONAL VALUE PER SERVING:**
Calories: 95 /kcal; Carbs: 9 g; Protein: 10 g; Fat: 2 g.

## GREEN MACHINE PROTEIN SHAKE

*Prep time:* 5 mins

*Cooking time:* 0 mins

*Total time:* 5 mins

*Servings:* 2

**INGREDIENTS:**

- ½ medium banana
- 1½ cups water
- 2 loose handfuls spinach
- ½ small Granny Smith apple
- ¼ avocado, peeled
- 1 small handful fresh parsley
- ¼ cup unflavored protein powder
- Juice of 1 lemon

**DIRECTIONS:**

1. Put the water, apple, banana, parsley, spinach, lemon juice, avocado, and protein powder in a blender and blend until smooth.
2. Pour the shake into two glasses and serve.

**NUTRITIONAL VALUE PER SERVING:**
Calories: 133 /kcal; Carbs: 16 g; Protein: 10 g; Fat: 5 g.

## CHOCOLATE RASPBERRY TRUFFLE PROTEIN SHAKE

Prep time: 5 mins

Cooking time: 0 mins

Total time: 5 mins

Servings: 2

### INGREDIENTS:

1. 1 cup low-fat milk
2. 2 tsp. unsweetened cocoa powder
3. ¼ cup chocolate protein powder
4. ½ cup frozen raspberries
5. 1 tsp. vanilla extract

### DIRECTIONS:

1. Put the milk, cocoa powder, protein powder, raspberries and vanilla in a blender and mix well. On high, blend until smooth.
2. Pour the shake into two glasses and serve.

### NUTRITIONAL VALUE PER SERVING:

Calories: 285 /kcal; Carbs: 33 g; Protein: 27 g; Fat: 5 g.

## BERRY BLISS PROTEIN SHAKE

Prep time: 5 mins

Cooking time: 0 mins

Total time: 5 mins

Servings: 2

Ingredients:

- 1 cup low-fat milk
- ¼ cup vanilla protein powder
- ½ cup low-fat, plain Greek yogurt
- 1 small handful spinach
- 1 cup frozen mixed berries
- 1 tbsp. freshly squeezed lemon juice
- 1 tsp. vanilla extract

### DIRECTIONS:

1. Mix the milk, protein powder, yogurt, spinach, berries, vanilla, and lemon juice all together in a blender. On high, blend until smooth.
2. Pour the shake into two glasses and serve.

### NUTRITIONAL VALUE PER SERVING:

Calories: 206 /kcal; Carbs: 24 g; Protein: 18 g; Fat: 4 g.

## PINA COLADA PROTEIN SHAKE

Prep time: 5 mins

Cooking time: 0 mins

Total time: 5 mins

Servings: 2

Ingredients:

- 1 cup frozen pineapple chunks
- 1½ cups unsweetened coconut milk
- 1 tsp. coconut extract
- ½ cup low-fat cottage cheese
- 4 or 5 ice cubes
- ¼ cup vanilla protein powder

### DIRECTIONS:

1. Put the cottage cheese, coconut milk, coconut extract, pineapple, protein powder, and ice in a blender and mix well. On high, blend until smooth.
2. Pour the shake into two glasses and serve.

### NUTRITIONAL VALUE PER SERVING:

Calories: 195 /kcal; Carbs: 18 g; Protein: 14 g; Fat: 5 g.

## PUMPKIN NUT SMOOTHIE

Prep time: 5 mins

Cooking time: 0 mins

Total time: 5 mins

Servings: 2

### INGREDIENTS:

- 1 cup soy milk
- 2 tbsp. unsweetened creamy peanut butter
- 1 cup unsweetened pumpkin purée
- ¼ cup peeled and chopped apple

### DIRECTIONS:

1. Blend the peanut butter, soy milk, pumpkin purée, and apple for 30 to 60 seconds on

FULL LIQUID DIET

medium speed in a blender.
2. Pour into two glasses and have a drink.

**NUTRITIONAL VALUE PER SERVING:**
Calories: 150 /kcal; Carbs: 13 g; Protein: 6 g; Fat: 6 g.

## VERY BERRY SMOOTHIE

**Prep time:** 5 mins

**Cooking time:** 0 mins

**Total time:** 5 mins

**Servings:** 1

**INGREDIENTS:**

- ¾ cup raspberries
- 1 orange, peeled and sectioned
- ¾ cup almond milk
- ¾ cup blueberries
- 2 tbsp. unflavored protein powder

**DIRECTIONS:**

1. Blend or process all the ingredients together in a blender or food processor.
2. Blend until you get the right texture.

**NUTRITIONAL VALUE PER SERVING:**
Calories: 275 /kcal; Carbs: 10 g; Protein: 21 g; Fat: 6 g.

## MATCHA MANGO SMOOTHIE

**Prep time:** 5 mins

**Cooking time:** 0 mins

**Total time:** 5 mins

**Servings:** 2

**INGREDIENTS:**

- 2 cups cubed mango
- 2 tsp. turmeric powder
- 2 tbsp. matcha powder
- 2 tbsp. honey
- 2 cups almond milk
- 1 cup crushed ice

**DIRECTIONS:**

1. Combine all the ingredients in a blender. Mix until it's smooth.
2. Serve right away.

**NUTRITIONAL VALUE PER SERVING:**
Calories: 285 /kcal; Carbs: 60 g; Protein: 4 g; Fat: 3 g

PUREE DIET

## ITALIAN CHICKEN PUREE

**Prep time:** 5 mins

**Cooking time:** 0 mins

**Total time:** 5 mins

**Servings:** 1

### INGREDIENTS:

- 1 tsp. Italian seasoning
- ¼ cup canned chicken
- 1/8 tsp. salt
- 1½ tbsp. tomato sauce
- 1/8 tsp. pepper

### DIRECTIONS:

1. Put all of the ingredients into a small blender and mix them until they are well combined and the mixture looks soft.
2. Put in a bowl and heat for 30 seconds and serve.

### NUTRITIONAL VALUE PER SERVING:

Calories: 104 /kcal; Carbs: 3 g; Protein: 4 g; Fat: 13 g.

## ENCHILADA BEAN PUREE

**Prep time:** 5 mins

**Cooking time:** 0 mins

**Total time:** 5 mins

**Servings:** 1

### INGREDIENTS:

- ½ cup black beans, rinsed
- 2 tbsp. roasted red pepper, finely chopped
- 1½ tbsp. red enchilada sauce, divided
- 1 tbsp. unflavored protein powder
- 2 tbsp. chicken broth

### DIRECTIONS:

1. In a small sauce pan, heat the black beans, 2 tablespoons of enchilada sauce, and the red pepper over medium heat.
2. Add broth.
3. Blend the ingredients well with a hand blender. OR put everything in a blender and mix it well.
4. Move the pureed beans to a bowl. Let it cool for a minute, then add protein powder and 1/2 tsp more enchilada sauce. Serve.

### NUTRITIONAL VALUE PER SERVING:

Calories: 187 /kcal; Carbs: 25 g; Protein: 19 g; Fat: 1 g.

## ROSEMARY CHICKEN AND BLUE CHEESE PUREE

**Prep time:** 3 mins

**Cooking time:** 15 mins

**Total time:** 18 mins

**Servings:** 8

### INGREDIENTS:

- 2 tbsp. raw sunflower seeds
- 1 clove garlic, minced
- 8 oz. lean ground chicken
- 1 cup chickpeas, drained and rinsed
- 1 oz. reduced fat blue cheese, crumbled
- 1 tsp. apple cider vinegar
- 2 tbsp. fresh rosemary, chopped, chopped
- 2 tbsp. low fat plain Greek yogurt

### DIRECTIONS:

1. In a skillet, toast sunflower seeds over medium heat for two to three minutes, stirring them every so often, until they are golden brown. Take out and put away.
2. Over medium-high heat, heat 2 tablespoons of water in the same pan. Add the garlic and cook for 1 minute, stirring often, until the smell is nice. Add chicken. Cook for 6–8 minutes, stirring to break up the meat, until it is done. Add 1 tablespoon of water at a time as the water evaporates to keep the pan from dehydrating.
3. Stir the chicken while you add the rosemary and chickpeas. Cook for 2 to 3 minutes, until hot.
4. Greek yogurt, Blue cheese, and apple cider vinegar should be mixed together in a small bowl.
5. Take the chicken off the heat. Mix in the blue cheese cream sauce as you stir. Add toasted sunflower seeds on top.
6. Mix the ingredients in a food processor until they are smooth.

### NUTRITIONAL VALUE PER SERVING:

Calories: 104 /kcal; Carbs: 6 g; Protein: 9 g; Fat: 4 g.

## MEDITERRANEAN CHICKEN PUREE

**Prep time:** 2 mins

**Cooking time:** 4 mins

**Total time:** 6 mins

**Servings:** 8

### INGREDIENTS:

- 12 oz. lean ground chicken
- 2 tsp. za'atarl
- 1 tbsp. tahini
- 1 tbsp. parsley, chopped
- ¼ cup chickpeas, drained and rinsed

### DIRECTIONS:

1. Over medium-high heat, warm up 2 tablespoons of water in a pan. Add the chicken and cook for another 5–7 minutes, breaking it up as you stir, until it's done. If the pan starts to dry out, add 1 tablespoon of water at a time.
2. Whisk together tahini, 3 tablespoons of water, and za'atar in a small bowl.
3. To the chicken, add the sauce.
4. At the same time that the sauce and chickpeas were added to the chicken,
5. Take it off the heat and add the parsley.
6. Mixture should be put in a food processor and run until smooth.

### NUTRITIONAL VALUE PER SERVING:
Calories: 89 /kcal; Carbs: 2 g; Protein: 4 g; Fat: 9 g.

## GINGER GARLIC TOFU PUREE

**Prep time:** 2 mins

**Cooking time:** 4 mins

**Total time:** 6 mins

**Servings:** 8

### INGREDIENTS:

- 16 oz. firm tofu, cubed
- 1 tbsp. coconut aminos
- 1 clove garlic, minced
- 1 tbsp. ginger, minced

### DIRECTIONS:

1. In a skillet on medium-high heat, mix ginger, coconut aminos, garlic, and 1/4 cup water. Get it to boil.
2. Add the tofu and heat it for 3–4 minutes, stirring every so often. If the pan starts to dry out, add 1 tablespoon of water at a time.
3. Mixture should be put in a food processor and run until smooth.

### NUTRITIONAL VALUE PER SERVING:
Calories: 61 /kcal; Carbs: 3 g; Protein: 7 g; Fat: 3 g.

## MEXICAN EGG PUREE

**Prep time:** 13 mins

**Cooking time:** 13 mins

**Total time:** 26 mins

**Servings:** 8

### INGREDIENTS:

- ½ lb. loose turkey sausage
- 1 tbsp. full fat plain Greek yogurt
- 6 Eggs
- ½ tsp. Paprika
- 1 tsp. Cumin
- 2 tbsp. Cilantro, chopped
- ¼ cup black beans, drained and rinsed

### DIRECTIONS:

1. Mix eggs, cumin, Greek yogurt, and paprika together really well in a bowl. Set aside.
2. Warm turkey sausage in a sauté pan over medium heat. Stirring to break up the meat, cook for 5–6 minutes, or until the meat is cooked through.
3. Turn the heat down to medium-low. Add the egg mixture and cook for 2 to 3 minutes, moving the rubber spatula around all the time.
4. Add the black beans and heat them for 1 minute.
5. Add the cilantro and 2 tablespoons of water to a food processor or blender. Blend until it's smooth.

### NUTRITIONAL VALUE PER SERVING:
Calories: 128 /kcal; Carbs: 3 g; Protein: 12 g; Fat: 7 g.

### INGREDIENTS:

## CHIMICHURRI CHICKEN PUREE

**Prep time:** 13 mins

**Cooking time:** 13 mins

**Total time:** 26 mins

**Servings:** 5

### INGREDIENTS:

- ½ lb. Lean ground chicken
- ¼ tsp. Dried oregano
- ½ tsp. Paprika
- 2 tbsp. Cilantro
- ¼ cup Parsley
- 2 tsp. Apple cider vinegar
- 2 Cloves garlic, peeled

### DIRECTIONS:

1. Heat 2 tablespoons of water in a sauté pan over medium-high heat. Add chicken, oregano and paprika. Cook for 6–8 minutes, stirring to break up the chicken, until it is done. Add 1 tablespoon of water at a time as the water evaporates to keep the pan from dehydrating.
2. Mix the apple cider vinegar, parsley, garlic, cilantro, and 3 tablespoons of water in a blender or food processor. Pulse until the food is finely chopped.
3. Mix the chimichurri into the pan.
4. Bring it back to the food processor and run it until its smooth.

### NUTRITIONAL VALUE PER SERVING:
Calories: 47 /kcal; Carbs: 0.5 g; Protein: 6 g; Fat: 2 g.

## CHICKEN AND BLACK BEAN MOLE PUREE

**Prep time:** 12 mins

**Cooking time:** 12 mins

**Total time:** 24 mins

**Servings:** 8

### INGREDIENTS:

- 1 clove garlic, Minced
- 1 cup black beans, rinsed and drained
- ½ lb. lean ground chicken
- ¼ cup low sodium chicken broth
- ½ tbsp. raw cacao powder
- 3 tbsp. raw almonds, soaked
- ¼ tsp. dried oregano
- ½ tsp. paprika
- ¼ tsp. coriander
- ¼ tsp. cumin
- 2 tbsp. cilantro, chopped
- ⅛ tsp. cinnamon
- ¼ tsp. garlic powder

### DIRECTIONS:

1. Heat 2 tablespoons of water in a sauté pan over medium-high heat. Add the garlic and cook for 1 minute, stirring often.
2. Add the chicken and stir it around for 6–8 minutes, until it is cooked all the way through. Add 1 tablespoon of water at a time as the water evaporates to keep the pan from dehydrating.
3. Mix 2 tablespoons of water, almonds that have been soaked, paprika, chicken broth, cacao, oregano, coriander, cumin, garlic powder, and cinnamon in a blender or food processor. Mix until it's smooth.
4. Add the black beans and sauce to the chicken and bring to a simmer. Put the mixture and cilantro in a blender or food processor and pulse until it is smooth.

### NUTRITIONAL VALUE PER SERVING:
Calories: 109 /kcal; Carbs: 9 g; Protein: 9 g; Fat: 4 g.

## CARIBBEAN PORK PUREE

**Prep time:** 7 mins

**Cooking time:** 7 mins

**Total time:** 14 mins

**Servings:** 8

### INGREDIENTS:

- 1 tsp. garlic powder
- ½ tsp. dried parsley
- 1 tsp. dried thyme
- ¼ tsp. allspice
- ½ tsp. paprika
- 1 tbsp. apple cider vinegar
- ¾ lb. lean ground pork
- ¼ cup cilantro, chopped
- ¼ cup black beans

### DIRECTIONS:

1. In a large skillet, heat the thyme, garlic powder, paprika, parsley, and all spice over medium heat for two to three minutes, until the combination is fragrant.
2. Raise the heat to medium-high and add 2 tablespoons of water and the pork. Cook for 5–7 minutes, breaking up the meat as you stir, until it's done. If the pan starts to dry out, add 1 tsp of water.
3. Add black beans and apple cider vinegar. Cook beans for 1–2 minutes to warm them up. Take it off the heat and add the cilantro.
4. Put the mixture in a food processor and blend it until it is smooth.

### NUTRITIONAL VALUE PER SERVING:
Calories: 65 /kcal; Carbs: 3 g; Protein: 10 g; Fat: 2 g.

## MOROCCAN FISH PUREE

**Prep time:** 10 mins

**Cooking time:** 3 mins

**Total time:** 13 mins

**Servings:** 8

### INGREDIENTS:

- 1 tsp. paprika
- ¼ tsp. cinnamon
- 1 tsp. cumin
- 1 tsp. apple cider vinegar
- ¼ tsp. turmeric
- 8 oz. tilapia fillets
- 1 clove garlic, minced
- 1 cup chickpeas, drained and rinsed
- 1/3 cup light coconut milk
- 2 tbsp. cilantro, chopped

### DIRECTIONS:

1. Over medium heat, toast cumin, paprika, turmeric and cinnamon in a large skillet. Toast until fragrant.
2. Add garlic, 2 tablespoons of water, and apple cider vinegar. Cook for 1 to 2 minutes, or until the garlic smells good.
3. Turn the heat up to high. Fish, chickpeas and coconut milk should be added at this point. Bring to a boil, then turn the heat down to a simmer and cook for 4–6 minutes, or until the fish is done. Cooking times can change based on how thick the fish is. Fish should be clear and have scales.
4. Take it off the heat and add the cilantro.
5. Mix the ingredients in a food processor until they are smooth.

### NUTRITIONAL VALUE PER SERVING:

Calories: 66 /kcal; Carbs: 7 g; Protein: 8 g; Fat: 2 g.

## CREAMY SHRIMP SCAMPI PUREE

**Prep time:** 8 mins

**Cooking time:** 5 mins

**Total time:** 13 mins

**Servings:** 8

### INGREDIENTS:

- 2 tbsp. olive oil
- 1 lb. shrimp
- 4 cloves garlic, minced
- ¼ cup parsley, chopped
- 2 tbsp. low fat plain Greek yogurt

### DIRECTIONS:

1. Olive oil should be heated over medium-high heat in a large sauté pan.
2. Dry the shrimp and put them in a hot pan. Cook for about 3 minutes, turning once, until just pink. Add the garlic and cook for one more minute, until it smells good
3. Move to a bowl that can handle heat. Mix in the parsley and Greek yogurt to coat the shrimps.
4. Add the mixture in a food processor until they are smooth.

### NUTRITIONAL VALUE PER SERVING:

Calories: 91 /kcal; Carbs: 1 g; Protein: 14 g; Fat: 4 g.

## RICOTTA AND WHITE BEAN PUREE

**Prep time:** 2 mins

**Cooking time:** 4 mins

**Total time:** 6 mins

**Servings:** 8

### INGREDIENTS:

- ¾ cup fat free ricotta
- 16 Oz. cannellini beans with liquid
- 2 tbsp. parsley, chopped
- 1 clove garlic, minced

### DIRECTIONS:

1. In a small pot over medium-high heat, mix garlic with beans and their liquid. Bring to a boil, then turn down the heat and let it cook for 3–4 minutes, or until the garlic smells good.
2. Put the mixture of beans in a bowl. Stir in the ricotta and parsley to mix them together.
3. Mix the ingredients in a food processor until they are smooth.

### NUTRITIONAL VALUE PER SERVING:

Calories: 60 /kcal; Carbs: 9.5 g; Protein: 5 g; Fat: 0.2 g.

## TURKEY TACOS WITH BEANS PUREE

**Prep time:** 10 mins

**Cooking time:** 21 mins

**Total time:** 31 mins

**Servings:** 8

### INGREDIENTS:

- 1 clove garlic, minced
- ¼ cup low sodium chicken broth
- 1 cup pinto beans, rinsed and drained
- ¼ tsp. mild chili powder
- 2 tbsp. cilantro, chopped
- ¼ tsp. garlic powder
- ¼ tsp. cumin
- ¼ tsp. paprika
- ½ lb. lean ground turkey

### DIRECTIONS:

1. Heat 2 tablespoons of water in a sauté pan over medium heat. Add garlic and stir fry 1 minute, until fragrant. Bring to a boil the chicken broth

and pinto beans you just added. Turn the heat down to medium-low and let it cook for 5 minutes.
2. You can mash the beans with the back of a fork or potato masher. Continue cooking for further 3-4 minutes, until liquid evaporates. Take it off the heat and add two tablespoons of chopped cilantro.
3. For the turkey, heat garlic powder, chili powder, cumin and paprika in a sauté pan. Toast 1 minute.
4. Add 2 tablespoons of water and turkey. Cook for 6–8 minutes, stirring to break up the meat, until it is done. Add 1 tablespoon of water at a time as the water evaporates to keep the pan from dehydrating.
5. In a blender or food processor, pulse the beans and turkey until they are smooth.

#### NUTRITIONAL VALUE PER SERVING:
Calories: 68 /kcal; Carbs: 5 g; Protein: 10 g; Fat: 1 g.

## SESAME TUNA SALAD PUREE

*Prep time:* 5 mins

*Cooking time:* 0 mins

*Total time:* 5 mins

*Servings:* 4

#### INGREDIENTS:
- 1 tbsp. coconut aminos
- 1 tsp. apple cider vinegar
- 1 tbsp. tahini
- 15 oz. chunk light tuna in water
- 2 tbsp. full fat plain greek yogurt
- 2 tbsp. parsley, chopped
- 2 tbsp. sesame seeds

#### DIRECTIONS:
1. Whisk the tahini, coconut aminos, Greek yogurt and apple cider vinegar, together in a bowl until the mixture is smooth.
2. Stir the tuna and sesame seeds together to mix them together and break up the tuna. Add the parsley and mix it in.
3. Mix the ingredients in a food processor until they are smooth.

#### NUTRITIONAL VALUE PER SERVING:
Calories: 78 /kcal; Carbs: 1 g; Protein: 11 g; Fat: 3 g.

## TURKEY CHILI PUREE

*Prep time:* 15 mins

*Cooking time:* 10 mins

*Total time:* 25 mins

*Servings:* 6

#### INGREDIENTS:
- 2 tbsp. olive oil
- 1 onion, chopped
- 1½ tbsp. chili powder
- 1 lb. lean ground turkey
- 28 oz. crushed tomato
- 1½ tsp. cumin
- 1 can kidney beans, rinsed and drained
- 1 cup chicken broth
- Salt and pepper to taste

#### DIRECTIONS:
1. On the Instant Pot's sauté setting, heat the oil and onion. Cook until softened.
2. Add turkey and spices. Saute the turkey until it turns brown.
3. Add broth and crushed tomatoes and stir. Close the lid and cook for 10 minutes on high.
4. Once done, open the valve. Stir in kidney beans and give it a god mix.
5. In a blender or food processor, pulse the beans and turkey until they are smooth.

#### NUTRITIONAL VALUE PER SERVING:
Calories: 111 /kcal; Carbs: 4 g; Protein: 3 g; Fat: 2 g.

## COCONUT MILK FLAN

*Prep time:* 5 mins + chilling time

*Cooking time:* 5 mins

*Total time:* 10 mins + chilling time

*Servings:* 1

#### INGREDIENTS:
- ½ cup light unsweetened coconut milk
- 1 tbsp. plain gelatin powder
- 1 tsp. stevia
- 2 tsp. vanilla extract

#### DIRECTIONS:
1. Heat the coconut milk for 1 to 2 minutes in a small saucepan. Then, add the stevia and vanilla extract and stir until they are dissolved.
2. Sprinkle the gelatin in and keep stirring so that the entire gelatin dissolves. Take off the heat.
3. Put the mixture in a blender and blend it for about 30 seconds or until it becomes foamy. Pour into a small jar or cup.
4. Let the dessert firm up for about an hour in the refrigerator.
5. Serve, and enjoy.

**NUTRITIONAL VALUE PER SERVING:**

Calories: 130 /kcal; Carbs: 5 g; Protein: 6 g; Fat: 7 g.

## HERBY TEMPEH PUREE

_Prep time: 10 mins_

_Cooking time: 20 mins_

_Total time: 30 mins_

_Servings: 2_

**INGREDIENTS:**

- 2 large garlic cloves, skins on
- 4 kale leaves, stems removed
- 250g plain tempeh, crumbled
- 1/2 cup fresh basil leaves
- 1/2 cup Italian parsley
- Juice and zest of one lemon
- 1/2 cup unsalted cashew nuts
- 2 tbsp. extra virgin olive oil
- 2 tbsp. nutritional yeast
- Salt and pepper, to taste
- 1/2 cup water, plus extra as needed

**DIRECTIONS:**

1. Preheat the oven to 350°F-180°C.
2. Put the garlic on a baking sheet and roast it for 20 minutes.
3. While the garlic cloves are roasting, put the rest of the ingredients in a food processor and pulse until smooth, adding a drop or two of water if needed to help the mixture come together.
4. Once the garlic cloves have been roasted, take off the skins and put them in the food processor and combine well.
5. Add salt and pepper to taste and serve.

**NUTRITIONAL VALUE PER SERVING:**

Calories: 110 /kcal; Carbs: 11 g; Protein: 20 g; Fat: 5 g.

## SPICY TOFU PUREE

_Prep time: 5 mins_

_Cooking time: 15 mins_

_Total time: 20 mins_

_Servings: 4_

**INGREDIENTS:**

- 12 oz. block steamed silken tofu
- 1 tbsp. olive oil
- ½ tsp. chili powder
- ½ tsp. garlic powder
- ¼ tsp. garlic powder
- ¼ tsp. turmeric
- ½ tsp. salt

**DIRECTIONS:**

1. Add a few inches of water to a boil in a pot. Put tofu in a basket for steaming.
2. Cover and steam for about 15 minutes, until the food is done.
3. Put steamed tofu and spices in a blender.
4. Add water and olive oil until the mixture is the consistency you want.

**NUTRITIONAL VALUE PER SERVING:**

Calories: 80 /kcal; Carbs: 7 g; Protein: 12 g; Fat: 8 g.

## SPICY CAULIFLOWER PUREE

_Prep time: 10 mins_

_Cooking time: 20 mins_

_Total time: 30 mins_

_Servings: 2_

**INGREDIENTS:**

- 2 cups broccoli, chopped
- 1 tbsp. olive oil
- 2 cups cauliflower, chopped
- 1 tsp. dry mint, ground
- ½ cup skim milk
- ½ tsp. Italian seasoning
- 1 tbsp. fresh parsley, chopped
- ½ tsp. salt
- ¼ tsp. ground cumin

**DIRECTIONS:**

1. Add water in a deep pot and add cauliflower in it with a pinch of salt. Cook the cauliflower for 15 minutes and then drain.
2. In a food processor, put cooked cauliflower, milk, broccoli, Italian seasoning, parsley, salt, mint, and cumin.
3. Blend slowly, adding olive oil a little at a time, until everything is pureed.

**NUTRITIONAL VALUE PER SERVING:**

Calories: 75 /kcal; Carbs: 5 g; Protein: 10 g; Fat: 3 g.

## CAULIFLOWER AND BEEF PUREE

_Prep time: 10 mins_

_Cooking time: 30 mins_

_Total time: 40 mins_

_Servings: 4_

**INGREDIENTS:**

- 8 oz. lean ground beef
- ½ cup cauliflower, chopped
- ¾ cup chicken broth
- 1 tbsp. fresh thyme, chopped
- 1 tbsp. fresh parsley, chopped
- Salt to taste
- 1 clove garlic, minced
- Cooking spray

**DIRECTIONS:**

1. Blanch cauliflower in a medium pot of boiling water for about 10 to 15 minutes, or until it is soft. Set aside.
2. Spray cooking spray on a pan. Add the ground beef to a pan with a medium heat and brown it.
3. Once the meat is browned, add herbs and half of the chicken broth. Cover and cook for 20 minutes.
4. Put the cauliflower, cooked beef, and broth in a blender.
5. Blend until smooth, adding more chicken broth until the consistency is right.
6. Strain the puree to get rid of any big chunks.

### NUTRITIONAL VALUE PER SERVING:

Calories: 120 /kcal; Carbs: 12 g; Protein: 22 g; Fat: 10 g.

## ITALIAN STYLE CHICKEN PUREE

**Prep time: 10 mins**

**Cooking time: 0 mins**

**Total time: 10 mins**

**Servings: 4**

### INGREDIENTS:

- 8 oz. boiled chicken breast, shredded
- 1 cup chicken broth
- ½ tsp. garlic powder
- ¼ cup parmesan cheese, grated
- 1 clove garlic
- 1 tbsp. oregano
- Salt to taste
- 1 tbsp. fresh parsley, chopped

### DIRECTIONS:

1. Put the half of the chicken broth, cooked chicken, and the rest of the ingredients in a blender.
2. Blend until smooth, adding more broth until you get the right consistency.
3. Strain the puree to get rid of any big chunks. Serve hot.

### NUTRITIONAL VALUE PER SERVING:

Calories: 76 /kcal; Carbs: 5 g; Protein: 18 g; Fat: 5 g.

## HEARTY BEEF AND POTATO PUREE

**Prep time: 10 mins**

**Cooking time: 25 mins**

**Total time: 35 mins**

**Servings: 6**

### INGREDIENTS:

- 8 oz. lean ground beef
- ¼ cup potatoes, chopped
- ¼ cup carrot, chopped
- 2 tbsp. cheddar cheese, shredded
- ¼ cup canned pumpkin puree
- 1 tsp. tomato paste
- 1 cup chicken broth
- Salt to taste
- 1 tbsp. parsley, chopped
- 1 clove garlic
- Cooking spray

### DIRECTIONS:

1. Grease a pot using cooking spray. Carrots and potatoes should be cooked in a pan for about 5 minutes over medium heat.
2. Add the ground beef to the pot and sauté. Once the meat is browned, add the garlic, parsley, tomato paste, pumpkin puree, salt, and half of the chicken broth.
3. Cover and cook for 20 minutes. Mix in the cheese near the end.
4. Put everything into a blender. Blend until smooth, adding the rest of the chicken broth to get the right texture.
5. Strain the puree to get rid of any big chunks. Serve hot.

### NUTRITIONAL VALUE PER SERVING:

Calories: 120 /kcal; Carbs: 8 g; Protein: 15 g; Fat: 6 g.

## CHICKEN AND PUMPKIN PUREE

**Prep time: 10 mins**

**Cooking time: 0 mins**

**Total time: 10 mins**

**Servings: 4**

### INGREDIENTS:

- 8 oz. boiled chicken breast, shredded
- 1 cup skim milk
- ¼ cup cheddar cheese, shredded
- ½ tsp. Dijon mustard
- ½ cup canned pumpkin puree
- Salt to taste
- 1 tbsp. fresh chives, chopped

### DIRECTIONS:

1. Cooked chicken, skim milk, pumpkin puree, mustard, cheese, salt, chives and half of the chicken broth should be put into a blender.
2. Blend until smooth, adding more broth until you get the right consistency.
3. Strain the puree to get rid of any big chunks. Serve hot.

### NUTRITIONAL VALUE PER SERVING:

Calories: 79 /kcal; Carbs: 4 g; Protein: 21 g; Fat: 4 g.

## ITALIAN TOMATO AND BEEF PUREE

**Prep time:** 10 mins

**Cooking time:** 20 mins

**Total time:** 30 mins

**Servings:** 6

### INGREDIENTS:

- 12 oz. lean ground beef
- 1 cup tomatoes, crushed
- ½ cup chicken broth
- 1 clove garlic
- 2 tbsp. parmesan cheese
- 1 tsp. oregano
- 1 bay leaf
- ¼ cup carrot, chopped
- 1 tbsp. fresh thyme, chopped
- Salt to taste
- ¼ cup onion, chopped
- Cooking spray

### DIRECTIONS:

1. Grease a pot using a cooking spray. Cook the carrots and onion over medium heat until fragrant.
2. Put the ground beef in the pot and cook it until it is brown. Add the oregano, tomatoes, thyme, bay leaf, garlic, salt, and half of the chicken broth once the meat has been browned.
3. Cover and cook for 20 minutes. Add the parmesan near the end.
4. Put everything into a blender. Blend until smooth, adding the rest of the chicken broth to get the right texture.
5. Strain the puree to get rid of any big chunks. Serve hot.

### NUTRITIONAL VALUE PER SERVING:

Calories: 121 /kcal; Carbs: 7 g; Protein: 11 g; Fat: 6 g.

## THAI STYLE CHICKEN BLENDED PUREE

**Prep time:** 10 mins

**Cooking time:** 0 mins

**Total time:** 10 mins

**Servings:** 4

### INGREDIENTS:

- 8 oz. boiled chicken breast, shredded
- 1 clove garlic
- 1 cup chicken broth
- 1 tbsp. green onion, chopped
- 2 tbsp. fresh ginger, grated
- 1 tbsp. soy sauce
- ½ tsp. vinegar
- ¼ cup powdered peanut butter

### DIRECTIONS:

1. Cooked chicken, soy sauce, garlic, ginger powder, green onion, vinegar, and half of the chicken broth should be put in a blender.
2. Blend until smooth, adding more broth until you get the right consistency.
3. Strain the puree to get rid of any big chunks. Serve warm.

### NUTRITIONAL VALUE PER SERVING:

Calories: 74 /kcal; Carbs: 3 g; Protein: 11 g; Fat: 2 g.

## LEMON SALMON PUREE

**Prep time:** 10 mins

**Cooking time:** 0 mins

**Total time:** 10 mins

**Servings:** 2

### INGREDIENTS:

- 6 oz. canned pink salmon
- ½ tsp. lemon juice
- 2 tbsp. Greek yogurt
- 2 tbsp. shallots, chopped
- salt to taste
- ½ tbsp. fresh chives, chopped
- 1 tbsp. olive oil

### DIRECTIONS:

1. Put yogurt, salmon, chives, lemon juice, shallots, olive oil and salt in a blender.
2. Blend until smooth. If needed, add water to get the consistency you want.
3. Strain the puree to get rid of any big chunks. Serve hot or at room temperature, depending on what you like.

### NUTRITIONAL VALUE PER SERVING:

Calories: 60 /kcal; Carbs: 4 g; Protein: 21 g; Fat: 3 g.

## PUREED SALMON WITH DILL AND CREAM CHEESE

**Prep time:** 5 mins

**Cooking time:** 0 mins

**Total time:** 5 mins

**Servings:** 1

### INGREDIENTS:

- 1 smoked salmon fillet
- 1 tbsp. roughly chopped dill
- Juice and zest of 1 lemon
- 2 tbsp. reduced fat cream cheese

### DIRECTIONS:

1. Blend all of the ingredients in a mini food processor until you get a smooth puree.

### NUTRITIONAL VALUE PER SERVING:

Calories: 89 /kcal; Carbs: 8 g; Protein: 23 g; Fat: 5 g.

## LEMONY MUSTARD PUREE

**Prep time: 10 mins**

**Cooking time: 0 mins**

**Total time: 10 mins**

**Servings: 4**

### INGREDIENTS:

- 8 oz. boiled chicken breast, shredded
- 2 tbsp. Dijon mustard
- ¾ cup chicken broth
- 1 tsp. brown sugar
- 2 tbsp. lemon juice
- salt to taste

### DIRECTIONS:

1. Put half of the chicken broth, lemon juice, mustard, salt, brown sugar, and cooked chicken in a blender.
2. Blend until smooth, adding more broth until you get the right consistency.
3. Strain the puree to get rid of any big chunks. Serve hot.

### NUTRITIONAL VALUE PER SERVING:

Calories: 76 /kcal; Carbs: 11 g; Protein: 22 g; Fat: 5 g.

## WORCESTERSHIRE AND CREAM CHICKEN PUREE

**Prep time: 10 mins**

**Cooking time: 0 mins**

**Total time: 10 mins**

**Servings: 4**

### INGREDIENTS:

- 8 oz. boiled chicken breast, shredded
- 1 tbsp. Worcestershire sauce
- 1 cup chicken broth
- ½ cup skim milk
- ½ cup fat-free half half cream
- salt to taste

### DIRECTIONS:

1. Cooked chicken, Worcestershire sauce, half-and-half, salt, milk, and half of the chicken broth should all be put in a blender.
2. Blend until smooth, adding more broth until you get the right consistency.
3. Strain the puree to get rid of any big chunks. Serve warm.

### NUTRITIONAL VALUE PER SERVING:

Calories: 69 /kcal; Carbs: 7 g; Protein: 12 g; Fat: 5 g.

## INDIAN CURRY CHICKEN PUREE

**Prep time: 10 mins**

**Cooking time: 0 mins**

**Total time: 10 mins**

**Servings: 4**

### INGREDIENTS:

- 8 oz. boiled chicken breast, shredded
- 2 tbsp. Greek yogurt
- ½ cup skim milk
- 1 cup chicken broth
- ½ tbsp. curry powder
- ½ cup tomatoes, chopped
- Salt to taste
- 1 clove garlic

### DIRECTIONS:

1. In a blender or food processor, add yogurt, cooked chicken, salt, tomatoes, milk, curry powder and half of the chicken broth.
2. Blend until smooth, adding more broth until you get the right consistency.
3. Strain the puree to get rid of any big chunks.

### NUTRITIONAL VALUE PER SERVING:

Calories: 75 /kcal; Carbs: 7 g; Protein: 12 g; Fat: 4 g.

## PARMESAN TILAPIA PUREE

**Prep time: 10 mins**

**Cooking time: 0 mins**

**Total time: 10 mins**

**Servings: 4**

### INGREDIENTS:

- 8 oz. steamed tilapia fillet, chopped
- 1 tbsp. pesto
- ¾ cup chicken broth
- 2 tbsp. parmesan cheese
- 1 tsp. lemon juice
- Salt and pepper, to taste
- ¼ cup chopped tomatoes

### DIRECTIONS:

1. Put steamed tilapia, pesto, tomatoes, and Parmesan cheese, half of the chicken broth, salt, lemon juice, and pepper in a blender or food processor.
2. Blend until smooth, adding more broth until you get the right consistency.
3. Strain the puree to get rid of any big chunks. Serve warm.

### NUTRITIONAL VALUE PER SERVING:

Calories: 67 /kcal; Carbs: 6 g; Protein: 12 g; Fat: 6 g.

## CRAB SHALLOT PUREE

**Prep time: 10 mins**

**Cooking time: 5 mins**

**Total time: 15 mins**

**Servings: 4**

### INGREDIENTS:

- 6 oz. can crab meat
- 2 tbsp. mayonnaise
- 1 cup chicken broth
- 2 tbsp. shallots, chopped
- ½ tsp. Old Bay seasoning

### DIRECTIONS:

1. Heat the chicken broth in a pot.
2. Put mayonnaise, crab meat, spices, shallots, and half of the chicken broth in a blender.
3. Blend until smooth, adding more broth until you get the right consistency.
4. Strain the puree to get rid of any big chunks. Serve warm.

### NUTRITIONAL VALUE PER SERVING:

Calories: 78 /kcal; Carbs: 6 g; Protein: 17 g; Fat: 6 g.

## CAULIFLOWER AND CHEESE MASH

**Prep time: 10 mins**

**Cooking time: 15 mins**

**Total time: 25 mins**

**Servings: 6**

### INGREDIENTS:

- 1 cauliflower head, finely chopped
- 1 cup sour cream
- 1 cup cheddar cheese, shredded
- Salt and pepper, to taste
- 2 cloves garlic

### DIRECTIONS:

1. Blanch cauliflower in a medium pot of boiling water for about 10 to 15 minutes, or until it is soft. Drain.
2. Put sour cream, cooked cauliflower, garlic, cheese, salt, and pepper in a blender.
3. Blend until smooth. If needed, add warm water to get the consistency you want.
4. Strain the puree to get rid of any big chunks. Serve warm.

### NUTRITIONAL VALUE PER SERVING:

Calories: 90 /kcal; Carbs: 11 g; Protein: 17 g; Fat: 8 g.

## CREAMY LEMON SHRIMP PUREE

**Prep time: 10 mins**

**Cooking time: 5 mins**

**Total time: 15 mins**

**Servings: 4**

### INGREDIENTS:

- 8 oz. frozen shrimp, chopped
- 2 tbsp. lemon juice
- ¼ cup parmesan cheese
- ¼ cup sour cream
- ¼ cup cream cheese
- 2 tbsp. mayonnaise
- 1 clove garlic, minced
- ¼ tsp. red pepper flakes

### DIRECTIONS:

1. Cook the shrimp, garlic, red pepper flakes and lemon juice for 5 minutes in a pan.
2. Put sautéed shrimp, sour cream, cream cheese, Parmesan, and mayonnaise in a blender.
3. Blend until smooth. Add warm water until you achieve the right consistency.
4. Strain the puree to get rid of any big chunks. Serve warm.

### NUTRITIONAL VALUE PER SERVING:

Calories: 100 /kcal; Carbs: 10 g; Protein: 14 g; Fat: 6 g.

## JALAPENO BEAN PUREE

**Prep time: 10 mins**

**Cooking time: 0 mins**

**Total time: 10 mins**

**Servings: 4**

### INGREDIENTS:

- 15 oz. canned pinto beans
- ¼ tsp. paprika
- 3 oz. canned jalapeno peppers
- ¼ tsp. sugar
- ¼ tsp. onion powder
- Salt to taste
- 1 tbsp. white vinegar

### DIRECTIONS:

1. In a blender, add jalapenos, beans, spices and vinegar.
2. Blend until smooth in a blender or food processor adding warm water until you get the right consistency.

### NUTRITIONAL VALUE PER SERVING:

Calories: 68 /kcal; Carbs: 10 g; Protein: 19 g; Fat: 5 g.

## PEAR AND RICOTTA PUREE

*Prep time:* 5 mins

*Cooking time:* 0 mins

*Total time:* 5 mins

*Servings:* 2

### INGREDIENTS:

- ½ cup ricotta
- 3 pieces canned pear
- 2 tbsp. plain, protein yogurt
- 1/4 tsp. cinnamon + extra for sprinkling on top
- 1/2 tsp. vanilla essence

### DIRECTIONS:

1. Use a mini food processor or stick blender to blend or process all the ingredients together until they are completely smooth.
2. To serve, spoon into ramekins and sprinkle with more cinnamon.

### NUTRITIONAL VALUE PER SERVING:

Calories: 90 /kcal; Carbs: 7 g; Protein: 21 g; Fat: 4 g.

## CHICKEN PUREE

*Prep time:* 5 mins

*Cooking time:* 0 mins

*Total time:* 5 mins

*Servings:* 1

### INGREDIENTS:

1. 1/2 cup cooked chicken
2. 1 tsp. Italian seasoning
3. 3 tbsp. tomato sauce
4. Salt and pepper to taste

### DIRECTIONS:

1. Put all the ingredients in a blender or food processor. You could also use a fork to mix them by hand.
2. Once everything is mixed well and soft, now heat it for 30 seconds in the microwave and serve warm.

### NUTRITIONAL VALUE PER SERVING:

Calories: 121 /kcal; Carbs: 6 g; Protein: 19 g; Fat: 3 g.

## BLACK BEAN AND RED PEPPER PUREE

*Prep time:* 10 mins

*Cooking time:* 5 mins

*Total time:* 15 mins

*Servings:* 1

### INGREDIENTS:

- 1 cup canned black beans, rinsed and drained
- 4 tbsp. chopped roasted red pepper
- 3 tbsp. chicken broth
- 3 tbsp. enchilada sauce

### DIRECTIONS:

1. Put the beans, half of the enchilada sauce, and the peppers in a pan and cook them over medium heat.
2. After these are done cooking, pour in the chicken broth.
3. Turn off the heat and use a regular blender or an immersion blender to mix the ingredients.
4. Before serving, put the puree in a bowl and add the remaining enchilada sauce.

### NUTRITIONAL VALUE PER SERVING:

Calories: 132 /kcal; Carbs: 5 g; Protein: 22 g; Fat: 7 g.

## SCRAMBLED EGG PUREE

*Prep time:* 5 mins

*Cooking time:* 5 mins

*Total time:* 10 mins

*Servings:* 1

### INGREDIENTS:

- 1 egg
- Salt and pepper, to taste

### DIRECTIONS:

1. Heat up a pan or skillet and whisk the egg in a small bowl before pouring it into the pan.
2. Add pepper and salt to taste, and use a spatula to move the egg scramble around as it cooks.

### NUTRITIONAL VALUE PER SERVING:

Calories: 67 /kcal; Carbs: 3 g; Protein: 25 g; Fat: 5 g.

## PUREED EGG SALAD

**Prep time:** 5 mins

**Cooking time:** 0 mins

**Total time:** 5 mins

**Servings:** 1

### INGREDIENTS:

- 2 hard-boiled egg
- Salt and pepper, to taste
- 2 tbsp. tomatoes diced
- 1½ tbsp. green onion chopped
- 1 tsp. olives, sliced
- 2 tbsp. cottage cheese
- 2 tsp. reduced-fat mayonnaise

### DIRECTIONS:

1. Everything but the cheese should be mixed together in a bowl.
2. Use a blender or food processor to mix the ingredients until they are smooth and creamy.
3. Add the cheese, fold gently and serve it cold.

### NUTRITIONAL VALUE PER SERVING:

Calories: 112 /kcal; Carbs: 6 g; Protein: 32 g; Fat: 6 g.

## TANGY CHICKEN PUREE

**Prep time:** 5 mins

**Cooking time:** 0 mins

**Total time:** 5 mins

**Servings:** 1

### INGREDIENTS:

- 1 cup canned chicken
- 2 tbsp. reduced-fat mayonnaise
- 2 tbsp. Greek yogurt
- Salt & Pepper, to taste
- ½ tsp. onion powder

### DIRECTIONS:

1. Put the chicken, mayonnaise, yogurt, salt, pepper, and onion powder in a food processor and pulse it until it is smooth.

### NUTRITIONAL VALUE PER SERVING:

Calories: 89 /kcal; Carbs: 4 g; Protein: 17 g; Fat: 4 g.

## BASIC FISH PUREE

**Prep time:** 5 mins

**Cooking time:** 0 mins

**Total time:** 5 mins

**Servings:** 1

### INGREDIENTS:

- 1 tbsp. green onions chopped
- 1 cup canned tuna, drained well
- Salt and pepper to taste
- 1 tbsp. reduced-fat mayonnaise

### DIRECTIONS:

1. Put the tuna into a food processor and blend it until it is smooth.
2. Add the salt, mayonnaise, and pepper to the processed fish and garnish with green onions and enjoy.

### NUTRITIONAL VALUE PER SERVING:

Calories: 77 /kcal; Carbs: 6 g; Protein: 18 g; Fat: 2 g.

## PUREED SALMON

**Prep time:** 5 mins

**Cooking time:** 15 mins

**Total time:** 20 mins

**Servings:** 3

### INGREDIENTS:

- ½ cup water
- 1 oz. onion, sliced
- ½ oz. dry white wine
- 1 ½ tsp. salt
- ½ lemon, sliced
- 2 spring dill
- 3 oz. boneless and skinless, salmon fillets
- 1 oz. cream
- 2 spring parsley

### DIRECTIONS:

1. In a saucepan, combine water, onion, wine, salt, lemon, pepper, parsley, and dill.
2. Bring to a boil, then turn down the heat, cover, and let it cook for 10 minutes.
3. Add the salmon fillet, cover the pot, and cook on low heat for 5 minutes, or until the fish is easy to flake.
4. Add cream to the mixture and blend in a food processor or blender.

### NUTRITIONAL VALUE PER SERVING:

Calories: 116 /kcal; Carbs: 5 g; Protein: 23 g; Fat: 6 g.

## LEEK AND BROCCOLI TOFU PUREE

**Prep time:** 10 mins

**Cooking time:** 10 mins

**Total time:** 20 mins

**Servings:** 6

### INGREDIENTS:

- 1 tbsp. olive oil
- 1 tbsp. dried mixed herbs
- 1 leek, thinly sliced
- 300g spinach, thinly sliced
- 1 head broccoli, finely chopped
- 1/2 cup vegetable stock
- 1/3 cup green pesto
- 300g firm tofu, crumbled
- 1½ cups frozen peas
- salt and pepper, to taste

### DIRECTIONS:

1. In a large pan over medium heat, heat the oil. Add the herbs and leeks and cook for 5 minutes, or until the leek is soft.
2. Add the spinach, broccoli, pesto, and stock and stir for another 3–4 minutes, or until the spinach is wilted.
3. Add the frozen peas and the crumbled tofu, and stir to mix.
4. Add salt and pepper to your taste.
5. Once it's cool, put it in a blender and blend it until it's a smooth puree.

### NUTRITIONAL VALUE PER SERVING:

Calories: 98 /kcal; Carbs: 6 g; Protein: 22 g; Fat: 7 g.

## CAULIFLOWER ALMOND PUREE

**Prep time:** 10 mins

**Cooking time:** 25 mins

**Total time:** 35 mins

**Servings:** 4

### INGREDIENTS:

- 2 tbsp. almond oil
- ¼ tsp. ground nutmeg
- ¼ tsp. black pepper
- 1 leek, light green and white parts, sliced
- 2 stalks celery, chopped
- 4 cups cauliflower florets
- 1 quart chicken broth, low-sodium
- ¾ tsp. kosher salt

### DIRECTIONS:

1. In a large pot, heat the almond oil over medium heat.
2. Add celery and cook, stirring occasionally, until the celery begins to soften.
3. Now add the leek and cook until celery and leek are tender.
4. Add the steamed cauliflower to the vegetable mixture and add stock, salt, nutmeg and pepper to the vegetables mixture and boil it.
5. Cook it for about 10 minutes, or until the cauliflower is tender. In a food processor or blender, puree the soup and serve.

### NUTRITIONAL VALUE PER SERVING:

Calories: 200 /kcal; Carbs: 14 g; Protein: 17 g; Fat: 14 g.

## STRAWBERRY PROTEIN PARFAIT

**Prep time:** mins

**Cooking time:** mins

**Total time:** mins

**Servings:** 2

### INGREDIENTS:

- ¼ cup plain Greek Yogurt
- 2 tbsp. sugar free whipped topping
- 1 tsp. strawberry Instant gelatin
- 1 scoop Vanilla Protein Powder

### DIRECTIONS:

1. In a bowl, mix the Greek yogurt, gelatin powder, protein powder, and whipped topping. Whisk until everything is well mixed.
2. Serve and enjoy.

### NUTRITIONAL VALUE PER SERVING:

Calories: 78 /kcal; Carbs: 1 g; Protein: 8 g; Fat: 2 g.

## BUTTERNUT SQUASH PUREE

**Prep time:** 10 mins

**Cooking time:** 30 mins

**Total time:** 40 mins

**Servings:** 8

### INGREDIENTS:

- 1 butternut squash
- 2 tbsp. maple syrup
- ¼ cup of butter
- Dash of salt

### DIRECTIONS:

1. Cut the squash in half and use a spoon to get the seeds out.
2. Put both halves, cut sides down, on a baking sheet and fill the pan with water.
3. Bake at 350°F-180°C for 30 minutes, or until the squash is soft enough to pierce with a fork. Take it out of the oven.
4. Put pieces of butter in a mixing bowl. With a spoon, scrape the squash flesh out of the skin and put it on top of the butter.

5. Add some salt and maple syrup.
6. Puree in a blender until it's smooth and tasty!

**NUTRITIONAL VALUE PER SERVING:**
Calories: 95 /kcal; Carbs: 11 g; Protein: 1 g; Fat: 5 g.

## CHEESY CAULIFLOWER PUREE

Prep time: 10 mins

Cooking time: 15 mins

Total time: 25 mins

Servings: 2

**INGREDIENTS:**

- 1 head, medium Cauliflower, raw
- 1 tbsp. Butter, unsalted
- 2 oz. low-fat cheddar cheese
- 2 tbsp. low-fat Whipping Cream

**DIRECTIONS:**

1. Clean and trim the cauliflower, then break it into small pieces.
2. Add 2 tablespoons of cream and 1 tablespoon of butter to a bowl that can go in the microwave.
3. Cook on high for six minutes.
4. Mix the cream and butter to coat the cauliflower. Heat on high for another six minutes.
5. Take it out of the microwave and put it and the cheese in a high-speed blender or food processor. Blend until it's smooth.
6. Salt and pepper can be added to taste. You can change the amount of cream and butter to suit your taste.

**NUTRITIONAL VALUE PER SERVING:**
Calories: 280 /kcal; Carbs: 15 g; Protein: 13 g; Fat: 21 g.

## PEPPER PUMPKIN PUREE

Prep time: 5 mins

Cooking time: 15 mins

Total time: 20 mins

Servings: 24

**INGREDIENTS:**

- 2 long yellow peppers
- 1 cup white vinegar
- 6 oz. tomato paste
- 1 dry jalapeno pepper
- 1 cup pumpkin, grated

**DIRECTIONS:**

1. In a pan, roast the pepper.
2. Bring the vinegar and pumpkin to a boil in a sauce pan. Put the dry pepper above the pumpkin puree to make it a little bit softer Add the tomato paste and cook for 5 more minutes.
3. Put all the ingredients in a food processor and blend them until they are a smooth puree.

**NUTRITIONAL VALUE PER SERVING:**
Calories: 13/kcal; Carbs: 3 g; Protein: 0 g; Fat: 0 g.

## VEGETABLE PUREE

Prep time: 10 mins

Cooking time: 10 mins

Total time: 20 mins

Servings: 12

**INGREDIENTS:**

- 3 cups water
- 2 beef bouillon cube
- 2 cups chicken stock
- ½ cup cabbage, fresh, chopped
- 1 cup cooked onion
- 1 cup turnips, cubes
- 1 cup winter squash, cubes
- 2 stalks celery, raw, large
- 1 lb. mixed vegetables, frozen
- ½ tsp. ginger, ground,
- 1 tsp. garlic powder,
- 10 oz. spinach, frozen

**DIRECTIONS:**

1. Put all of the ingredients into a stockpot and heat on low for about an hour. It might take a bit more time. Just keep boiling until it tastes good.
2. Then put it all in a blender and mix it.
3. Enjoy!

**NUTRITIONAL VALUE PER SERVING:**
Calories: 76 /kcal; Carbs: 14 g; Protein: 3 g; Fat: 1 g.

## CORN PUREE

Prep time: 15 mins

Cooking time: 25 mins

Total time: 40 mins

Servings: 2

**INGREDIENTS:**

- 1 half and half cream
- 1 cup sweet corn, fresh
- ½ cup corn meal
- 1 tbsp. unsalted butter
- Salt to taste

DIRECTIONS:

1. Put sweet corn in a blender and blend it until it is a smooth puree. Bring the half-and-half to a boil in a large pot.
2. Whisk in the corn meal and butter keep cooking and stirring it until it gets thicker. Add salt to

your taste and serve.

**NUTRITIONAL VALUE PER SERVING:**
Calories: 320 /kcal; Carbs: 36 g; Protein: 7 g; Fat: 8 g.

## CHICKEN RICOTTA PUREE

**Prep time:** 5 mins

**Cooking time:** 0 mins

**Total time:** 5 mins

**Servings:** 3

**INGREDIENTS:**
- 3 cups cooked chicken
- ½ cup chicken broth
- Salt and Pepper, to taste
- ½ cup ricotta

**DIRECTIONS:**
1. Put the chicken, broth, ricotta, salt and pepper in a food processor and pulse it until it is smooth.

**NUTRITIONAL VALUE PER SERVING:**
Calories: 222 /kcal; Carbs: 9 g; Protein: 25 g; Fat: 11 g.

## EGGS PUREE DELIGHT

**Prep time:** 1 mins

**Cooking time:** 3 mins

**Total time:** 4 mins

**Servings:** 1

**INGREDIENTS:**
- 2 medium eggs
- Black pepper, to taste
- ¼ cup tomato juice
- 1 tbsp. salsa

**DIRECTIONS:**
1. Spray non-stick cooking spray on a skillet or shallow saucepan.
2. Whisk the eggs and tomato juice together and then add salsa and stir well.
3. Pour into a hot skillet and sprinkle with freshly ground black pepper.
4. Let it cook until it starts to look like an omelet, then stir it. Stir the eggs every now and then until they are done.
5. Put the mixture in a bowl and eat it.

**NUTRITIONAL VALUE PER SERVING:**
Calories: 220 /kcal; Carbs: 9 g; Protein: 23 g; Fat: 13 g.

## GINGER CARROT PUREE

**Prep time:** 5 mins

**Cooking time:** 20 mins

**Total time:** 25 mins

**Servings:** 5

**INGREDIENTS:**
- 2 tbsp. extra virgin olive oil
- 2 tbsp. ginger root, grated
- 2 cup carrots, chopped
- 1 cup onions, chopped
- 4 pears, cored
- 1 tbsp. butter
- 3 cup vegetable broth
- salt and pepper to taste

**DIRECTIONS:**
1. In a medium sauce pan over medium-high heat, cook the onion and ginger in the olive oil for a few minutes, stirring every so often.
2. Cook for a few more minutes after adding the carrots and pears. Add enough broth to cover the mixture, and let it cook on low heat until the carrots are soft.
3. Use a hand blender to make the mixture smooth. Add butter and salt, and pepper as you like.

**NUTRITIONAL VALUE PER SERVING:**
Calories: 190 /kcal; Carbs: 30 g; Protein: 14 g; Fat: 8 g.

## WHITE BEAN PUREE

**Prep time:** 5 mins

**Cooking time:** 0 mins

**Total time:** 5 mins

**Servings:** 3

**INGREDIENTS:**
- 19 oz. canned white beans

**DIRECTIONS:**
1. Drain. Rinse beans. Puree. You might need to add one or two tablespoons of water.

**NUTRITIONAL VALUE PER SERVING:**
Calories: 160 /kcal; Carbs: 1 g; Protein: 26 g; Fat: 11 g.

## STRAWBERRY PUREE

Prep time: 3 mins

Cooking time: 0 mins

Total time: 3 mins

Servings: 6

### INGREDIENTS:

- ½ oz. water
- 2 cups strawberry

### DIRECTIONS:

1. Blend until smooth.

### NUTRITIONAL VALUE PER SERVING:

Calories: 23 /kcal; Carbs: 0 g; Protein: 0 g; Fat: 0 g.

## CARROT PUREE

Prep time: 10 mins

Cooking time: 10 mins

Total time: 20 mins

Servings: 6

### INGREDIENTS:

- 2 lb. carrots peeled, chopped

### DIRECTIONS:

1. Steam the carrots until soft, mash for about 10 minutes, then puree in a blender. If required then add water some water while blending.

### NUTRITIONAL VALUE PER SERVING:

Calories: 58 /kcal; Carbs: 0 g; Protein: 13 g; Fat: 2 g.

## BLACKBERRY PUREE

Prep time: 5 mins

Cooking time: 0 mins

Total time: 5 mins

Servings: 8

### INGREDIENTS:

- 1½ cup blackberries, fresh
- ½ cup grapes, seedless
- 6 strawberries, fresh
- 1½ tbsp. honey
- 6 oz. fat-free vanilla yogurt

### DIRECTIONS:

1. Blend all ingredients in a blender or a food processor. Chill before serving.

### NUTRITIONAL VALUE PER SERVING:

Calories: 48 /kcal; Carbs: 12 g; Protein: 2 g; Fat: 0 g.

## SPINACH PUREE

Prep time: 5 mins

Cooking time: 20 mins

Total time: 25 mins

Servings: 10

### INGREDIENTS:

- 10 oz. spinach, fresh
- 1 clove garlic
- ½ tsp. salt
- 2 cups water

### DIRECTIONS:

1. Add the spinach, garlic, salt and water in a saucepan and steam it for 20 minutes. Blend it in a blender or food processor and serve.

### NUTRITIONAL VALUE PER SERVING:

Calories: 13 /kcal; Carbs: 2 g; Protein: 2 g; Fat: 0 g.

## ZUCCHINI PUREE

Prep time: 10 mins

Cooking time: 50 mins

Total time: 1 hour

Servings: 2

### INGREDIENTS:

- 2 cups zucchini, diced
- 5 whole mushrooms
- 1/3 onion, big chunks
- ½ lemon, juice
- ¼ cup low sodium chicken broth

### DIRECTIONS:

1. Set oven temperature to 400°F-200°C. Spread the vegetables out on a baking sheet and use olive oil cooking spray to lightly coat them. Season with salt and pepper to taste and roast the vegetables for 45 minutes, or until zucchini is tender.
2. Put all of the vegetables and other ingredients in a blender and blend until the consistency you want is reached.
3. Use a small pot to heat up the puree for 5–10 minutes and serve.

### NUTRITIONAL VALUE PER SERVING:

Calories: 53 /kcal; Carbs: 11 g; Protein: 3 g; Fat: 0 g.

## MANGO PUREE

**Prep time:** 5 mins

**Cooking time:** 0 mins

**Total time:** 5 mins

**Servings:** 1

### INGREDIENTS:

- 1 mango, peeled and diced
- 1 tbsp. water
- 4 tsp. Splenda

### DIRECTIONS:

1. Combine all ingredients in a blender or food processor and blend until smooth.

### NUTRITIONAL VALUE PER SERVING:

Calories: 8/kcal; Carbs: 2 g; Protein: 0 g; Fat: 0 g.

## BUFFALO SHRIMP PUREE

**Prep time:** 5 mins

**Cooking time:** 0 mins

**Total time:** 5 mins

**Servings:** 2

### INGREDIENTS:

- 2 tbsp. blue cheese crumbles
- 3 oz. cooked shrimp
- 2 tbsp. hot buffalo sauce

### DIRECTIONS:

1. In a mini food processor, put shrimp, hot sauce and blue cheese and blend.
2. Serve cold or heat in the microwave.

### NUTRITIONAL VALUE PER SERVING:

Calories: 87 /kcal; Carbs: 1 g; Protein: 12 g; Fat: 3 g.

## BROCCOLI PUREE

**Prep time:** 10 mins

**Cooking time:** 25 mins

**Total time:** 35 mins

**Servings:** 9

### INGREDIENTS:

- 2 lb. broccoli, chopped
- ¼ cup carrots sliced
- 1 medium onion, chopped
- 2 cups water
- 1 clove garlic, minced
- 1 can fat free chicken broth
- Salt and pepper to taste
- 1 can fat free evaporated milk

### DIRECTIONS:

1. Put the first six ingredients in a large stock pot. Boil for 20 minutes while stirring every so often.
2. Make sure to stir the vegetables because the liquid won't cover them all.
3. Move to a blender and puree, and then put back in the pot. Add salt and pepper and canned milk. Keep cooking for 5 more minutes on medium-low heat.

Serve and enjoy.

### NUTRITIONAL VALUE PER SERVING:

Calories: 101 /kcal; Carbs: 18 g; Protein: 8 g; Fat: 1 g.

## SWEET POTATO PUREE

**Prep time:** 5 mins

**Cooking time:** 0 mins

**Total time:** 5 mins

**Servings:** 2

### INGREDIENTS:

- 2 tbsp. salted butter
- 2 medium sweet potato, steamed
- 1 tbsp. half and half cream

### DIRECTIONS:

- In a mini food processor add butter, cream and mashed sweet potatoes and blend.
- Serve cold or heat in the microwave.

### NUTRITIONAL VALUE PER SERVING:

Calories: 214 /kcal; Carbs: 42 g; Protein: 3 g; Fat: 6 g.

## APPLE PEAR PUREE

**Prep time:** 30 mins

**Cooking time:** 15 mins

**Total time:** 45 mins

**Servings:** 8

Ingredients:

- 4 medium pears
- 4 medium apples

DIRECTIONS:

1. Peel, core, and chop pears and apples.
2. Put in a pot and heat on low to medium low for about 10 minutes, or until soft.
3. Blend in a food processor or blender and serve.

### NUTRITIONAL VALUE PER SERVING:

Calories: 89 /kcal; Carbs: 23 g; Protein: 1 g; Fat: 1 g.

## CHICKEN BEAN PUREE

Prep time: 10 mins

Cooking time: 1 hour

Total time: 1 hour 10 mins

Servings: 6

### INGREDIENTS:

- 32 oz. chicken stock
- 2 tbsp. olive oil
- 3 cups of white beans, soaked
- 3 cloves of garlic (more, if you like)
- 1 medium onion, chopped
- Salt and pepper, to taste

### DIRECTIONS:

1. In a pot with a thick bottom, heat the olive oil. Cook chopped onion in oil until it becomes clear and starts to brown.
2. Add the garlic and spices and stir with a wooden spoon until the garlic smells good. Bring the beans and stock to a boil, and then turn the heat down to a simmer.
3. Cook the beans until they are very soft, and then puree them with an immersion blender.

### NUTRITIONAL VALUE PER SERVING:

Calories: 200 /kcal; Carbs: 31 g; Protein: 10 g; Fat: 5 g.

## AVOCADO PUREE

Prep time: 5 mins

Cooking time: 0 mins

Total time: 5 mins

Servings: 1

### INGREDIENTS:

- 2 avocados
- 3 tbsp. Fat Free Ranch dressing

### DIRECTIONS:

1. Blend them in a food processor until smooth.

### NUTRITIONAL VALUE PER SERVING:

Calories: 40 /kcal; Carbs: 3 g; Protein: 2 g; Fat: 3 g.

## SPINACH ALMOND MILK PUREE

Prep time: 5 mins

Cooking time: 10 mins

Total time: 15 mins

Servings: 6

### INGREDIENTS:

- 2 medium onions
- 2-4 cloves garlic
- 1lb. fresh spinach
- 1 tbsp. curry powder
- 1 inch peeled ginger
- Salt to taste
- 2½ cups almond milk

### DIRECTIONS:

1. Add all the ingredients into a steam blender and cook for 10 minutes.
2. Blend until steam start rising.
3. Serve and enjoy.

### NUTRITIONAL VALUE PER SERVING:

Calories: 60 /kcal; Carbs: 10 g; Protein: 3 g; Fat: 1 g.

## CHICKEN CHILI PUREE

Prep time: 5 mins

Cooking time: 0 mins

Total time: 5 mins

Servings: 4

### Ingredients:

- 1 can baked beans
- 2 tbsp. chilli sauce
- 1 can cooked chicken

### DIRECTIONS:

1. In a mini food processor, put chicken, chilli sauce and baked beans and blend.
2. Serve cold or heat in the microwave.

### NUTRITIONAL VALUE PER SERVING:

Calories: 80 /kcal; Carbs: 15 g; Protein: 6 g; Fat: 1 g.

## EDAMAME PUREE

Prep time: 5 mins

Cooking time: 10 mins

Total time: 15 mins

Servings: 5

### INGREDIENTS:

- 3 garlic cloves
- 2 tbsp. water
- 2 tbsp. olive oil
- 1 cup Edamame beans, cooked
- Salt and pepper, to taste
- ½ tbsp. lemon juice

### DIRECTIONS:

1. Put edamame beans and garlic cloves that have been roughly chopped into a blender. To make the puree smoother, add olive oil and water.
2. Add salt, pepper, and lemon juice to get the taste you want.

**NUTRITIONAL VALUE PER SERVING:**

Calories: 75 /kcal; Carbs: 5 g; Protein: 6 g; Fat: 4 g.

## AVOCADO TOMATO PUREE

*Prep time: 20 mins*

*Cooking time: 30 mins*

*Total time: 50 mins*

*Servings: 4*

**INGREDIENTS:**

- 3 avocado
- 4 mushrooms
- 1 full crown broccoli
- 5 baby bell peppers
- 750 ml tomato puree
- Salt and pepper, to taste
- 2 tbsp. olive oil

**DIRECTIONS:**

1. All of the vegetables, except for the avocado, should be cooked in a deep pan with olive oil and salt and pepper.
2. Once they are cooked, add the tomato puree, cover the pan, and cook on low heat for 5 to 10 minutes. Now add the avocados and blend the puree.

**NUTRITIONAL VALUE PER SERVING:**

Calories: 300 /kcal; Carbs: 23 g; Protein: 15 g; Fat: 21 g.

## PEACH PUREE

*Prep time: 10 mins*

*Cooking time: 15 mins*

*Total time: 25 mins*

*Servings: 2*

**INGREDIENTS:**

- 2 large peaches, skins removed
- 2 tbsp. sweetener, low-calorie
- ¼ cup water

**DIRECTIONS:**

1. Peel peaches after boiling them. Cut it up and put it in a small pot with water. Heat over medium-low heat for about 15 minutes, or until some of the liquid has cooked down.
2. Add sweetener and blend until you get the right texture.

**NUTRITIONAL VALUE PER SERVING:**

Calories: 16 /kcal; Carbs: 0 g; Protein: 4 g; Fat: 0 g.

## MUSHY PEA PUREE

*Prep time: 5 mins*

*Cooking time: 5 mins*

*Total time: 10 mins*

*Servings: 4*

**INGREDIENTS:**

- 24 oz. frozen peas, about 5 cups
- 1½ vegetable stock, no salt added
- 2 garlic cloves, sliced in half
- 2 tbsp. lemon juice
- 1½ cups flat-leaf parsley
- 8 mint leaves

**DIRECTIONS:**

- Put the peas, stock and garlic in a medium saucepan and turn the heat to high. Bring to a boil and simmer for two minutes.
- Take it off the heat and add the parsley, mint and lemon juice. Puree in a blender or food processor.

**NUTRITIONAL VALUE PER SERVING:**

Calories: 150 /kcal; Carbs: 0 g; Protein: 28 g; Fat: 11 g.

## APPLE PUREE

*Prep time: 5 mins*

*Cooking time: 3 mins*

*Total time: 8 mins*

*Servings: 1*

**INGREDIENTS:**

- 1 Medium Granny Smith Apple
- ¼ cup Water
- 1 tbsp. Ground Cinnamon
- 12 drops of Vanilla Cream Stevia

**DIRECTIONS:**

1. All of the ingredients should be put into a food processor and pulsed until smooth. Pour into a bowl and heat for 3 minutes on high.

**NUTRITIONAL VALUE PER SERVING:**

Calories: 112 /kcal; Carbs: 3 g; Protein: 1 g; Fat: 1 g.

## CHEESY EGG PUREE

**Prep time: 5 mins**

**Cooking time: 5 mins**

**Total time: 10 mins**

**Servings: 1**

### INGREDIENTS:

- 1 large egg
- 1 tbsp. ricotta cheese
- ½ oz. fat free milk
- 1 tsp. butter, unsalted

### DIRECTIONS:

1. Whisk the egg, milk, and cheese together in a bowl. Melt butter in pan on very low heat pour the mixture into the pan.
2. Whisk eggs constantly until they are smooth and pureed.

### NUTRITIONAL VALUE PER SERVING:

Calories: 98 /kcal; Carbs: 1 g; Protein: 9 g; Fat: 6 g.

## CURRIED BROCCOLI PUREE

**Prep time: 15 mins**

**Cooking time: 10 mins**

**Total time: 25 mins**

**Servings: 2**

### INGREDIENTS:

- 2 cups vegetable broth
- 2 cups chopped broccoli
- 1 cup water
- ¼ cup chopped onions
- 1 clove garlic
- 1 tbsp. rolled oats
- ½ block firm tofu, low-fat
- 2 tbsp. nutritional yeast
- ½ tsp. black pepper
- 1 tbsp. yellow curry powder
- ½ tsp. salt
- 1 tsp. cinnamon

### DIRECTIONS:

1. In a saucepan, bring water and broth to a slow boil.
2. Add the onions, broccoli, and oats. Cover and cook for about 10 minutes, or until the broccoli is very soft.
3. Put the cooked mixture, nutritional yeast, garlic, tofu, salt, curry powder, pepper, and cinnamon in a blender
4. Blend until smooth.

### NUTRITIONAL VALUE PER SERVING:

Calories: 230 /kcal; Carbs: 30 g; Protein: 25 g; Fat: 3 g.

SOFT FOOD DIET

## BEST CHOCOLATE PORRIDGE

**Prep time:** 5 mins

**Cooking time:** 3 mins

**Total time:** 8 mins

**Servings:** 2

### INGREDIENTS:

- 3 tbsp. porridge oats
- 1 Small square, dark unsweetened chocolate
- 1 tbsp. chocolate protein powder
- 1 tbsp. low-calorie sweetener
- 1 cup skimmed milk
- Fresh blackberries, for serving

### DIRECTIONS:

1. Put oats, protein powder, milk and chocolate in a bowl. Mix well, put in a microwave-safe dish, and cook for 2 minutes. Stir, and cook for another 20 to 30 seconds. Mix in the sweetener you want, and then put the mixture in a bowl to serve.
2. Add a few blackberries and some chopped chocolate to the top.
3. Enjoy!

### NUTRITIONAL VALUE PER SERVING:
Calories: 324 /kcal; Carbs: 12 g; Protein: 8 g; Fat: 5 g.

## CHOCOLATE CHIA PUDDING

**Prep time:** 10 mins

**Cooking time:** 0 mins

**Total time:** 10 mins

**Servings:** 4

### INGREDIENTS:

- 2 cups unsweetened soy milk
- ¼ cup unsweetened cocoa powder
- 10 drops liquid stevia
- ¼ tsp. vanilla extract
- ¼ tsp. ground cinnamon
- ½ cup fresh raspberries, for garnish
- ½ cup chia seeds

### DIRECTIONS:

1. Put soy milk, cocoa powder, stevia, vanilla and cinnamon in a small bowl. Whisk well until everything is mixed together.
2. Add chia seeds and stir.
3. Divide the mixture in four small dishes.
4. Cover it and put it them in the fridge for 1 hour.
5. When it's done, put raspberries on top and enjoy!

### NUTRITIONAL VALUE PER SERVING:
Calories: /kcal; Carbs: g; Protein: g; Fat: g.

## PUMPKIN CUSTARD

**Prep time:** 5 mins

**Cooking time:** 3 mins

**Total time:** 8 mins

**Servings:** 1

### INGREDIENTS:

- ½ cup canned pumpkin puree
- ½ tsp. vanilla extract
- 1 whole egg
- 1 tsp. brown sugar
- ½ tsp. pumpkin pie spice

### DIRECTIONS:

1. In a small bowl, mix all the ingredients well.
2. Pour into ramekin or a small mug that has been sprayed with cooking spray.
3. Heat it in a microwave for 2 1/2 to 3 minutes, or until the custard is firm.

### NUTRITIONAL VALUE PER SERVING:
Calories: 123 /kcal; Carbs: 11 g; Protein: 7 g; Fat: 5 g.

## LEMON-BLACKBERRY FROZEN YOGURT

**Prep time:** 10 mins

**Cooking time:** 0 mins

**Total time:** 10 mins

**Servings:** 4

### INGREDIENTS:

- 4 cups frozen blackberries
- 1 lemon, juiced
- ½ cup low-fat plain Greek yogurt
- Fresh mint leaves, for garnish
- 2 tsp. liquid stevia

### DIRECTIONS:

1. Add yogurt, blackberries, lemon juice, and stevia to your food processor and blend well until smooth.
2. Serve with fresh mint leaves on top and enjoy right away.

**NUTRITIONAL VALUE PER SERVING:**

Calories: 68 /kcal; Carbs: 15 g; Protein: 3 g; Fat: 0 g.

## CREAMY CAULIFLOWER DISH

**Prep time:** 10 mins

**Cooking time:** 5 mins

**Total time:** 15 mins

**Servings:** 4

**INGREDIENTS:**

- ½ tsp. pepper
- ½ tsp. garlic salt
- 4 tsp. extra virgin olive oil
- 1/3 cup low-fat buttermilk
- 1 tsp. salted butter
- Large head of cauliflower
- 3 cloves garlic

**DIRECTIONS:**

1. Break the cauliflower into tiny florets and put them in a large bowl that can go in the microwave. Add a quarter cup of water and garlic to the bowl.
2. Microwave cauliflower for 5 minutes, or until it is soft.
3. Crush the garlic cloves with a garlic press, put them in a food processor, and then add them to the cauliflower.
4. Add pepper, butter, garlic salt, buttermilk, and two teaspoons of olive oil.
5. Process until the mixture is smooth and creamy.
6. Pour the rest of the olive oil on top and serve.

**NUTRITIONAL VALUE PER SERVING:**

Calories: 113 /kcal; Carbs: 13 g; Protein: 5 g; Fat: 6 g.

## BEETROOT AND BUTTERBEAN HUMMUS

**Prep time:** 5 mins

**Cooking time:** 0 mins

**Total time:** 5 mins

**Servings:** 4

**INGREDIENTS:**

- 2 tbsp. Fat-Free Greek yogurt
- Salt and pepper, to taste
- 1 tbsp. extra-virgin olive oil
- 1-2 cloves garlic, crushed
- Bunch of chives, chopped
- 8 oz. cooked beetroot
- 14 oz. butterbeans, drained and rinsed

**DIRECTIONS:**

1. Cut the beets into small cubes.
2. Add the pepper, salt, oil, butterbeans, yogurt, garlic and chives in a food processor.
3. Blend the ingredients until you get a nice puree.
4. Combine the beetroot cubes with the prepared blitz gently.
5. Serve and enjoy!

**NUTRITIONAL VALUE PER SERVING:**

Calories: 80 /kcal; Carbs: 10 g; Protein: 4 g; Fat: 2 g.

## RAISIN AND OATS MUG CAKES

**Prep time:** 10 mins

**Cooking time:** 1 mins

**Total time:** 11 mins

**Servings:** 1

**INGREDIENTS:**

- 1½ tbsp. flour
- ½ tbsp. raisins
- 1½ tbsp. almond milk
- 1/16 tsp. salt
- ¼ tsp. baking powder
- 1/8 tsp. baking soda
- ½ tbsp. canola oil
- 1/8 tsp. hazelnut extract
- 1/8 tsp. vanilla extract
- ¼ tsp. baking powder
- ¾ tbsp. oats
- 1 tsp. lemon juice

**DIRECTIONS:**

1. Mix all the ingredients in an oven safe mug and cook for 1 minute.
2. Let it cool down, serve it, and enjoy.

**NUTRITIONAL VALUE PER SERVING:**

Calories: 185 /kcal; Carbs: 39 g; Protein: 8 g; Fat: 1.7 g.

## BUFFALO CHICKEN DIP

**Prep time:** 25 mins

**Cooking time:** 20 mins

**Total time:** 45 mins

**Servings:** 12

**INGREDIENTS:**

- 2-3 chicken breasts, cooked and shredded
- 1 cup cheddar cheese
- 1 cup mozzarella cheese
- 8 oz. whipped cream cheese
- 1 cup plain Greek yogurt, fat-free
- 1 tbsp. ranch seasoning
- ½ cup buffalo wing sauce
- Chives for garnish

**DIRECTIONS:**

1. Mix the chicken and all ingredients in a mixing bowl.
2. Put in a baking dish and bake at 350°F -180°C for 15 to 20 minutes.
3. Garnish it with chives and enjoy.

**NUTRITIONAL VALUE PER SERVING:**

Calories: 208 /kcal; Carbs: 2 g; Protein: 25 g; Fat: 10 g.

## PEANUT BUTTER PROTEIN BITES

Prep time: 20 mins + chilling time

Cooking time: 0 mins

Total time: 20 mins + chilling time

Servings: 10

**INGREDIENTS:**

- 1 cup old fashioned rolled oats
- ¾ cup smooth natural peanut butter
- 1 cup vanilla protein powder
- 1 tbsp. ground flaxseed
- 2 tbsp. Ground flaxseed
- 1 tsp. vanilla extract
- 1 tbsp. chia seeds
- ¾ tsp. stevia baking blend
- ¼ cup dark chocolate chips
- 1 tbsp. water

**DIRECTIONS:**

1. Put oats, peanut butter, protein powder, chia seeds, vanilla, flaxseed, chocolate chips, water and stevia in a bowl and mix them all together.
2. Put it in the fridge for 30 minutes.
3. Make balls out of the mixture, eat, and enjoy!

**NUTRITIONAL VALUE PER SERVING:**

Calories: 181 /kcal; Carbs: 11 g; Protein: 11 g; Fat: 10 g.

## EGG WHITE SCRAMBLE

Prep time: 5 mins

Cooking time: 5 mins

Total time: 10 mins

Servings: 2

**INGREDIENTS:**

- 1/4 cup non-fat cottage cheese
- Pinch of dried herbs
- Nonstick cooking spray
- 2 egg whites, lightly beaten
- Salt and black pepper, to taste

**DIRECTIONS:**

1. With a fork, break up the curds in a medium bowl of cottage cheese. Beat the egg whites until smooth, and then add them.
2. Spray a small skillet that doesn't stick with cooking spray and put it over medium heat. Add the egg mixture, sprinkle on the herbs, and stir gently for 4 to 5 minutes, or until the eggs are done.
3. Mix the cooked eggs with a fork until you get the consistency you want. Add salt and pepper to taste, and serve right away. Enjoy.

**NUTRITIONAL VALUE PER SERVING:**

Calories: 85 /kcal; Carbs: 2 g; Protein: 15 g; Fat: 1 g.

## HAM AND SWISS EGGS

Prep time: 5 mins

Cooking time: 5 mins

Total time: 10 mins

Servings: 2

**INGREDIENTS:**

- 1 tsp. butter
- 2 tbsp. skim milk
- 4 eggs, lightly beaten
- ¼ cup shredded Swiss cheese
- Salt and black pepper, to taste
- ¼ cup finely minced cooked ham

**DIRECTIONS:**

1. Whisk the eggs and milk together until they are well mixed, and then add salt and pepper to taste. Melt butter in a skillet on medium-high heat and add egg mixture. Cook and stir for 5 minutes, or until the eggs are set and cooked all the way through.
2. Add ham and cheese to the eggs and stir until everything is mixed well and the eggs are hot. Season the eggs with salt and pepper to your taste, and serve them right away. Enjoy.

**NUTRITIONAL VALUE PER SERVING:**

Calories: 238 /kcal; Carbs: 2 g; Protein: 20 g; Fat: 16 g.

## GREEK YOGURT BARK

Prep time: 10 mins + chilling time

Cooking time: 0 mins

Total time: 10 mins + chilling time

Servings: 6

**INGREDIENTS:**

- ¼ cup sliced almonds
- 1½ cups vanilla Greek yogurt, low-fat
- 4 strawberries, sliced
- ½ cup blueberries

**DIRECTIONS:**

1. Put parchment paper on a baking sheet.
2. Spread Greek yogurt in a thin, even layer on a baking sheet that has been lined.

**SOFT FOOD DIET**

3. Add strawberries, blueberries, and thin slices of almonds to the top.
4. Cover the baking sheet with aluminum foil and put it in the freezer until the bark is completely frozen, which usually takes 8 hours.

**NUTRITIONAL VALUE PER SERVING:**
Calories: 97 /kcal; Carbs: 10 g; Protein: 9 g; Fat: 2 g.

## TROPICAL PORRIDGE

*Prep time: 5 mins*

*Cooking time: 5 mins*

*Total time: 10 mins*

*Servings: 1*

**INGREDIENTS:**
- 1 cup coconut milk
- 1/2 cup diced ripe mango
- 4 tbsp. breakfast porridge mix
- 1 small banana, diced

**DIRECTIONS:**
1. In a small saucepan over medium heat, bring the coconut milk to a boil. Mix the porridge mix into the milk and stir until it is smooth.
2. Turn down the heat and let the porridge simmer, uncovered, for about 2 minutes, until it gets thicker.
3. Take the porridge off the heat and mix in the mango and banana. Enjoy!

**NUTRITIONAL VALUE PER SERVING:**
Calories: 172 /kcal; Carbs: 34 g; Protein: 3 g; Fat: 3 g.

## PORRIDGE WITH BERRIES

*Prep time: 5 mins*

*Cooking time: 5 mins*

*Total time: 10 mins*

*Servings: 1*

Ingredients:
- 4 tbsp. breakfast porridge mix
- 1 cup water
- 1 tbsp. lemon juice
- ½ cup frozen mixed berries

### DIRECTIONS:
1. In a small saucepan, combine water, lemon juice and berries. Bring to a boil over medium heat, stirring every so often and gently crushing the berries to the desired consistency.
2. Stir the porridge mix in the pot until it is smooth.
3. Turn down the heat and let the porridge simmer, uncovered, for about 2 minutes, while stirring every now and then. Serve right away, and enjoy.

**NUTRITIONAL VALUE PER SERVING:**
Calories: 95 /kcal; Carbs: 20 g; Protein: 3 g; Fat: 0 g.

## MEAT LOAF

*Prep time: 10 mins NB*

*Cooking time: 1 hour*

*Total time: 1 hour 10 mins*

*Servings: 8*

**INGREDIENTS:**
- 1½ lb. lean ground beef
- 8 oz. tomato sauce, no salt added
- 1 egg
- ¼ cup onion, chopped
- 2 tbsp. Unflavored protein powder
- ¼ tsp. salt
- ¼ cup green pepper, chopped
- ¼ tsp. oregano, dried
- ¼ tsp. pepper
- 1 tsp. mustard
- 1/3 cup ketchup

**DIRECTIONS:**
1. Mix together everything except for the mustard, ketchup, and brown sugar.
2. Put into a loaf pan. Now in small bowl mix mustard, ketchup, and brown sugar together, then spread it on top of the meat loaf.
3. Bake for 1 hour at 350°F-180°C.
4. Let it sit for 10 minutes and then divide it into 8 slices and serve.

**NUTRITIONAL VALUE PER SERVING:**
Calories: 160 /kcal; Carbs: 7 g; Protein: 5 g; Fat: 21 g.

## CURRY CHICKEN LENTIL SOUP

*Prep time: 10 mins*

*Cooking time: 18 mins*

*Total time: 28 mins*

*Servings: 4*

**INGREDIENTS:**
- 1 tbsp. olive oil
- 2 medium carrots, diced
- 1 onion, peeled and diced
- 4 cups chicken stock
- 1 cup red lentils, rinsed and picked over
- 1 tbsp. minced garlic
- 2 tsp. ground cumin
- 1 lb. chicken breast
- salt and black pepper to taste
- 1 tsp. curry powder

**DIRECTIONS:**
1. Use the Instant Pot's "Saute" setting. Add olive oil. When the pan is hot, add the onion and cook

it for 5 minutes. Then, put in the carrots and garlic. Cook for one minute.
2. Then add the chicken, lentils, spices and chicken stock. Change the function to "Manual" and set it for 10 minutes. When done, carefully take off the lid when the pressure has gone down.
3. Take the chicken out of the pot and shred it. Put it back in the pot and stir.
4. Adjust salt and pepper to taste, and serve.

**NUTRITIONAL VALUE PER SERVING:**

Calories: 143 /kcal; Carbs: 6 g; Protein: 8 g; Fat: 5 g.

## STRAWBERRIES WITH WHIPPED YOGURT

**Prep time:** 10 mins

**Cooking time:** 0 mins

**Total time:** 10 mins

**Servings:** 2

**INGREDIENTS:**

- 1 cup plain Greek yogurt
- 1 cup sliced strawberries
- 4 tbsp. heavy cream

**DIRECTIONS:**

1. Pulse the strawberries in a blender or food processor as needed until they are the consistency you want, and then set them aside.
2. In a medium bowl with high sides, beat the cream and yogurt with an electric hand mixer until the mixture thickens and stiff peaks form, about 5 minutes.
3. Strawberries should be put into two bowls, topped with whipped yogurt, and eaten right away.

**NUTRITIONAL VALUE PER SERVING:**

Calories: 210 /kcal; Carbs: 14 g; Protein: 5 g; Fat: 16 g.

## GAZPACHO

**Prep time:** 15 mins + chilling time

**Cooking time:** 5 mins

**Total time:** 20 mins + chilling time

**Servings:** 5

**INGREDIENTS:**

- 2 tbsp. vegetable oil
- 1 small yellow onion, diced
- 1 small red bell pepper, diced
- 2 large tomatoes, peeled and diced
- 1 small cucumber, peeled and diced
- 2 garlic cloves, minced
- 1 tbsp. balsamic vinegar
- 1 tbsp. lime juice
- 1 tsp. kosher salt, plus more to taste
- 1 tbsp. chopped fresh basil leaves
- black pepper, to taste
- 1/2 tsp. ground cumin

**DIRECTIONS:**

1. In a medium saucepan, heat the oil over medium heat and sauté the red pepper and onion for about 5 minutes, stirring every now and then, until the vegetables are softened. Add the garlic and cook for another minute while stirring all the time.
2. Take the pan off the heat and stir in the tomatoes, lime juice, cucumber, basil, vinegar, salt, cumin, and pepper to taste.
3. If you want, you can pour the mixture into a blender and pulse it until it's the consistency you want, or you can use an immersion blender.
4. Put soup in the fridge for about 2 hours, or until it's completely cold. Serve and enjoy.

**NUTRITIONAL VALUE PER SERVING:**

Calories: 124 /kcal; Carbs: 14 g; Protein: 2 g; Fat: 8 g.

## CARROT PUDDING

**Prep time:** 10 mins

**Cooking time:** 20 mins

**Total time:** 30 mins

**Servings:** 4

**INGREDIENTS:**

- 2/3 cup carrot puree
- 1 tsp. lemon zest
- 4 cups of coconut milk
- 2 tbsp. cornstarch + 4 tbsp. water, mixed together
- 1 tsp. vanilla paste
- 1 whole egg

**DIRECTIONS:**

1. Put the carrot and milk in a pot, set it over low heat, cover it, and cook until small bubbles form.
2. Whisk the cornstarch slurry, egg, and lemon zest together in a bowl. Slowly pour the mixture into the pan.
3. Cover and cook for an additional 15 minutes.
4. Divide among dessert bowls and serve!

**NUTRITIONAL VALUE PER SERVING:**

Calories: 159 /kcal; Carbs: 18 g; Protein: 4 g; Fat: 10 g.

## ROASTED VEGETABLE QUINOA AND CHICKPEA SALAD

Prep time: 10 mins

Cooking time: 35 mins

Total time: 45 mins

Servings: 1

### INGREDIENTS:
- 1 cup vegetable broth
- 1 summer squash, chopped
- ½ cup quinoa
- 1 tsp. dried oregano
- 1 cup cooked chickpeas
- 1 tbsp. dried basil
- ½ cup zucchini, diced
- ½ cup finely chopped tomatoes
- ½ cup eggplants, diced

### DIRECTIONS:
1. Bake all vegetables for about 30 minutes in the oven.
2. When the vegetables are in the oven, put the broth and quinoa in a pan and let it boil.
3. Boil it until all the broth is absorbed.
4. Now, mix all roasted vegetables, chickpeas, quinoa and all the spices in a salad bowl.
5. Your salad is done and ready to eat.

### NUTRITIONAL VALUE PER SERVING:
Calories: 100 /kcal; Carbs: 10 g; Protein: 7 g; Fat: 2 g.

## FANCY SCRAMBLED EGGS

Prep time: 5 mins

Cooking time: 5 mins

Total time: 10 mins

Servings: 4

### INGREDIENTS:
- 4 whole eggs
- 1/8 tsp. pepper
- 1/8 tsp. salt
- 2 tbsp. red bell pepper, chopped
- 1 garlic clove, chopped
- 2 tbsp. olive oil
- 1½ tsp. chives, chopped

### DIRECTIONS:
1. Mix pepper, eggs, and salt in a bowl.
2. Add red bell pepper, oil, and garlic in a large skillet and cook for 5 minutes over medium heat.
3. Add chives and egg mixture to skillet.
4. Stir eggs while cooking them over low heat for 4 to 5 minutes, or until the eggs are done.
5. Serve and enjoy.

### NUTRITIONAL VALUE PER SERVING:
Calories: 199 /kcal; Carbs: 2 g; Protein: 15 g; Fat: 13 g.

## CHEESECAKE COTTAGE CHEESE

Prep time: 5 mins +chilling time

Cooking time: 0 mins

Total time: 5 mins + chilling time

Servings: 2

### INGREDIENTS:
- 1 tsp. vanilla extract
- 1 cup low-fat cottage cheese
- 2 tsp. brown sugar
- 2 tbsp. whipped cream cheese

### DIRECTIONS:
1. Mix cream cheese, cottage cheese, brown sugar, and vanilla extract together in a bowl. Blend well.
2. Serve and enjoy with your favorite fruit.

### NUTRITIONAL VALUE PER SERVING:
Calories: 128 /kcal; Carbs: 11 g; Protein: 12 g; Fat: 4 g.

## LOADED BAKED POTATO SOUP

Prep time: 10 mins

Cooking time: 15 mins

Total time: 25 mins

Servings: 4

### INGREDIENTS:
- 1 tbsp. canola oil
- ½ cup chopped onion
- 2 slices bacon, cut in half
- 4 cups reduced-sodium chicken broth
- ½ cup reduced-fat sour cream
- ½ cup shredded Cheddar cheese, divided
- 1½ lb. russet potatoes, diced
- ¼ cup snipped chives
- ¼ tsp. freshly ground pepper

### DIRECTIONS:
1. In a large saucepan, heat the oil over medium heat. Add the bacon and cook for 4 to 5 minutes, turning it every so often, until it is crispy. Add the onion to the pan and stir it for 2 to 3 minutes, until it starts to soften. Potatoes and broth go in next. Get it to boil. Turn down the heat to a simmer and cook for 12 to 15 minutes, or until the potatoes are soft.
2. Using a slotted spoon, move about half of the potatoes to a bowl and mash them until almost smooth but still a little bit chunky. Add the mashed potatoes, sour cream, 1/4 cup of cheese, and pepper to the pan. Cook and stir for 1 to 2 minutes, until cheese melts and the soup is hot

all the way through. Serve with crumbled bacon, chives, and the remaining cheese.

**NUTRITIONAL VALUE PER SERVING:**

Calories: 328 /kcal; Carbs: 37 g; Protein: 14 g; Fat: 14 g.

## MIXED BERRY SHORTCAKE YOGURT CRUMBLE

Prep time:  5 mins

Cooking time:  5 mins

Total time:  10 mins

Servings: 2

**INGREDIENTS:**

1. 2 tbsp. almond flour
2. ¼ tsp. stevia
3. ½ tsp. ground cinnamon
4. 2 tbsp. frozen or fresh diced strawberries
5. 1 tsp. vanilla extract
6. ½ tbsp. unsalted butter
7. 1 cup nonfat plain Greek yogurt
8. 2 tbsp. frozen or fresh blueberries

**DIRECTIONS:**

1. Put the cinnamon, almond flour and stevia in a small bowl and mix them together.
2. Mix the almond flour mixture and butter together in a small skillet over medium heat. While the butter melts, stir the food often for 1 to 2 minutes. Once the butter's moisture has been absorbed and the mixture starts to get a little crisp and clumpy, take it off the heat. Set aside the almond flour mixture in a separate bowl and clean the skillet carefully.
3. Put the blueberries and strawberries in the pan and cook them for 2 to 3 minutes, stirring often, until they are soft. Take off the heat.
4. In a small bowl, mix the vanilla extract with the yogurt. Stack the fruit, yogurt, and almond flour mixture in two bowls and enjoy.

**NUTRITIONAL VALUE PER SERVING:**

Calories: 147 /kcal; Carbs: 11 g; Protein: 14 g; Fat: 7 g.

## BANANA BRULE YOGURT PARFAIT

Prep time:  5 mins

Cooking time:  2 mins

Total time:  7 mins

Servings: 1

**INGREDIENTS:**

- Nonstick cooking spray
- 1 tsp. brown sugar
- ¼ cup banana slices
- Dash ground cinnamon
- 1 cup nonfat plain Greek yogurt

**DIRECTIONS:**

1. Spray cooking spray on a small pan. Put it over a medium flame.
2. Put the slices of banana in the pan. Spread the brown sugar over the slices of banana. Cook for 1–2 minutes, stirring often, until everything is toasty. Turn off the heat.
3. Put the yogurt in a bowl, and then pour the banana mixture on top. Sprinkle cinnamon on top and eat right away.

**NUTRITIONAL VALUE PER SERVING:**

Calories: 168 /kcal; Carbs: 20 g; Protein: 24 g; Fat: 0 g.

## YOGURT POPSICLES

Prep time:  5 mins + chilling time

Cooking time:  0 mins

Total time:  5 mins + chilling time

Servings: 6

**INGREDIENTS:**

- 1 cup mixed berry
- 1 cup Greek yogurt
- ½ cup regular or instant oats
- ½ cup skim milk

**DIRECTIONS:**

1. Mix the yogurt and milk together.
2. Put some of the mix into each of your Popsicle molds.
3. Fill each mold with a few berries.
4. Add 1 tbsp. oats into each mold.
5. Put a wooden ice cream stick in each mold, and put the popsicles in the freezer.
6. Before serving run a little hot water over the mound until the popsicles come loose.

**NUTRITIONAL VALUE PER SERVING:**

Calories: 75 /kcal; Carbs: 11 g; Protein: 5 g; Fat: 0.6 g.

## NO OATS CEREAL

Prep time:  5 mins + chilling time

Cooking time:  2 mins

Total time:  7 mins + chilling time

Servings: 2

**INGREDIENTS:**

- 1 cup nonfat plain Greek yogurt
- 1 tbsp. chia seeds
- 6 tbsp. almond flour
- ¼ tsp. stevia
- 1 tbsp. unsweetened peanut butter powder
- ¼ cup fresh or frozen strawberries, diced

1. DIRECTIONS:
2. Mix the yogurt, chia seeds, almond flour, stevia and peanut butter powder in a pint-size

canning jar. Set aside.
3. Heat a pan over medium heat. Put the strawberry slices in the pan. Cook for 1 to 2 minutes over medium heat, or until the strawberries get soft.
4. Add the strawberries into the jar and mix them well with the other ingredients.
5. Put the jar in the fridge after you have tightly sealed it. Let the mixture sit for at least 8 hours or overnight to set.

### NUTRITIONAL VALUE PER SERVING:

Calories: 232 /kcal; Carbs: 14 g; Protein: 19 g; Fat: 13 g.

## CINNAMON FLAX AND ALMOND CAKES

**Prep time:** 5 mins

**Cooking time:** 20 mins

**Total time:** 25 mins

**Servings:** 4

### INGREDIENTS:

- 4 tbsp. flax meal
- 4 tbsp. unsweetened almond milk
- 4 tbsp. almond flour
- 2 tsp. brown sugar
- 2 large eggs
- 1 tsp. vanilla extract
- 1 tsp. ground cinnamon
- Nonstick cooking spray
- ¼ tsp. stevia

### DIRECTIONS:

1. Mix the flax meal, almond flour, almond milk, brown sugar, eggs, vanilla extract, cinnamon, and stevia with a fork or whisk in a large mixing bowl to make a batter.
2. Coat a large pan with cooking spray that doesn't stick, and heat it over medium heat.
3. To make small round cakes, take a heaping tablespoon of batter and spread it out. Cook for 2 to 3 minutes for each side, or until golden brown. When the cake is ready to be turned over, little bubbles will begin to form on the top.
4. Keep doing this until all of the batter is cooked. About 8 small cakes should come out of this recipe.

### NUTRITIONAL VALUE PER SERVING:

Calories: 117 /kcal; Carbs: 7 g; Protein: 7 g; Fat: 8 g.

## COCONUT ALMOND CAKES

**Prep time:** 5 mins

**Cooking time:** 20 mins

**Total time:** 25 mins

**Servings:** 4

### INGREDIENTS:

- Nonstick cooking spray
- ½ cup unsweetened coconut milk
- 1 cup almond flour
- 2 tsp. vanilla extract
- 2 large eggs
- 1 tsp. baking powder
- 1 tsp. ground cinnamon
- ¼ tsp. salt
- ½ tsp. stevia

### DIRECTIONS:

1. Spray a large pan with cooking spray that doesn't stick, and heat it over medium heat.
2. While the skillet heats up, put the almond flour, eggs, coconut milk, cinnamon, vanilla extract, stevia, baking powder, and salt in a medium bowl and beat well until everything is mixed together.
3. For each cake, about 2 tablespoons of the mixture of ingredients should be put into the pan. Cook each side for 1 to 2 minutes, or until golden brown.
4. Repeat with the rest of the batter, making sure to leave at least an inch between each cake if you are cooking more than one at the same time.
5. Take the cakes off the heat and eat them plain or with whatever topping you like.

### NUTRITIONAL VALUE PER SERVING:

Calories: 209 /kcal; Carbs: 17 g; Protein: 9 g; Fat: 7 g.

## SHRIMP CAULIFLOWER CHOWDER

**Prep time:** 10 mins

**Cooking time:** 25 mins

**Total time:** 35 mins

**Servings:** 4

### INGREDIENTS:

- 1½ cups small salad shrimp
- 1 cup cauliflower rice
- 1 cup diced yellow onion
- 1 tbsp. extra-virgin olive oil
- ¼ tsp. salt
- ½ cup water
- ½ cup unsweetened almond milk
- ½ cup light canned coconut milk, unsweetened
- Dash freshly ground black pepper
- 4 tbsp. nutritional yeast

### DIRECTIONS:

1. Heat the oil in a medium saucepan over medium heat. Cook the onion, stirring it often, for 5 to 7 minutes, or until it is almost clear.
2. Mix in the riced cauliflower, salt and water. Cook, stirring every now and then, for 6 to 8 minutes, until the cauliflower is soft and the water has been absorbed.
3. Stir well after adding the almond milk, coconut milk, pepper and nutritional yeast to the pot. Simmer for about 1 to 2 minutes over low to medium heat. Take off the heat.
4. Pour the mixture into a blender and process it on low for one to two minutes until it is smooth.
5. Pour the blended mixture back into the pan and then add the shrimp. Cook on low to medium heat for 5 - 6 minutes, until the shrimp are cooked all the way through. Take it off the heat and serve.

### NUTRITIONAL VALUE PER SERVING:

Calories: 133 /kcal; Carbs: 6 g; Protein: 14 g; Fat: 6 g.

## SEAFOOD CAKES

**Prep time:** 5 mins

**Cooking time:** 15 mins

**Total time:** 20 mins

**Servings:** 8

### INGREDIENTS:

- ½ cup canned baby shrimp
- 2 tbsp. coconut aminos, plus more for dipping
- 4 tbsp. almond flour
- 2 tbsp. light unsweetened canned coconut milk
- 2 tbsp. unsweetened almond milk
- ½ tsp. garlic powder
- ½ tsp. ginger powder
- ½ tsp. chopped parsley or dried
- ¼ tsp. salt
- 1 large egg
- 1/3 cup finely diced yellow onion
- 1 tbsp. extra-virgin olive oil
- Nonstick cooking spray

### DIRECTIONS:

1. Mix the shrimp, almond flour, almond milk, coconut aminos, egg, coconut milk, ginger powder, garlic powder, parsley, and salt together in a large mixing bowl. Mix well, and then put to the side.
2. Over medium heat, heat the oil in a medium-sized pan. Cook the onion for about 5 minutes, or until it starts to look a little bit clear. Take it off the heat and add it to the shrimp and combine it well.
3. Put one or two heaping tablespoons of the shrimp mixture in the same pan and spread it out with the back of a spoon. Repeat with the rest of the shrimp mixture to make eight shrimp cakes.
4. Cook the shrimp cakes until each side is golden brown for about for 3 to 4 minutes on each side. If necessary, cook the shrimp cakes in batches. If the cakes are sticking to the pan, lightly spray the pan with cooking spray.
5. Take the cakes off the heat and serve them with more coconut aminos on the side to dip them in.

### NUTRITIONAL VALUE PER SERVING:

Calories: 124 /kcal; Carbs: 5 g; Protein: 7 g; Fat: 9 g.

## LENTIL AND VEGETABLE SOUP

**Prep time:** 15 mins

**Cooking time:** 1 hour

**Total time:** 1 hour 15 mins

**Servings:** 12

### INGREDIENTS:

- 3 tbsp. olive oil
- 3 garlic cloves
- 1 Spanish onion, chopped
- 1 carrot, chopped
- 2 celery sticks, chopped
- 1 lb. lentils
- 6 oz. smoked ham, chopped
- 1 bay leaf
- 12½ cup stock
- 4 tomatoes, peeled and chopped
- 1½ tsp. sweet paprika
- 4 fresh parsley sprigs
- Salt and pepper to taste
- 4 tbsp. sherry vinegar

### DIRECTIONS:

1. In a pot, heat oil. Add the garlic, onion, carrot and celery, and cook over low heat for 5 to 7 minutes, until the vegetables are soft.
2. Add the ham and cook for another 3 minutes, stirring every so often. Take out and set aside cooked food.

**SOFT FOOD DIET**

3. Add lentils, a bay leaf, stock, and parsley to the pot. Turn up the heat to medium and let it boil. Turn down the heat and let it simmer for 30 minutes.
4. Add the tomatoes and return the ham and vegetables to the pot. Simmer it for another 30 minutes after stirring.
5. Take out the parsley and bay leaf and throw them away. Mix in the paprika and vinegar, and then add salt and pepper to taste. Heat for 2–3 minutes, then pour into warmed soup bowls and serve right away.

**NUTRITIONAL VALUE PER SERVING:**
Calories: 191 /kcal; Carbs: 24 g; Protein: 13 g; Fat: 5 g.

## BACON AND AVOCADO SALAD

**Prep time: 10 mins**

**Cooking time: 0 mins**

**Total time: 10 mins**

**Servings: 1**

**INGREDIENTS:**
- 1 tbsp. olive oil-based mayonnaise
- 1 cup cooked bacon
- 1 tbsp. lemon juice
- 2 tbsp. low-fat Greek yogurt
- 1 cup avocado, diced
- Pepper to taste

**DIRECTIONS:**
1. Mix the liquid-based ingredients together in a bowl to make salad dressing.
2. Now add in the avocado and bacon to make a salad.
3. Add pepper and your salad is done and ready to eat.

**NUTRITIONAL VALUE PER SERVING:**
Calories: 90 /kcal; Carbs: 12 g; Protein: 6 g; Fat: 1 g.

## BUTTERNUT SQUASH SOUP

**Prep time: 10 mins**

**Cooking time: 30 mins**

**Total time: 40 mins**

**Servings: 4**

**INGREDIENTS:**
- 5 lb. butternut squash
- ½ onion, diced
- 32 oz. almond milk
- 1 tsp. olive oil
- 1 tsp. garlic
- 1 tsp. ginger, minced
- 2 scoops unflavored protein powder
- salt and pepper for taste
- Paprika for garnish

**DIRECTIONS:**
1. In a saucepan, cook an onion in olive oil over medium heat until the onion is clear. Then add the ginger and garlic and cook for another minute.
2. Once the squash is soft, add the almond milk, broth, and spices. Bring to a boil, and then let it simmer for 15 minutes or until the squash is soft.
3. You can use an immersion blender or a regular blender to blend. Once the temperature is below 140F-60°C add protein powder.

**NUTRITIONAL VALUE PER SERVING:**
Calories: 123 /kcal; Carbs: 8 g; Protein: 9 g; Fat: 6 g.

## CAULIFLOWER GARLIC SOUP

**Prep time: 10 mins**

**Cooking time: 20 mins**

**Total time: 30 mins**

**Servings: 4**

**INGREDIENTS:**
- 1½ tbsp. extra virgin olive oil
- 1 onion, chopped
- 1 head cauliflower, cut into florets
- 2 cups vegetable broth
- 2 tsp. of garlic, minced
- Salt and pepper to taste
- 1 cup unsweetened coconut milk
- 4 scoops unflavored protein powder
- 2 tbsp. green onion, chopped
- 4 tbsp. nutritional yeast

**DIRECTIONS:**
1. In a saucepan, heat the olive oil over medium heat. Cook the onion for 3 minutes. Then add the garlic and cook for two minutes more.
2. Bring to a boil the broth and cauliflower. Once boiling, turn the heat down to a simmer and cook the cauliflower for about 15 minutes, or until it is soft.
3. Use and immersion blender to blend the soup. Then add nutritional yeast, salt, and pepper and mix well.
4. Once the temperature is below 140 F, add protein powder that has no flavor. If you want, you can add green onions on top as garnish.

**NUTRITIONAL VALUE PER SERVING:**
Calories: 219 /kcal; Carbs: 14 g; Protein: 27 g; Fat: 6 g.

## BABY ARUGULA AND PARMESAN SALAD

Prep time: 10 mins

Cooking time: 0 mins

Total time: 10 mins

Servings: 1

### INGREDIENTS:

- 1 tbsp. olive oil based mayonnaise
- 1 cup baby arugula
- 1 tbsp. lemon juice
- 2 tbsp. low fat Greek yogurt
- ½ cup parmesan cheese
- Pepper to taste

### DIRECTIONS:

1. Mix the liquid-based ingredients together in a bowl to make salad dressing.
2. Now, add the Parmesan cheese and baby arugula and mix everything together to make a salad.
3. Add pepper and your salad is ready to eat.

### NUTRITIONAL VALUE PER SERVING:

Calories: 124 /kcal; Carbs: 11 g; Protein: 5 g; Fat: 4 g.

## HIGH PROTEIN TOMATO SOUP

Prep time: 10 mins

Cooking time: 20 mins

Total time: 30 mins

Servings: 4

### INGREDIENTS:

- 1 tsp. olive oil
- 28 oz. crushed tomatoes
- 1 tsp. minced garlic
- 1 tsp. Italian seasonings
- 14 oz. diced tomatoes
- 4 scoops unflavored protein powder
1. ¼ cup Parmesan cheese
2. Basil, for garnish
3. Salt and pepper to taste
4. Cottage cheese, for garnish

### DIRECTIONS:

1. For 30 seconds, cook garlic in olive oil over medium heat.
2. Add tomatoes that have been crushed and cut up, Italian seasoning, and cheese. Cover and cook for 20 min.
3. Once it's done cooking, add protein powder when the temperature drops below 140 F-60°C.
4. Top it with basil and cottage cheese and serve.

### NUTRITIONAL VALUE PER SERVING:

Calories: 157 /kcal; Carbs: 9 g; Protein: 24 g; Fat: 3 g.

## CHICKEN SALAD

Prep time: 10 mins

Cooking time: 0 mins

Total time: 10 mins

Servings: 1

### INGREDIENTS:

- 1 tbsp. olive oil based mayonnaise
- 2 tbsp. low fat Greek yogurt
- 1 tbsp. lemon juice
- Pepper to taste
- Salt to taste
- ½ cup cooked chicken, cubes

### DIRECTIONS:

1. Mix the liquid-based ingredients together in a bowl to make a paste.
2. Now add the chicken and mix everything together to make a salad.
3. You can add salt and pepper to your taste.
4. Your salad is done and ready to eat.

### NUTRITIONAL VALUE PER SERVING:

Calories: 121 /kcal; Carbs: 4 g; Protein: 5 g; Fat: 2 g.

## GREENS SOUP

Prep time: 20 mins

Cooking time: 8 mins

Total time: 28 mins

Servings: 4

### INGREDIENTS:

- 2 onions, chopped
- 12 oz. chicken sausage
- 4 cups of chicken broth
- 2 tsp. of minced garlic

- 15 oz. black eyed peas, drained and rinsed
- 2 bunches of Swiss chard, chopped
- 10 oz. can diced tomatoes
- 15 oz. can white beans, drained and rinsed
- 1/4 tsp. salt
- 1/2 tsp. onion powder
- 1/4 tsp. garlic powder
- 1/4 tsp. crushed red pepper
- 1 bay leaf
- 1/4 tsp. paprika

### DIRECTIONS:

1. Put everything in the Instant Pot. For 8 minutes, cook on high. Allow 3–5 minutes to slowly release the pressure. Enjoy.

### NUTRITIONAL VALUE PER SERVING:

Calories: 145 /kcal; Carbs: 8 g; Protein: 7 g; Fat: 5 g.

## CLASSIC TUNA SALAD

**Prep time:** 10 mins

**Cooking time:** 0 mins

**Total time:** 10 mins

**Servings:** 1

### INGREDIENTS:

- 1 tbsp. olive oil based mayonnaise
- 2 tbsp. low fat Greek yogurt
- 1 tbsp. lemon juice
- Pepper to taste
- Salt to taste
- 1 tbsp. Dijon mustard
- ½ cup cooked tuna
- 1 tbsp. finely chopped pickles
- 1 tbsp. red onion, chopped

### DIRECTIONS:

1. Mix the liquid-based ingredients together in a bowl to make a paste.
2. Now add the chopped pickles, tuna cubes, and chopped onion and mix to make a salad.
3. You can add salt and pepper to your taste.
4. Your salad is done and ready to eat.

### NUTRITIONAL VALUE PER SERVING:

Calories: 99 /kcal; Carbs: 5 g; Protein: 3 g; Fat: 2 g.

## TOMATO, CUCUMBER AND BASIL SALAD

**Prep time:** 10 mins

**Cooking time:** 0 mins

**Total time:** 10 mins

**Servings:** 1

### INGREDIENTS:

- 1 tbsp. olive oil based mayonnaise
- 1 red onion, chopped
- 1 tbsp. lemon juice
- Pepper to taste
- 2 tbsp. low fat Greek yogurt
- 1 tbsp. Dijon mustard
- 1 cup tomatoes, chopped
- ½ cup cucumber cubes
- ½ cup finely chopped basil

### DIRECTIONS:

1. Mix the liquid-based ingredients together in a bowl to make a paste.
2. Now add the cucumber, tomato, chopped onion and basil and mix to make a salad.
3. Add pepper and your salad is done and ready to eat.

### NUTRITIONAL VALUE PER SERVING:

Calories: 112 /kcal; Carbs: 12 g; Protein: 7 g; Fat: 3 g.

## TACO SOUP

**Prep time:** 5 mins

**Cooking time:** 15 mins

**Total time:** 20 mins

**Servings:** 4

### INGREDIENTS:

- 1 onion, finely chopped
- 2 tbsp. taco seasonings
- 1 lb. lean ground turkey meat
- 8 oz. tomato sauce
- 1/2 cup black beans, drained
- 14 oz. diced tomato
- 1/2 cup kidney beans, drained

### DIRECTIONS:

1. In a saucepan, cook the ground turkey, onions, and spices over medium heat. Then add chopped tomatoes, beans, tomato sauce. After 10 minutes, add the beans. Keep cooking until the beans are warm.
2. Serve with sides of your choice.

### NUTRITIONAL VALUE PER SERVING:

Calories: 132 /kcal; Carbs: 8 g; Protein: 6 g; Fat: g.4

## SHRIMP SALAD

**Prep time:** 10 mins

**Cooking time:** 5 mins

**Total time:** 15 mins

**Servings:** 4

### INGREDIENTS:

- ½ lemon
- 1 cucumber, chopped
- 1 tsp. dried thyme
- 1 lb. shrimps

- 1 tbsp. dried basil
- ½ cup seafood sauce
- 3 tbsp. low fat Greek yogurt
- ½ cup lettuce, diced
- 1 bay leaf
- ½ cup olive oil based mayonnaise

### DIRECTIONS:

1. Fill a saucepan with water and boil it with bay leaf, thyme, shrimp, lemon juice, and dried basil.
2. Once the shrimp has been done, drain it and let it cool.
3. Mix the Greek yogurt, seafood sauce and mayonnaise in a big bowl.
4. Now add the lettuce and cucumber.
5. Put the shrimp on top of the salad after they have cooled.
6. Your salad is done and ready to eat.

### NUTRITIONAL VALUE PER SERVING:

Calories: 111 /kcal; Carbs: 5 g; Protein: 6 g; Fat: 6 g.

## CINNAMON SPICE CEREAL

**Prep time:** 5 mins + chilling time

**Cooking time:** 0 mins

**Total time:** 5 mins + chilling time

**Servings:** 1

### INGREDIENTS:

- ¾ cup nonfat plain Greek yogurt
- 3 tbsp. almond flour
- 4 tbsp. unsweetened almond milk
- 1 tbsp. chia seeds
- 2 tbsp. quick oats
- ¼ tsp. stevia
- 1 tsp. ground cinnamon

### DIRECTIONS:

1. Mix the yogurt, almond flour, almond milk, oats, cinnamon, chia seeds, and stevia together in a pint-size canning jar.
2. Close the bag tightly and put it in the fridge. Let the oat mixture sit for at least 8 hours or overnight to set.

### NUTRITIONAL VALUE PER SERVING:

Calories: 336 /kcal; Carbs: 26 g; Protein: 27 g; Fat: 17 g.

## CUCUMBER, AVOCADO, BLACK BEAN, CORN AND TOMATO SALAD

**Prep time:** 10 mins

**Cooking time:** 0 mins

**Total time:** 10 mins

**Servings:** 2

### INGREDIENTS:

- 1 tbsp. olive oil based mayonnaise
- 1 cup corn
- 1 tbsp. lemon juice
- 2 tbsp. low fat Greek yogurt
- 1 cup black beans
- ½ cup cucumber, cubes
- Pepper to taste
- 1 cup tomatoes, chopped
- 1 tbsp. Dijon mustard
- ½ cup avocado, finely chopped

### DIRECTIONS:

1. Mix the liquid-based ingredients together in a bowl to make a paste.
2. Now add the cucumber, tomato, corn, avocado, and black beans and mix to make a salad.
3. Add pepper and your salad is done and ready to eat.

### NUTRITIONAL VALUE PER SERVING:

Calories: 123 /kcal; Carbs: 8 g; Protein: 11 g; Fat: 2 g.

## ITALIAN HERB MUFFINS

**Prep time:** 5 mins

**Cooking time:** 12 mins

**Total time:** 17 mins

**Servings:** 4

### INGREDIENTS:

- Nonstick cooking spray
- 8 tbsp. almond flour
- 1 large egg
- ¼ cup shredded Parmesan cheese
- 1 tsp. Italian seasoning
- 1 tsp. garlic powder
- ¼ tsp. salt
- 1 tsp. baking powder

### DIRECTIONS:

1. Set the oven temperature to 350°F-180°C. Put four cupcake liners in a muffin tin and spray the liners with cooking spray.
2. Mix the garlic powder, parmesan cheese, Italian seasoning, almond flour, baking powder, salt and egg in a large bowl. Mix well until everything is mixed in.
3. Fill the cups with heaping tablespoons of the mixture until all of the batter is used.
4. Bake for about 12 minutes, or until the tops are golden brown.

### NUTRITIONAL VALUE PER SERVING:

Calories: 128 /kcal; Carbs: 5 g; Protein: 7 g; Fat: 10 g.

## CAULIFLOWER TOTS

*Prep time:* 5 mins

*Cooking time:* 15 mins

*Total time:* 20 mins

*Servings:* 4

### INGREDIENTS:

- ½ cup almond flour
- 1 cup cauliflower rice
- ½ cup shredded mozzarella cheese
- 1 tbsp. cornstarch
- 1 large egg
- ¼ tsp. salt

### DIRECTIONS:

- Get the oven ready at 400°F-200°C. Set aside a large baking sheet that has been lined with parchment paper.
- Mix the cauliflower rice, mozzarella cheese, almond flour, cornstarch, egg, and salt together in a large bowl. Mix well until everything is mixed in.
- Put heaping tablespoons of the mixture about an inch apart on the baking sheet until all of the batter is used. About 16 tots should come out of this recipe.
- Bake for 13 to 15 minutes, or until the edges are brown and crispy.

### NUTRITIONAL VALUE PER SERVING:
Calories: 152 /kcal; Carbs: 6 g; Protein: 9 g; Fat: 11 g.

## ALMOND CRUSTED MOZZARELLA STRIPS

*Prep time:* 10 mins

*Cooking time:* 6 mins

*Total time:* 16 mins

*Servings:* 3

### INGREDIENTS:

- 1 tbsp. cornstarch
- ½ tsp. Italian seasoning
- 8 tbsp. almond flour
- 2 large eggs
- ¼ tsp. salt
- 1 tbsp. extra-virgin olive oil
- 6 light mozzarella sticks

### DIRECTIONS:

1. The cornstarch should be put on a small plate. Mix the Italian seasoning, almond flour, and salt together on a separate small plate. In a small bowl, beat the eggs, and put them between the two plates.
2. The mozzarella sticks should be cut in half. Coat each mozzarella stick lightly in cornstarch, then soak and coat in the egg, and afterwards coat well in the almond flour mixture. Coat each piece of mozzarella well with the batter so that the cheese is completely surrounded by the mixture and doesn't spill out onto the baking sheet while it's baking. Put each piece of mozzarella that has been coated on a large plate. Repeat until each piece of mozzarella is covered.
3. Wrap the plate of mozzarella sticks in plastic wrap and put it in the freezer for about 2 hours.
4. Get the oven ready at 400°F-200°C. Put parchment paper on a baking sheet.
5. Put the mozzarella pieces on the baking sheet about 1 inch apart.
6. Use a basting brush to lightly coat each side of each piece of mozzarella with oil.
7. Bake for 4 to 6 minutes, until the crust turns a little bit golden. Keep a close eye on the cheese to make sure it doesn't start to spread.

### NUTRITIONAL VALUE PER SERVING:
Calories: 182 kcal; Carbs: 4 g; Protein: 11 g; Fat: 15 g.

## CHEESY CHICKEN AND BROCCOLI CASSEROLE

*Prep time:* 12 mins

*Cooking time:* 25 mins

*Total time:* 37 mins

*Servings:* 8

### INGREDIENTS:

- ½ tbsp. olive oil
- 2 cups broccoli florets, chopped
- 1 cup red bell pepper, sliced
- ¼ cup fat-free plain Greek yogurt
- 2 cups chicken breasts, cooked and shredded
- ½ cup shredded cheddar cheese
- 1 egg
- 2 tbsp. cilantro, chopped

### DIRECTIONS:

1. Turn the oven on to 400°F-200°C. Coat a small casserole dish with butter. Set aside.
2. Over medium-high heat, heat the olive oil in a pan. Add the bell pepper and cook it for 4 minutes, stirring every so often, until it is soft. Add the broccoli and cook for another minute or two. Take it off the heat and let it cool for five minutes.
3. Whisk the Greek yogurt and egg together in a medium bowl until they are smooth. Mix in the cheddar to combine.
4. Mix in the chicken and broccoli.
5. Spread the mixture evenly in the casserole dish that has been ready.
6. Put the casserole in the oven and bake for 20 to 25 minutes, or until it is golden brown and bubbling.
7. Add cilantro as a garnish and serve.

### NUTRITIONAL VALUE PER SERVING:
Calories: 189 /kcal; Carbs: 2 g; Protein: 22 g; Fat: 7 g.

## SALMON AND FENNEL EN PAPILLOTE

**Prep time: 5 mins**

**Cooking time: 20 mins**

**Total time: 25 mins**

**Servings: 4**

### INGREDIENTS:

- 7 salmon fillets
- 1 tsp. salt-free lemon pepper
- ½ tbsp. olive oil
- 1 lemon, sliced into rounds
- 1 bulb fennel, thinly sliced
- 4 sheets of parchment paper
- 1 tbsp. dill, chopped

### DIRECTIONS:

1. Turn the oven on to 350°F-180°C.
2. Bend each piece of parchment paper in half, then open it up and lay it flat on a clean counter.
3. Pat salmon dry. Use olive oil, and then sprinkle lemon pepper on it. Put each salmon fillet on a piece of parchment paper so that it is above the fold. Add lemon slices, fennel, and dill to the top.
4. Each piece of parchment paper should be folded over the salmon. Start folding at one corner of the edge that has been folded to make a pouch around the salmon that is sealed. Keep going until the whole thing is sealed, tucking the last edge under.
5. Put the packets of parchment on a baking sheet. Put the fish in the oven for 18–20 minutes, or until it is fully cooked. Cooking times will depend on how thick the fish is.
6. Carefully open each bag and let the steam escape. Serve and enjoy.

### NUTRITIONAL VALUE PER SERVING:

Calories: 155 /kcal; Carbs: 5 g; Protein: 19 g; Fat: 6 g.

## CHICKEN PATTIES

**Prep time: 7 mins**

**Cooking time: 20 mins**

**Total time: 27 mins**

**Servings: 8**

### INGREDIENTS:

- ½ cup chickpeas, drained and rinsed
- 1 cup spinach, finely sliced
- 16 oz. lean ground chicken
- 2 oz. reduced fat feta cheese
- 1 egg
- ½ tsp. dried oregano
- 2 cloves garlic, minced
- 1 tbsp. parsley, chopped
- ½ tsp. paprika

### DIRECTIONS:

1. Turn the oven on to 350°F-180°C. Coat a baking sheet with oil. Set aside.
2. Pulse chickpeas in a food processor until they are in small pieces.
3. Mix the chickpeas, spinach, ground chicken, feta, egg, garlic, oregano, paprika, and parsley in a large bowl. Mix until everything is well-blended.
4. Make 8 patties, each about ¼ cup in size. Place on a baking sheet that has been prepared.
5. Put them in the oven and bake for 18–20 minutes, turning them over halfway through, until they are done.
6. Serve and enjoy.

### NUTRITIONAL VALUE PER SERVING:

Calories: 112 /kcal; Carbs: 1 g; Protein: 14 g; Fat: 6 g.

## ITALIAN MEATLOAF

**Prep time: 15 mins**

**Cooking time: 50 mins**

**Total time: 1 hour 5 mins**

**Servings: 8**

### INGREDIENTS:

- 2 cloves garlic, minced
- ¼ cup red onions, small diced
- 16 oz. lean ground beef
- ½ cup zucchini, small diced
- ¼ cup almond flour
- 8 oz. lean ground turkey
- 1 egg
- 2 tbsp. grated parmesan
- 1 tsp Italian seasoning, no salt added
- ¾ cup diced tomatoes, no salt added

### DIRECTIONS:

1. Turn the oven on to 400°F-200°C. Put parchment paper in a loaf pan. Set aside.
2. Over medium-high heat, bring 2 tablespoons of water to a boil in a large pan. Add the onions and cook for 3–4 minutes, until they become clear. Add zucchini and sauté 3-4 minutes, until just soft. Add the garlic and cook for 30 seconds, until it smells good.
3. Take out and put somewhere to cool. If the pan starts to dry out, add 1 tablespoon of water at a time.
4. Mix the cooled vegetables, turkey, beef, Parmesan, almond flour and egg together in a large bowl until everything is mixed together.
5. Move to a loaf pan.
6. Crushed tomatoes should go on top.
7. Put the pan in the oven and bake for 30–40 minutes, or until the loaf is cooked properly.
8. Let it rest for 10 minutes, cut the loaf into slices and serve.

### NUTRITIONAL VALUE PER SERVING:

Calories: 175 /kcal; Carbs: 3 g; Protein: 26 g; Fat: 6 g.

## CRANBERRY CHICKEN SALAD

*Prep time: 5 mins*

*Cooking time: 0 mins*

*Total time: 5 mins*

*Servings: 8*

### INGREDIENTS:
- ¼ cup low-fat cottage cheese
- 1 tbsp. lemon juice
- ¼ tbsp. low-fat Greek yogurt
- ¼ cup celery, chopped
- 2 cups chicken breasts, boiled and shredded
- ¼ cup fresh cranberries, chopped
- ¼ cup carrots, shredded
- 2 tbsp. dill, chopped and divided
- 2 tbsp. parsley, chopped

### DIRECTIONS:
1. Whisk Greek yogurt, cottage cheese, and lemon juice together in a large bowl until smooth.
2. Add shredded chicken, carrots, celery, parsley, cranberries, and half of the dill. Stir until the mixture is smooth.
3. Serve with the rest of the dill on top.

### NUTRITIONAL VALUE PER SERVING:
Calories: 126 /kcal; Carbs: 2 g; Protein: 21 g; Fat: 3 g.

## SPINACH AND MUSHROOM EGG CUPS

*Prep time: 5 mins*

*Cooking time: 25 mins*

*Total time: 30 mins*

*Servings: 6*

### INGREDIENTS:
- 12 large eggs, divided
- ½ cup shredded cheddar
- 3 tbsp. low fat plain Greek yogurt
- 2 oz. spinach, chopped
- 3 oz. mushrooms, chopped

### DIRECTIONS:
1. Turn the oven on to 350°F-180°C. Grease a muffin pan with cooking spray. Set aside.
2. Separate the yolks from the whites of 8 eggs. Put the yolks in a separate bowl to use in another recipe and put the whites in a large bowl. Add 4 more whole eggs and Greek yogurt to the mix. Mix until it's smooth.
3. Now add mushrooms, cheese, and spinach and stir to combine.
4. Pour the mixture into 8 muffin cups. Put them to oven and bake 22-25 minutes, until set and golden.
5. Cool for a few minutes, and then carefully take out of the muffin tin.
6. Serve and enjoy.

### NUTRITIONAL VALUE PER SERVING:
Calories: 120 /kcal; Carbs: 2 g; Protein: 13 g; Fat: 6 g.

## CREAMY TUSCAN SHRIMP

*Prep time: 10 mins*

*Cooking time: 6 mins*

*Total time: 16 mins*

*Servings: 8*

### INGREDIENTS:
- 1 tbsp. unsalted butter
- 3 cloves garlic, minced
- 8 oz. shrimp, peeled & deveined
- 3 tbsp. low-fat plain Greek yogurt
- 2 cups baby arugula
- 1 tsp salt-free Italian seasoning
- ¾ cup salt added diced tomatoes
- 2 tbsp. parsley, chopped

### DIRECTIONS:
1. Melt the butter in a large pan over medium-high heat.
2. Add the shrimp and cook for 1 to 2 minutes, until they turn pink.
3. Add the garlic and cook for another minute, or until the shrimp is done and the garlic smells good.
4. Stir in the arugula until it wilts.
5. Add Greek yogurt, diced tomatoes, half of the parsley, and Italian seasoning. Stir to mix, then cook for 1–2 minutes, until everything is cooked.
6. Serve the shrimp with the rest of the parsley on top.

### NUTRITIONAL VALUE PER SERVING:
Calories: 55 /kcal; Carbs: 2 g; Protein: 7 g; Fat: 2 g.

## BRAISED COLLARDS WITH PORK AND BEANS

*Prep time: 10 mins*

*Cooking time: 45 mins*

*Total time: 55 mins*

*Servings: 8*

### INGREDIENTS:
- 1 tbsp. olive oil
- 1 clove garlic, minced
- ¼ cup onion, chopped
- 3 cups collard greens, chopped
- 8 oz. lean ground pork
- ½ cup low sodium chicken broth
- 1 tbsp. apple cider vinegar
- 1 cup no salt added pinto beans

### DIRECTIONS:
1. Olive oil should be in a large pot over medium-

high heat.
2. Add the onion and cook it for 3–4 minutes, until it becomes clear. Add the garlic and cook for 30 seconds, until it smells good.
3. Add the pork and cook for 5–7 minutes, stirring every so often to break it up, until it's cooked all the way through.
4. Add collard greens, 1/2 cup water, apple cider vinegar, chicken broth, and pinto beans. Bring to a boil, then turn the heat down to medium-low and let it simmer for 25–35 minutes, or until the collards are soft.
5. Serve and enjoy.

### NUTRITIONAL VALUE PER SERVING:

Calories: 87 /kcal; Carbs: 8 g; Protein: 9 g; Fat: 3 g.

## DEVILED EGG AND BACON

**Prep time:** 8 mins

**Cooking time:** 0 mins

**Total time:** 8 mins

**Servings:** 8

### INGREDIENTS:

- 8 Eggs, hard boiled and peeled
- ½ cup Low-fat plain Greek yogurt
- 1 tbsp. Dijon mustard
- 2 tbsp. Dill, chopped
- 3 tbsp. chickpeas, rinsed and drained
- 2 Slices bacon, cooked and crumbled
- ¼ tsp. Paprika

### DIRECTIONS:

1. Cut each egg from center. Remove the yolks with care. Half of the yolks should be discarded and the other half should be put in a food processor. Add Greek yogurt, chickpeas, Dijon mustard, and half of the dill. Blend until it's smooth.
2. Cut a thin slice off the bottom of each egg white so that it can sit flat. Put together on a plate.
3. Put prepared the egg yolk mixture into each egg white with a spoon or a pipe. Sprinkle paprika on top, and then add crumbled bacon and the rest of the dill.
4. Serve and enjoy.

### NUTRITIONAL VALUE PER SERVING:

Calories: 77 /kcal; Carbs: 2 g; Protein: 8 g; Fat: 3 g.

## PORK TACO SOUP

**Prep time:** 10 mins

**Cooking time:** 17 mins

**Total time:** 27 mins

**Servings:** 8

### INGREDIENTS:

- 1 tsp. cumin
- ½ tsp. paprika
- ½ tsp. onion powder
- ¼ tsp. dried oregano
- 1 tbsp. olive oil
- ½ tsp. garlic powder
- ½ cup black beans, no salt added
- ½ lb. lean ground pork
- 1 cup chicken broth, low sodium
- ½ cup pinto beans, no salt added
- ¼ cup low-fat plain greek yogurt
- 1 cup zucchini, chopped
- ¼ cup cilantro, chopped

### DIRECTIONS:

1. Roast cumin, garlic powder, paprika, onion powder and oregano in a medium pot over medium heat for 2-3 minutes, stirring often, until fragrant.
2. Raise the temperature to medium-high. Stir in the olive oil and heat for 1 minute.
3. Add the pork and cook for 5–7 minutes, stirring every so often to break it up, until it's cooked all the way through.
4. Add chicken broth, pinto beans, black beans, and zucchini. Mix everything together, and then bring to a boil. Turn the heat down to medium-low and let the zucchini simmer for 4-5 minutes, or until it is soft.
5. Serve soup with 1/2 tablespoon of Greek yogurt and cilantro on top.

### NUTRITIONAL VALUE PER SERVING:

Calories: 100 /kcal; Carbs: 8 g; Protein: 10 g; Fat: 3 g.

## COCONUT CHICKEN SOUP

**Prep time:** 20 mins

**Cooking time:** 30 mins

**Total time:** 50 mins

**Servings:** 6

### INGREDIENTS:

- 1 lb. chicken breast, sliced
- 1 inch piece ginger, minced
- 1 red bell pepper, thinly sliced
- 1 cup pumpkin, cubed
- 1 tbsp. coconut oil
- Salt and pepper, to taste
- 2 garlic cloves, minced
- Handful cilantro leaves
- 1 small onion, thinly sliced
- 1 medium zucchini, diced
- 14 oz. lite coconut milk
- 1 small chili pepper, thinly sliced
- Juice of 1 lime
- 2 cups chicken broth

### DIRECTIONS:

1. Marinate the sliced chicken breast with salt and pepper to taste.
2. Heat the coconut oil in a large pot over high heat and then add the marinated chicken

breast and stir-fry for 4-5 minutes over high heat, or until the surface of the chicken is no longer pink.
3. Combine the minced ginger and garlic and chopped onion in the pot and stir-fry for a further 2-3 minutes. Stir in the chopped zucchini and cubed pumpkin. Add the sliced chilli pepper, chicken broth, coconut milk, bell pepper, and lime juice and give everything a thorough stir once more.
4. Bring to a boil, then reduce to a low heat, cover, and cook for 20 minutes, just until the pumpkin is completely cooked.
5. Remove from the heat and, if needed, season with more salt and pepper. Before serving garnish the soup with cilantro leaves.

### NUTRITIONAL VALUE PER SERVING:
Calories: 230 /kcal; Carbs: 12 g; Protein: 17 g; Fat: 13 g.

## BAKED FISH WITH ALMOND CHUTNEY

**Prep time:** 5 mins

**Cooking time:** 20 mins

**Total time:** 25 mins

**Servings:** 4

### INGREDIENTS:
- 1 lb. flaky white fish (flounder, tilapia, etc.)
- 2 tsp. lemon juice
- 1 tbsp. olive oil
- 1 tsp. coriander
- ½ cup no salt added diced tomatoes
- ½ cup sliced raw almonds

### DIRECTIONS:
1. Turn the oven on to 375°F-190°C.
2. Olive oil and lemon juice should be mixed together in a large casserole dish.
3. Dry fish with a paper towel. Put the fish in the casserole dish and turn it to coat it with the olive oil mixture. Spread out into one layer. Put the fish in the oven for 15 to 20 minutes, or until it is fully cooked. Cooking times will be different for different thicknesses.
4. Almonds, coriander and diced tomatoes should all be put into a food processor or high-speed blender and mixed together to prepare chutney.
5. Take the fish out of the oven and put the chutney on top. Return to oven for another 2–3 minutes, or until the fish is flaky and the chutney is warm.

### NUTRITIONAL VALUE PER SERVING:
Calories: 136 /kcal; Carbs: 2 g; Protein: 16 g; Fat: 7 g.

## TURKEY KALE MEATBALLS

**Prep time:** 10 mins

**Cooking time:** 30 mins

**Total time:** 40 mins

**Servings:** 5

### INGREDIENTS:
- 1 lb. lean ground turkey
- 1 tbsp. low sodium parmesan cheese
- 1½ cups baby kale, finely chopped
- ¼ cup low-fat plain Greek yogurt
- 1 egg
- 1 tsp. garlic powder
- 1 tsp. apple cider vinegar
- 2 tbsp. parsley, chopped
- 2 tbsp. dill, chopped

### DIRECTIONS:
1. Turn the oven on to 350°F-180°C. Coat a baking sheet with oil. Set aside.
2. Mix the turkey, Parmesan, kale, and egg in a large bowl. Roll the meat into 16 small balls. Place on a baking sheet that has been prepared. Put the pan in the oven and bake for 25 to 30 minutes, turning it over halfway through, until the food is done.
3. Mix together 1 tablespoon of hot water, apple cider vinegar, Greek yogurt, dill, garlic powder, and parsley in a small bowl with a whisk to make herbed sauce.
4. Serve meatballs with the prepared sauce and enjoy.

### NUTRITIONAL VALUE PER SERVING:
Calories: 172 /kcal; Carbs: 2 g; Protein: 32 g; Fat: 4 g.

## CROCKPOT CHICKEN CURRY

**Prep time:** 15 mins

**Cooking time:** 4 hours

**Total time:** 4 hour 15 mins

**Servings:** 6

### INGREDIENTS:
- 1 onion, diced
- 1 tsp. ginger root
- 5 garlic cloves
- 1½ tsp. salt
- 2 tomatoes
- 2 tsp. ground turmeric
- ½ tsp. cayenne pepper
- ½ cup Greek yogurt
- 1 tsp. garam masala
- 8 cups baby spinach
- 1 lb. boneless chicken
- 4 green cardamom pods
- 1 tsp. ground cinnamon
- 1 tbsp. whole cloves

**DIRECTIONS:**

1. Everything except the chicken, spinach, and whole spices should be ground up in a food processor. Make a nice paste that is smooth. Be patient, this could take a few minutes.
2. Put the chicken pieces in a slow cooker and pour the sauce you just made over them. Place whole spices in.
3. Cut the spinach into small pieces and add it in the last hour of cooking.
4. Cook on high for four hours, until the chicken is soft.
5. Serve and enjoy.

**NUTRITIONAL VALUE PER SERVING:**
Calories: 186 /kcal; Carbs: 8 g; Protein: 28 g; Fat: 4 g.

## EGG WHITE OMELET

**Prep time:** 10 mins

**Cooking time:** 10 mins

**Total time:** 20 mins

**Servings:** 1

**INGREDIENTS:**

- ½ onion, finely chopped
- 2 cups fresh baby spinach
- ¼ cup broccoli, small florets
- ¼ bell pepper, finely chopped
- ½ cup egg whites
- 4-5 grape tomatoes, cut in half
- 3 mushrooms, finely chopped
- pinch of cinnamon
- 3 slices apple, chopped
- salt and black pepper, to taste

**DIRECTIONS:**

1. Spray a medium-sized nonstick pan with nonstick spray and heat it to medium. Add the mushrooms and onion and cook for 3 to 5 minutes, or until the onion is soft. Add the bell pepper, apple, mushrooms and broccoli, to the skillet and cook for 1 to 2 minutes. Sea salt, ground pepper, and cinnamon should be sprinkled on top.
2. Add the spinach and cook and stir it until it is hot and has wilted. Toss in tomatoes.
3. Take it off the heat, cover it, and keep it warm.
4. Spray a little cooking spray on the same medium nonstick skillet and turn the heat to low or medium. Add the egg whites and cook for 2 minutes.
5. Spoon the vegetable mixture onto half of the omelet, fold the omelet over, slide it onto a plate, and add more salt and pepper to taste.

**NUTRITIONAL VALUE PER SERVING:**
Calories: 189 /kcal; Carbs: 25 g; Protein: 19 g; Fat: 1 g.

## CHERRY BERRY FROZEN GREEK YOGURT

**Prep time:** 10 mins

**Cooking time:** 0 mins

**Total time:** 10 mins

**Servings:** 4

**INGREDIENTS:**

- 24 oz. strawberry Greek yogurt
- ¼ cup unsweetened frozen strawberries
- 1 tsp. vanilla extract
- ¼ cup Splenda

**DIRECTIONS:**

1. In a bowl, mix the ingredients until they are well blended.
2. Pour into the bowl of your ice cream maker and follow the instructions that came with it. When it comes out of the machine, the ice cream will look like soft serve.
3. Serve and enjoy.

**NUTRITIONAL VALUE PER SERVING:**
Calories: 165 /kcal; Carbs: 28 g; Protein: 13 g; Fat: 0 g.

## CURRIED CAULIFLOWER SOUP

**Prep time:** 10 mins

**Cooking time:** 30 mins

**Total time:** 40 mins

**Servings:** 10

**INGREDIENTS:**

- 1 tsp. extra virgin olive oil
- 1 large head cauliflower, cut into 1-inch pieces
- 1 medium onion, diced
- 2 tbsp. curry powder
- 14-oz can light coconut milk
- 1 tsp. ground cumin
- 1 tsp. ground turmeric
- Salt to taste
- 1/4 tsp. ground cinnamon
- 1 tsp. stevia
- 1/4 cup chopped fresh cilantro

**DIRECTIONS:**

1. On low heat, warm the olive oil in a large pot. When the onion is golden, add it to the pan. Add the coconut milk, cauliflower, turmeric, curry powder, sugar, cumin, cinnamon, and salt to taste. Pour enough water on top to cover.
2. Bring to a low boil, then turn down the heat and simmer for about 10 minutes, or until the cauliflower is soft.
3. Use an immersion blender to mix the soup until it has the right texture. If you are using a blender with a stand, let the mixture cool for 20 minutes. Fill the blender with the soup. Put a clean, folded towel over the lid to hold it down firmly.

Blend the soup on low speed until it is smooth. If you want it hot, put it back in the pot and heat it up.
4. Pour the soup into bowls and top with cilantro to serve.

### NUTRITIONAL VALUE PER SERVING:

Calories: 55 /kcal; Carbs: 7 g; Protein: 1 g; Fat: 3 g.

## CURRIED LENTIL SOUP

**Prep time: 10 mins**

**Cooking time: 10 mins**

**Total time: 20 mins**

**Servings: 4**

### INGREDIENTS:

- 1 tsp. canola oil
- 1 tbsp. garlic, minced
- 1 cup chopped onion
- 2 cups fresh baby spinach
- ¼ tsp. salt
- 1½ tbsp. balsamic vinegar
- 1½ tbsp. curry powder
- 1 tbsp. ginger, minced
- 3 cups vegetable broth, low sodium
- 16 oz. package steamed lentils
- ¼ cup plain fat free Greek yogurt
- 1/8 tsp. cayenne pepper
- ¼ cup fresh cilantro
- ¼ tsp. pepper

### DIRECTIONS:

1. Put oil in the pan, add the onion, and cook for 3 minutes. Put in the garlic and ginger and cook for 1 minute. Add the cayenne pepper and curry powder and stir constantly for 30 seconds while cooking.
2. Mix in the lentils, broth, and vinegar. Turn up the heat and bring to a boil. Reduce the heat and let it cook for 5 minutes.
3. Use a hand-held blender to mix the lentils and water. Add in spinach, pepper and salt to the pot, stir till the spinach wilts.
4. Add 2 tablespoons of cilantro in the soup and mix.
5. Serve with the rest of the yogurt and cilantro on top.

### NUTRITIONAL VALUE PER SERVING:

Calories: 210 /kcal; Carbs: 35 g; Protein: 14 g; Fat: 2 g.

## CHICKEN AND BEAN BAKE

**Prep time: 10 mins**

**Cooking time: 45 mins**

**Total time: 55 mins**

**Servings: 6**

### INGREDIENTS:

- 2 cans of garbanzo beans
- 2 tsp. chopped fresh herbs
- 1/2 tsp. black pepper
- 1 cup green beans, fresh or frozen
- 1 tsp. fresh garlic, minced
- 1/2 tsp. kosher salt
- 2 tbsp. olive oil
- Red pepper flakes to taste
- 6 skinless chicken breasts

### DIRECTIONS:

1. Prepare materials first by draining and rinsing beans, chopping herbs, and mincing garlic.
2. On the bottom of a casserole dish, combine beans, garlic, herbs, salt, red pepper flakes, and pepper. Place the breasts on top and drizzle olive oil on chicken, and season with additional salt and pepper.
3. Bake for 45 minutes at 425°F-220°C in the oven.

### NUTRITIONAL VALUE PER SERVING:

Calories: 263 /kcal; Carbs: 22 g; Protein: 31 g; Fat: 7 g.

## WHITE VEGGIE SCRAMBLE

**Prep time: 10 mins**

**Cooking time: 5 mins**

**Total time: 15 mins**

**Servings: 1**

### INGREDIENTS:

- Spray canola oil
- 2 tbsp. chopped red and yellow peppers
- ½ tbsp. chopped red onion
- 3 egg whites
- ½ cup chopped spinach
- 1 tbsp. salsa

### DIRECTIONS:

1. Canola oil should be sprayed on a little frying pan. For two to three minutes, sauté the onion and pepper.
2. Add spinach and cover, and simmer for an additional two to three minutes or until tender.
3. Over medium heat, add the egg whites and stir until they are cooked.
4. If desired, fold in half and add tablespoon of salsa on top.

### NUTRITIONAL VALUE PER SERVING:

Calories: 110 /kcal; Carbs: 7 g; Protein: 14 g; Fat: 0 g.

## FRESH HUMMUS

**Prep time: 10 mins**

**Cooking time: 0 mins**

**Total time: 10 mins**

**Servings: 4**

### INGREDIENTS:

- 1 can of chickpeas
- ¼ cup tahini
- 1 large fresh lemon, juiced
- 2 tbsp. extra virgin olive oil
- 1-2 tbsp. water
- 1 large garlic clove, minced
- 1/2 tsp. ground cumin
- 1 tsp. sea salt
- Paprika, for garnish

### DIRECTIONS:

1. Tahini and lemon juice should be blended in a food processor. Combine thoroughly after mixing. When necessary, pause the operation, scrape the sides with a silicone spatula, and continue processing for another 30 to 45 seconds.
2. Combine the mixture with garlic, olive oil, cumin, and sea salt. Similar to step one, pause, scrape the sides if necessary, and then continue processing for another 30 to 60 seconds.
3. Blend in half a can of rinsed chickpeas before adding to the mixture. Once mixed, add the remaining half of the chickpeas and process again.
4. Add 1-2 tbsp. of water as required thinning out hummus if it's too thick or hasn't been totally processed, then processing for around 30 seconds to achieve the appropriate texture.
5. Place the hummus in a serving bowl and top with paprika and extra virgin olive oil. Serve with fresh vegetables or pitas. Refrigerate any leftover hummus in an airtight container.

### NUTRITIONAL VALUE PER SERVING:

Calories: 260 /kcal; Carbs: 22 g; Protein: 9 g; Fat: 17 g.

## KEY LIME PIE

**Prep time: 10 mins**

**Cooking time: 5 mins**

**Total time: 15 mins**

**Servings: 4**

### INGREDIENTS:

- 2 cups Jell-O - sugar free lime
- 2 scoops unflavored protein powder
- 1½ cup plain Greek yogurt
- ¼ cup water

### DIRECTIONS:

1. Water should be heated until it is warm but not boiling.
2. Pour the boiling water over the Jell-O crystals in a tall-sided bowl that has been filled with the powder. While you gather the other ingredients, let it sit there.
3. Blend the protein powder and plain yogurt in the bowl.
4. To set, pour into ramekins.
5. It's done, serve and enjoy.

### NUTRITIONAL VALUE PER SERVING:

Calories: 101 /kcal; Carbs: 4 g; Protein: 20 g; Fat: 0 g.

## BROCCOLI SOUP

**Prep time: 10 mins**

**Cooking time: 20 mins**

**Total time: 30 mins**

**Servings: 6**

### INGREDIENTS:

- 4 cups vegetable broth
- ¼ tsp. salt
- 1 onion, quartered
- 2½ lb. broccoli florets
- 1 cup milk, low-fat

### DIRECTIONS:

1. In a large saucepan, combine the broccoli, vegetable broth, and onion; bring to a boil above high heat. After a boil reduce heat and cover, and cook for 20 minutes, or until broccoli is soft.
2. In a blender, puree the soup and return it to the pot. Add milk and salt to the soup. If necessary, add more broth or water. Pour the soup into serving dishes and enjoy.

### NUTRITIONAL VALUE PER SERVING:

Calories: 90 /kcal; Carbs: 12 g; Protein: 7 g; Fat: 2 g.

## CREAMY TOMATO SOUP

**Prep time: 10 mins**

**Cooking time: 25 mins**

**Total time: 35 mins**

**Servings: 6**

### INGREDIENTS:

- 1 tbsp. organic canola oil
- 1/2 tsp. ground cumin
- 1½ cups chopped red onion
- 1/4 tsp. hot smoked paprika
- 3/8 tsp. salt
- 28 oz. chopped tomatoes
- 4 minced garlic cloves
- ¼ cup fat free milk
- 1 cup vegetable stock

### DIRECTIONS:

1. Over medium heat, warm a medium saucepan. Add canola oil, ground cumin, finely chopped red onion, salt, and hot smoked paprika in a skillet and cook for 8 minutes while stirring.
2. Now add 4 minced garlic cloves and further cook for 1 minute.
3. Add 1/2 cup vegetable stock and a 28 oz. can of diced tomatoes and simmer for 15 minutes on low heat.
4. Add 1/4 cup whole milk after removing from heat and blend it to the desired consistency using an immersion blender.
5. Serve and enjoy.

### NUTRITIONAL VALUE PER SERVING:
Calories: 92 /kcal; Carbs: 14 g; Protein: 3 g; Fat: 2 g.

## SPINACH AND MUSHROOM MUFFINS

**Prep time:** 10 mins

**Cooking time:** 40 mins

**Total time:** 50 mins

**Servings:** 15

### INGREDIENTS:

- 1/4 cup butter
- Salt and pepper, to taste
- 8 oz. mushrooms, sliced
- 5 oz. fresh spinach
- 2 cloves garlic, minced
- 2 tsp. baking powder
- 2/3 cup coconut flour
- 1/2 tsp. pepper
- ¾ tsp. salt
- 1/2 cup whipping cream
- 7 large eggs
- 1 cup grated cheese of choice

### DIRECTIONS:

1. Set the oven to 350°F-180°C and generously butter a muffin tray.
2. Melt butter in a skillet over medium heat. Add the sliced mushrooms once it is hot and melted. Stirring is not necessary after the first minute. Then, add salt and pepper to taste, and continue to cook for another 5 to 7 minutes, or until the mushrooms are golden brown.
3. After cooking the garlic for 30 seconds or until it becomes aromatic, add the fresh spinach and cook it for 1 minute or until just wilted. Place aside.
4. Mix the baking powder, coconut flour, salt, and pepper in a big bowl. Whisk in the eggs, cheese and whipping cream. Add the mixture of spinach and mushrooms.
5. Fill each muffin cup with batter until it is about 3/4 filled. Bake for 25 to 30 minutes, or until the pastry is puffy, firm to the touch, and light golden brown.

### NUTRITIONAL VALUE PER SERVING:
Calories: 148 /kcal; Carbs: 5 g; Protein: 6 g; Fat: 10 g.

## MEDITERRANEAN TOMATO FISH

**Prep time:** 10 mins

**Cooking time:** 30 mins

**Total time:** 40 mins

**Servings:** 4

### INGREDIENTS:

- 1 cup cherry tomatoes, sliced in half
- ¼ cup chopped Kalamata olives
- 2 cups fresh tomatoes, chopped
- 1 tsp. Italian seasoning
- Salt and pepper to taste
- ¼ cup capers
- 1 tbsp. olive oil
- 4 fish filets

### DIRECTIONS:

1. Set the oven to 400 °F-200°C.
2. Tomatoes should be simmered in a medium pot on medium high for 15-20 minutes, or until most of the liquid was boiled off and they had somewhat condensed.
3. Reduce heat to low, then stir in cherry tomatoes, olives, capers, spices, and anchovy paste.
4. Season fish with salt and pepper in a medium oven-safe skillet while the oil is heating up.
5. Sear the fish for 4-5 minutes with the skin side up until you have a lovely char.
6. Place fish in the oven for about 8 minutes, or until it appears to be thoroughly cooked.
7. Serve fish topped with tomato mixture.

### NUTRITIONAL VALUE PER SERVING:
Calories: 271 /kcal; Carbs: 13 g; Protein: 43 g; Fat: 7 g.

## SWEET POTATO TUNA SALA

**Prep time:** 5 mins

**Cooking time:** 0 mins

**Total time:** 5 mins

**Servings:** 2

### INGREDIENTS:

- ½ cup cherry tomatoes
- 1 tbsp. Dijon mustard
- ½ cup celery
- 1½ cup baked sweet potato chunks
- 5 oz. canned tuna
- 2½ tbsp. hummus
- 1 green scallion

### DIRECTIONS:

1. Put the tuna in a small dish after draining. To cut the lumps into smaller pieces, use a fork.
2. Mix in the celery, tomatoes, scallions, tomatoes, and sweet potato chunks. To moisten the tuna to your preferred consistency, add the hummus and mustard.

3. Add a pinch of freshly ground pepper and sea salt.
4. Serve and enjoy.

**NUTRITIONAL VALUE PER SERVING:**
Calories: 456 /kcal; Carbs: 69 g; Protein: 20 g; Fat: 8 g.

## ALMOND BANANA GREEK YOGURT

*Prep time:* 5 mins

*Cooking time:* 0 mins

*Total time:* 5 mins

*Servings:* 1

**INGREDIENTS:**
- 1 small banana
- 1 tbsp. honey
- 1 cup plain Greek nonfat yogurt
- 1 tbsp. raw sliced almonds

**DIRECTIONS:**
1. Bananas should be chopped finely and combined with yogurt.
2. Add honey and almond slices to your yogurt for a tasty garnish. Enjoy.

**NUTRITIONAL VALUE PER SERVING:**
Calories: 183 /kcal; Carbs: 42 g; Protein: 4 g; Fat: 4 g.

## PEANUT BUTTER BANANA ICE CREAM

*Prep time:* 10 mins

*Cooking time:* 0 mins

*Total time:* 10 mins

*Servings:* 1

**INGREDIENTS:**
- 1 cup vanilla soy milk
- 1 tbsp. peanut butter syrup, sugar free
- 2 tbsp. powdered peanut butter
- 1½ scoops whey protein powder, vanilla
- 1 banana

**DIRECTIONS:**
1. Blend the items thoroughly in a bowl. Incorporate into the bowl of your ice cream machine as directed by the manufacturer.
2. When ice cream is completed in the ice cream maker, it will resemble soft serve.

**NUTRITIONAL VALUE PER SERVING:**
Calories: 340 /kcal; Carbs: 42 g; Protein: 40 g; Fat: 5 g.

## BALSAMIC SALMON

*Prep time:* 10 mins

*Cooking time:* 8 mins

*Total time:* 18 mins

*Servings:* 2

**INGREDIENTS:**
- ½ tbsp. coconut oil
- 2 tbsp. balsamic vinegar
- ½ tbsp. honey
- 2 salmon fillets
- 1 tsp. red chili flakes

**DIRECTIONS:**
1. In a large skillet, heat the oil over medium to high heat. Season the fish with salt and pepper on both sides.
2. Cook the salmon in the skillet for 1 to 2 minutes on each side, or until it turns golden.
3. In a small bowl, combine the honey, vinegar, and red pepper flakes while the salmon is cooking. When the fish is fork-tender and the liquid has reduced and thickened, add the vinegar mixture to the skillet and simmer for about 5 minutes.

**NUTRITIONAL VALUE PER SERVING:**
Calories: 250 /kcal; Carbs: 8 g; Protein: 24 g; Fat: 15 g.

## SAVORY QUINOA MUFFINS

*Prep time:* 10 mins

*Cooking time:* 30 mins

*Total time:* 40 mins

*Servings:* 24

**INGREDIENTS:**
- ½ cup low-fat crumbled feta
- 4 cups cooked and cooled quinoa
- ¼ cup canola oil
- 2 large eggs
- 1 cup fresh spinach, chopped
- 2 cups all-purpose flour
- ¼ cup skim milk
- 1 tsp. salt
- 1½ tsp. baking powder
- 1/2 cup frozen peas
- ½ tsp. finely ground black pepper
- 1 zucchini, grated
- 1 tsp. chopped fresh dill

**DIRECTIONS:**
1. Set oven to 350°F-180°C. Use cooking spray to muffin pans. If preferred, cupcake liners are also an option.
2. Mix oil, milk, and eggs in a large bowl.
3. Combine the baking powder, flour, salt, and pepper in a separate, smaller dish. Add quinoa

and stir.
4. Once combined, add this mixture to the wet ingredients and whisk. Avoid overmixing.
5. Peas, dill, spinach, zucchini, and feta should be added now and stir just enough to mix.
6. Scoop the batter into the pan and bake for 30 minutes.

### NUTRITIONAL VALUE PER SERVING:
Calories: 98 /kcal; Carbs: 13 g; Protein: 3 g; Fat: 3 g.

## BROCCOLI CHEESE SOUP

**Prep time: 10 mins**

**Cooking time: 10 mins**

**Total time: 20 mins**

**Servings: 4**

### INGREDIENTS:
- 3 cups vegetable stock, unsalted
- 1 cup diced yellow onion
- 4 cups broccoli
- 1/2 tsp. salt
- 1/4 tsp. freshly ground black pepper
- 4 oz. shredded cheddar cheese, divided
- 1/4 + 1/8 cup fat free half-and-half
- 1 carrot, chopped
- 3 garlic cloves, minced
- 1/4 cup parsley leaves

### DIRECTIONS:
1. Mix the first seven ingredients together in a large pot and bring to a boil. Turn down the heat and let it cook for 10 minutes, or until the broccoli is soft.
2. Remove the pot from heat. Use a hand blender to blend the soup until it is smooth and creamy.
3. Mix in 2 ounces of cheese and 1/4 cup plus 1/8 cup of half-and-half. You don't need to turn on the stove again. The cheese will melt from the heat left over from the soup.
4. Top each bowl with the remaining 1 tablespoon of cheese and parsley.

### NUTRITIONAL VALUE PER SERVING:
Calories: 183 /kcal; Carbs: 16 g; Protein: 11 g; Fat: 6 g.

## CHICKPEA SOUP

**Prep time: 5 mins**

**Cooking time: 25 mins**

**Total time: 30 mins**

**Servings: 6**

### INGREDIENTS:
- 1 cup plum tomatoes with liquid
- ½ red bell pepper, diced
- 1 cup canned chickpeas, rinsed, drained
- ½ tsp. dried leaf basil
- 4 cups Chicken Broth
- 1 tsp. olive oil
- 1 garlic clove, minced
- 1 small onion, chopped
- 1 carrot, sliced
- 1 celery stalk, sliced
- Black pepper to taste

### DIRECTIONS:
1. Heat the oil in a nonstick skillet and sauté the celery, garlic and onion for 5 minutes. Mix together the remaining ingredients.
2. Bring to a boil, and then lower to a low heat and cook, covered, for 20 minutes.
3. Serve and enjoy.

### NUTRITIONAL VALUE PER SERVING:
Calories: 74 /kcal; Carbs: 13 g; Protein: 15 g; Fat: 1 g.

## TOMATO SOUP

**Prep time: 10 mins**

**Cooking time: 45 mins**

**Total time: 55 mins**

**Servings: 4**

### INGREDIENTS:
- 1 tbsp. butter
- Pinch of cayenne pepper
- 3 tbsp. snipped dill, for garnish
- 2 large garlic cloves, chopped
- 1 onion, finely chopped
- 28 oz. diced tomatoes
- 1/8 tsp. ground mace
- 1 tsp. dried thyme
- Salt and black pepper, to taste

### DIRECTIONS:
1. In a small Dutch oven, melt the butter over medium-high heat.
2. Cook the onions for until they are transparent and then add the garlic and sauté for further 5 to 6 minutes.
3. Toss in the tomatoes along with their juices, as well as the mace, thyme, and cayenne pepper to the pot. Bring to a boil, then reduce to a low heat and cook for 15 minutes, or until the onion and tomatoes are tender.
4. Allow the soup to rest, uncovered, for 20

minutes. Transfer the mixture to a blender and purée it to your preferred consistency, either pulpy or entirely smooth.
5. Sprinkle dill over each bowl before serving.

**NUTRITIONAL VALUE PER SERVING:**

Calories: 100 /kcal; Carbs: 18 g; Protein: 13 g; Fat: 3 g.

## SPINACH AND FETA CHEESE OMELET

*Prep time: 5 mins*

*Cooking time: 5 mins*

*Total time: 10 mins*

*Servings: 2*

**INGREDIENTS:**

- 2 cups spinach
- 3 eggs, beaten
- 1/2 bell pepper chopped
- 2 tsp. olive oil
- 1/2 cup chopped tomatoes
- 2 tbsp. minced onion
- 1/4 cup low-fat Feta cheese

**DIRECTIONS:**

1. On medium-high heat, heat the oil in a pan. Add the red bell pepper, onions, and tomatoes. Cook until soft, stirring often. Cook the spinach leaves until they are soft. Take the vegetables out of the pan.
2. Spray the pan with cooking spray and put the eggs in it. Cook the eggs for 2 minutes, or until the bottom of the pan shows that the eggs are starting to set. Using a spatula, gently lift the edges of the omelet to let the uncooked eggs flow to the edges and cook. Keep cooking for another 2 to 3 minutes, or until the omelet starts to look dry in the middle.
3. The feta cheese goes on top of the omelet, and the vegetable mixture goes in the middle. With a spatula, gently fold the egg. Let the omelet cook for another two minutes, or until the cheese melts to the right consistency. Put the omelet on a plate by sliding it out of the pan. Half it and serve.

**NUTRITIONAL VALUE PER SERVING:**

Calories: 215 /kcal; Carbs: 7 g; Protein: 13 g; Fat: 14 g.

## SUPER SCRAMBLE

*Prep time: 5 mins*

*Cooking time: 7 mins*

*Total time: 12 mins*

*Servings: 1*

**INGREDIENTS:**

- Non-stick cooking spray
- 2 tsp. red bell peppers, diced
- 2 white mushrooms
- 1/4 cup firm tofu
- 1/2 cup egg whites
- 3 tbsp. low fat cheddar cheese

**DIRECTIONS:**

1. Heat a pan on medium heat. Grease it with cooking spray and add peppers and mushrooms. Cook them for 2-3 minutes.
2. Put eggs and tofu in it. Scramble eggs over low heat with a wooden spoon for about 3–4 minutes, or until done.
3. Add cheese, and you're done.

**NUTRITIONAL VALUE PER SERVING:**

Calories: 190/kcal; Carbs: 5 g; Protein: 28 g; Fat: 7 g.

## CRAB CAKES

*Prep time: 15 mins*

*Cooking time: 10 mins*

*Total time: 25 mins*

*Servings: 8*

**INGREDIENTS:**

- 1 lb. lump crab meat
- ½ red bell pepper, finely chopped
- 1 tsp. Old Bay seasoning
- 2 eggs, slightly beaten
- 1½ cups bread crumbs
- 2 scallions, thinly sliced
- ¼ tsp. cayenne pepper
- 1 tbsp. fat-free mayonnaise
- 2 tsp. canola oil

**DIRECTIONS:**

1. Combine the bread crumbs, mayonnaise, crab, bell pepper, eggs, scallions, cayenne pepper and Old Bay seasoning in a medium mixing bowl and mix well.
2. Form the batter into eight circular cakes.
3. Heat the oil in a large pan over medium heat. Cook the crab cakes for 8 to 10 minutes, or till golden brown, flipping once in a while.

**NUTRITIONAL VALUE PER SERVING:**

Calories: 106 /kcal; Carbs: 5 g; Protein: 13 g; Fat: 3 g.

## APPLE CRUMBLE

*Prep time: 10 mins*

*Cooking time: 35 mins*

*Total time: 45 mins*

*Servings: 2*

**INGREDIENTS:**

- 2 small Granny Smith apples peeled and sliced
- 1/4 tsp. apple pie spice

- 4 tbsp. no-calorie sweetener, divided
- 1 tbsp. butter
- 1 tbsp. sliced almonds
- 1/2 cup high fiber cereal

### DIRECTIONS:

1. Set your oven's temperature to 350°F-180°C.
2. Spray a nonstick skillet using nonstick cooking spray and put it over medium heat. Add 3 tbsp. sweetener, apples and pie spice, and cook for about 3 minutes, or until the apples are soft. Pour the mixture into the ramekins.
3. Pulse the cereal, butter, almonds, and remaining 1 tbsp. sweetener in a mini-food processor until the ingredients are well mixed. Divide the mixture into both ramekins.
4. Bake for 35 minutes, or until the topping is golden brown and the filling is bubbling over it.

### NUTRITIONAL VALUE PER SERVING:

Calories: 212 /kcal; Carbs: 12 g; Protein: 18 g; Fat: 11 g.

## STRAWBERRY CHEESECAKE PUDDING PARFAIT

**Prep time:** 10 mins + chilling time

**Cooking time:** 0 mins

**Total time:** 10 mins + chilling time

**Servings:** 4

### INGREDIENTS:

- 1 box pudding mix, cheesecake
- 6 oz. plain Greek yogurt
- 1 oz. reduced fat cream cheese
- 5 tbsp. whipped cream, low-fat
- 11 oz. protein shake vanilla
- 1/4 tsp. lemon juice
- 10 strawberries hulled and sliced

### DIRECTIONS:

1. Mix the protein shake and instant pudding mix for about 2 minutes on medium speed in a mixing bowl.
2. Mix again, this time adding the cream cheese, Greek yogurt, and lemon juice. Put in the fridge for at least 2 hours.
3. To put it all together, put a few slices of strawberry in the bottom of a cup or bowl. On top, put/ 14 cup of pudding mixture and a small amount of whipped cream. Repeat.

### NUTRITIONAL VALUE PER SERVING:

Calories: 212 /kcal; Carbs: 15 g; Protein: 19 g; Fat: 10 g.

## AVOCADO EGG SALAD

**Prep time:** 10 mins

**Cooking time:** 0 mins

**Total time:** 10 mins

**Servings:** 2

### INGREDIENTS:

- 4 hard-boiled eggs
- 1 tbsp. dill pickle relish
- 1 large avocado
- Salt and pepper to taste
- 3 tbsp. fat-free mayonnaise
- 2 tbsp. minced onion
- ¼ tsp. paprika
- 2 lettuce leaves

### DIRECTIONS:

1. Cut hard-boiled eggs in half and take out the yolks.
2. Mix the yolk with the relish, fat-free mayonnaise, salt, pepper, and minced onion.
3. Chop the egg white into small pieces and cut the avocado into bite-sized pieces.
4. Pour the mayonnaise mixture over the top and gently stir to coat everything.
5. Spoon the mixture onto a leaf of lettuce and sprinkle with paprika. Serve.

### NUTRITIONAL VALUE PER SERVING:

Calories: 135 /kcal; Carbs: 4 g; Protein: 23 g; Fat: 1 g.

## CURRIED CHICKPEAS

**Prep time:** 15 mins

**Cooking time:** 5 hours

**Total time:** 5 hour 10 mins

**Servings:** 6

### INGREDIENTS:

- 1 lb. chickpeas, garbanzo beans
- 1 clove of garlic, minced
- 1 small onion, chopped
- 10 oz. light coconut milk
- 10 oz. vegetable stock
- 1/2 tbsp. each of coriander and cumin
- 4 cups water
- 3 tbsp. curry powder

### DIRECTIONS:

1. Put the onion and garlic in the bottom of the crockpot. Then put the chick peas on top.
2. Then put in all your spices and liquid.
3. Set your slow cooker to low and let it run for about 5 hours, or until the chickpeas are soft.

### NUTRITIONAL VALUE PER SERVING:

Calories: 212 /kcal; Carbs: 12 g; Protein: 25 g; Fat: 9 g.

## CINNAMON BUN PROTEIN OATMEAL

**Prep time:** 10 mins

**Cooking time:** 2 mins

**Total time:** 12 mins

**Servings:** 2

### INGREDIENTS:

- ½ cup quick oats
- 4 oz. boiling water
- 2 oz. skim milk
- No-calorie sweetener, to taste
- 1 scoop vanilla protein powder
- 1/8 tsp. salt
- dash of ground cinnamon
- 1 tbsp. sugar-free pancake syrup

### DIRECTIONS:

1. Mix the oats, protein powder, sweetener, and milk in a bowl until you have a thick meal. There shouldn't be any dry protein powder in the meal or on the edges of the bowls.
2. Gradually add the boiling water to the meal a little at a time, mixing after each addition. Do this until just a little bit of the oatmeal is under the water.
3. Heat about 90 seconds in the microwave.
4. Stir together the salt, pancake syrup, and cinnamon.
5. Serve and enjoy.

### NUTRITIONAL VALUE PER SERVING:
Calories: 115 /kcal; Carbs: 11 g; Protein: 22 g; Fat: 7 g.

## CHICKEN AND RICE SKILLET

**Prep time:** 10 mins

**Cooking time:** 20 mins

**Total time:** 30 mins

**Servings:** 6

### INGREDIENTS:

- 1 lb. chicken breasts, cooked and cubed
- 1 small onion, finely diced
- 2 cups cauliflower rice
- 1 green pepper, finely diced
- 1 can cheddar cheese soup
- 2 cans tomatoes
- 1 can black beans
- 1 tsp. minced garlic
- 2 tbsp. tomato paste
- ¼ tsp. ground cumin
- ¼ tsp. ground coriander

### DIRECTIONS:

1. Spray a pan with nonstick cooking spray and add the onions and peppers. Cook until the vegetables are soft, then add the garlic and spices and mix well.
2. Add the tomato paste, tomatoes and chicken. Simmer until about half of the liquid is gone.
3. Add the black beans and cauliflower rice. Stir well.
4. The last step is to add the cheese soup and mix it well. Let the mixture simmer on low to medium heat for about ten minutes, or until it is warm. Serve hot!

### NUTRITIONAL VALUE PER SERVING:
Calories: 245 /kcal; Carbs: 23 g; Protein: 26 g; Fat: 11 g.

## ITALIAN POACHED EGGS

**Prep time:** 10 mins

**Cooking time:** 12 mins

**Total time:** 22 mins

**Servings:** 4

### INGREDIENTS:

- 16 oz. Marinara Sauce
- 4 eggs
- pinch of salt
- 1/8 tsp. pepper
- 3-4 pieces jarred roasted red pepper, sliced
- 4 leaves fresh basil, torn

### DIRECTIONS:

1. Add marinara sauce and red pepper slices in a large pan and place it on medium high-heat.
2. Make a "well" with the back of a spoon and crack an egg into it. Do this again with the other three eggs.
3. Put salt and pepper on it.
4. Let eggs cook for about 12 minutes, or until you can shake the pan and see that the eggs are firm.
5. Take it off the heat, sprinkle it with torn basil, and put it in a bowl or plate.

### NUTRITIONAL VALUE PER SERVING:
Calories: 114 /kcal; Carbs: 4 g; Protein: 8 g; Fat: 6 g.

## FRIED EGGS ON PARMESAN CHEESE CRUST

**Prep time:** 5 mins

**Cooking time:** 5 mins

**Total time:** 10 mins

**Servings:** 1

### INGREDIENTS:

- 2 tbsp. shredded parmesan cheese
- ¼ tsp. each salt and pepper
- 1 tsp fresh thyme, chopped
- 2 eggs

### DIRECTIONS:

1. On medium heat, spread cheese in a circle on the bottom of a nonstick skillet.
2. Put two eggs on top of the pile. Cover. Cook the eggs until the yolks have set.
3. Take the lid off and sprinkle salt and pepper on top. Put on a plate.
4. Add herbs on top and serve.

**NUTRITIONAL VALUE PER SERVING:**
Calories: 186 /kcal; Carbs: 1 g; Protein: 16 g; Fat: 12 g.

## CHOCOLATE PROTEIN PUDDING

*Prep time:  5 mins*

*Cooking time:  0 mins*

*Total time:  5 mins*

*Servings: 1*

**INGREDIENTS:**
- 2 tbsp. chocolate protein powder
- 1 cup 0% fat, plain Greek yogurt

**DIRECTIONS:**
1. Put the ingredients in a bowl and stir them together with a small rubber spatula until the mixture is well blended.

**NUTRITIONAL VALUE PER SERVING:**
Calories: 67 /kcal; Carbs: 4 g; Protein: 13 g; Fat: 0 g.

## SOFT CRAB SALAD

*Prep time:  5 mins*

*Cooking time:  0 mins*

*Total time:  5 mins*

*Servings: 1*

**INGREDIENTS:**
- 2 oz. imitation crab
- 1/2 scoop unflavored protein powder
- 1 pinch seafood seasoning
- 1 tbsp. light mayonnaise
- 1 pinch dried dill

**DIRECTIONS:**
1. Cut the crab meat into tiny pieces.
2. Mix the light mayonnaise and the protein powder until they are well mixed. Add crab meat and seasonings and enjoy.

**NUTRITIONAL VALUE PER SERVING:**
Calories: 118 /kcal; Carbs: 8 g; Protein: 13 g; Fat: 5 g.

## SOFT CHICKEN SALAD

*Prep time:  5 mins*

*Cooking time:  0 mins*

*Total time:  5 mins*

*Servings: 1*

**INGREDIENTS:**
- 1 cup canned chicken, drained
- 1 tsp. taco seasoning
- 2 tsp. juice from jarred salsa
- 1 tbsp. light mayonnaise

**DIRECTIONS:**
1. Put chicken into a bowl. Break the chicken into smaller pieces with a fork. Stir in the mayo until it is well mixed and soft.
2. Add salsa juice and taco seasoning and mix well. Serve.

**NUTRITIONAL VALUE PER SERVING:**
Calories: 112 /kcal; Carbs: 2 g; Protein: 18 g; Fat: 4 g.

## ENCHILADA EGGS

*Prep time:  5 mins*

*Cooking time:  7 mins*

*Total time:  12 mins*

*Servings: 4*

Ingredients:
- 10 oz. enchilada sauce
- pinch of salt
- 4 eggs

DIRECTIONS:
1. Heat the enchilada sauce in a medium skillet until it starts to bubble.
2. Make a well for each egg in the sauce with a spoon. Break an egg and put it in the sauce. Do this again. Cover the pan for 7 minutes for yolks to be firm.
3. Spoon the eggs with just a little sauce onto serving plates and serve.

**NUTRITIONAL VALUE PER SERVING:**
Calories: 90 /kcal; Carbs: 4 g; Protein: 6 g; Fat: 5 g.

## CREAM OF MUSHROOM CHICKEN

**Prep time: 10 mins**

**Cooking time: 20 mins**

**Total time: 30 mins**

**Servings: 6**

### INGREDIENTS:

- 10 oz. can cream of mushroom soup, fat-free
- 1 lb. boneless, skinless chicken thighs
- Salt to taste
- Pepper to taste

### DIRECTIONS:

1. Turn oven on to 350°F-180°C.
2. Cut as much fat as you can off the chicken thighs with kitchen shears. Spread the chicken on a baking sheet and add salt and pepper to taste.
3. Spread cream of mushroom soup on the chicken thighs in an even layer. Bake for 20 minutes, or until the chicken is 165°F from the inside.
4. Take the chicken out of the oven and let cool. Cut it into tiny pieces and eat it slowly.

### NUTRITIONAL VALUE PER SERVING:

Calories: 114 /kcal; Carbs: 4 g; Protein: 16 g; Fat: 4 g.

## CREAMY DEVILED EGGS

**Prep time: 10 mins**

**Cooking time: 0 mins**

**Total time: 10 mins**

**Servings: 8**

### INGREDIENTS:

- 8 hard cooked eggs
- 2 tsp. yellow mustard
- ½ cup low-fat mayo
- 1/4 tsp. salt
- splash of pickle juice
- dash of pepper
- dash of paprika

### DIRECTIONS:

1. Cut eggs in half lengthwise. Take out the yolks and mash them in a bowl. Add pickle juice, mayonnaise, mustard and seasonings. Blend well.
2. Spoon the mixture into the middles of the egg whites. Add a pinch of paprika to make it look nice.

### NUTRITIONAL VALUE PER SERVING:

Calories: 72 /kcal; Carbs: 0 g; Protein: 6 g; Fat: 5 g.

# MAINTENANCE DIET RECIPES

# BREAKFAST RECIPES

## VEGGIE QUICHE MUFFINS

**Prep time:** 10 mins

**Cooking time:** 40 mins

**Total time:** 50 mins

**Servings:** 12

### INGREDIENTS:

- 1 cup green onion
- ¾ cup shredded cheddar
- 1 cup diced tomatoes
- 1 cup chopped broccoli
- 4 eggs
- 2 cups milk
- 1 tsp. oregano
- 1 cup pancake mix
- ½ tsp. pepper
- ½ tsp. salt

### DIRECTIONS:

1. Set the oven temperature to 375°F-190°C and lightly oil a 12-cup muffin tin
2. Sprinkle broccoli, tomatoes, onions, and cheddar into muffin cups.
3. Whisk the rest of the ingredients together in a medium bowl, and then pour it evenly over the vegetables.
4. Put in an oven that has already been heated for about 40 minutes, or until golden brown.
5. Let it sit for about 5 minutes to cool down, then serve. Enjoy!

### NUTRITIONAL VALUE PER SERVING:

Calories: 58 /kcal; Carbs: 3 g; Protein: 5 g; Fat: 3 g.

## STEEL CUT OAT BLUEBERRY PANCAKES

**Prep time:** 10 mins

**Cooking time:** 16 mins

**Total time:** 26 mins

**Servings:** 4

### INGREDIENTS:

- ½ cup oats
- 1½ cup water
- 1 cup flour
- 1/8 tsp. salt
- ½ tsp. baking soda
- ½ tsp. baking powder
- 1 cup milk
- 1 egg
- 1 cup frozen blueberries
- ½ cup Greek yogurt
- ¾ cup agave nectar

### DIRECTIONS:

1. Mix the oats, salt, and water in a medium saucepan, stir, and heat over high heat until the mixture boils.
2. Turn it down to low and let it cook for 10 minutes, or until the oats are soft. Set aside.
3. In a medium bowl, mix the rest of the ingredients, except for the agave nectar. Then, fold in the oats.
4. Warm up the griddle and grease it lightly. Pour 1/4 cup of batter for each pancake and it takes about 3 minutes to cook on each side.
5. Add agave to the top.

### NUTRITIONAL VALUE PER SERVING:

Calories: 257 /kcal; Carbs: 46 g; Protein: 14 g; Fat: 7 g.

## VERY BERRY MUESLI

**Prep time:** 10 mins + chilling time

**Cooking time:** 0 mins

**Total time:** 10 mins + chilling time

**Servings:** 2

### INGREDIENTS:

- 1 cup oats
- ½ cup milk
- 1 cup fruit flavored yogurt
- ½ cup dried raisins
- 1/8 tsp. salt
- ½ cup frozen blueberries
- ½ cup chopped apple
- ¼ cup chopped walnuts

### DIRECTIONS:

1. Mix the yogurt, salt, and oats well in a medium bowl, then tightly cover the mixture.
2. Put in the fridge for 6 hours to cool down.
3. Mix in the raisins and apples with a light hand.
4. Add the nuts, and it's ready to eat. Enjoy!

### NUTRITIONAL VALUE PER SERVING:

Calories: 198 /kcal; Carbs: 31 g; Protein: 6 g; Fat: 4 g.

## STRAWBERRY AND MUSHROOM SANDWICH

Prep time: 10 mins

Cooking time: 0 mins

Total time: 10 mins

Servings: 4

### INGREDIENTS:
- 8 oz. Cream cheese
- 1 tbsp. grated Lemon zest
- 1 tbsp. Honey
- 2 cups sliced Strawberries
- 4 sliced Portobello Mushrooms

### DIRECTIONS:
1. Put the honey, lemon zest, and cheese in a food processor and run it until the ingredients are fully mixed.
2. Spread the cheese mixture on mushrooms like butter.
3. Add strawberries to the top. Enjoy!

### NUTRITIONAL VALUE PER SERVING:
Calories: 180 /kcal; Carbs: 6 g; Protein: 2 g; Fat: 16 g.

## CAKE BATTER PROTEIN BALLS

Prep time: 5 mins

Cooking time: 0 mins

Total time: 5 mins

Servings: 4

### INGREDIENTS:
- 1 scoop vanilla protein powder
- 2 tbsp. almond butter
- 1/3 cup oats
- 1 tbsp. Almond milk
- 1/2 tsp. cake batter extract
- 1 dash sprinkles

### DIRECTIONS:
1. Combine all of the ingredients and roll them into four balls. Cool until you are ready to eat.

### NUTRITIONAL VALUE PER SERVING:
Calories: 101 /kcal; Carbs: 6 g; Protein: 9 g; Fat: 5 g.

## TURKEY SAUSAGE AND MUSHROOM STRATA

Prep time: 15 mins

Cooking time: 1 hour

Total time: 1 hour 15 mins

Servings: 12

### INGREDIENTS:
- 12 oz. chopped turkey sausage
- 8 oz. cubed ciabatta bread
- 4 oz. shredded cheddar
- 2 cups milk
- 12 oz. egg substitute
- 3 eggs
- 1 cup sliced mushroom
- ½ cup chopped green onion
- ½ tsp. pepper
- ½ tsp. paprika
- 2 tbsp. grated parmesan cheese

### DIRECTIONS:
1. Set oven to 400°F-200°C. Toast bread cubes for about 8 minutes by putting them flat on a baking sheet.
2. In the meantime, put sausage in a skillet over medium heat and let it cook while stirring until it is fully browned and broken up.
3. Mix Parmesan cheese, Pepper, salt, egg substitute, paprika, eggs, cheddar cheese, and milk together in a bowl with a whisk.
4. Add the rest of the ingredients and mix well to combine. Put the mixture in a large baking dish, preferably one that is 9x13 inches. Cover it tightly and let it sit in the fridge overnight.
5. Set the oven to 350°F, take the lid off the casserole dish, and bake until the strata is done and golden brown.
6. Slice it and serve.

### NUTRITIONAL VALUE PER SERVING:
Calories: 185 /kcal; Carbs: 9 g; Protein: 2 g; Fat: 18 g.

## SWEET MILLET CONGEE

Prep time: 15 mins

Cooking time: 1 hour

Total time: 1 hour 15 mins

Servings: 4

### INGREDIENTS:
- 1 cup millet
- 1 cup diced sweet potato
- 5 cups water
- 2 tbsp. stevia
- 1 tsp. cinnamon
- ¼ cup honey
- 1 diced apple

### DIRECTIONS:

1. Put the sweet potato, stevia, cinnamon, water, and millet in a deep pot and stir to mix.
2. Bring to a boil over high heat, then turn down the heat to low and let it simmer for an hour or until all the water is absorbed and the millet is done.
3. Add the rest of the ingredients, stir, and serve.

### NUTRITIONAL VALUE PER SERVING:

Calories: 136 /kcal; Carbs: 28 g; Protein: 3 g; Fat: 1 g.

## SMOOTHIE BOWL WITH GREEK YOGURT

**Prep time: 5 mins**

**Cooking time: 5 mins**

**Total time: 10 mins**

**Servings: 1**

### INGREDIENTS:

- ¾ cup low-fat milk
- 1 handful fresh spinach
- ¼ cup low-fat plain Greek yogurt
- ¼ cup frozen mixed berries
- ½ scoop vanilla protein powder
- ¼ cup fresh blueberries
- ¼ cup fresh raspberries
- 1 tsp. chia seeds
- 1 tbsp. sliced, slivered almonds

### DIRECTIONS:

1. Put the milk, spinach, yogurt, frozen berries and protein powder into a blender and mix well.
2. Blend at high speed for 3–4 minutes, or until the powder is completely mixed in and can't be seen.
3. The smoothie should go into a small bowl.
4. Add the blueberries, fresh raspberries, chia seeds and almonds to the smoothie to make it look nice.
5. Serve and enjoy.

### NUTRITIONAL VALUE PER SERVING:

Calories: 255 /kcal; Carbs: 21 g; Protein: 20 g; Fat: 10 g.

## BREAKFAST QUINOA BOWLS

**Prep time: 5 mins**

**Cooking time: 25 mins**

**Total time: 30 mins**

**Servings: 2**

### INGREDIENTS:

- 1 sliced peach
- 1 cup low fat milk
- 1/3 cup quinoa
- 2 tsp. natural stevia
- ½ tsp. vanilla extract
- 14 blueberries
- 12 raspberries
- 2 tsp. honey

### DIRECTIONS:

1. Stir 2/3 cup milk and quinoa together in a saucepan with natural stevia.
2. Bring to a boil over medium-high heat, then cover and lower the heat to a low simmer for another 20 minutes.
3. Grease the grill pan and grill peach slices on it. Set aside.
4. Warm up the rest of the milk in the microwave, and then set it aside.
5. Divide the cooked quinoa between 2 bowls and divide the rest of the ingredients between the bowls. Enjoy

### NUTRITIONAL VALUE PER SERVING:

Calories: 180 /kcal; Carbs: 36 g; Protein: 4 g; Fat: 4 g.

## PERFECT GRANOLA

**Prep time: 10 mins**

**Cooking time: 30 mins**

**Total time: 40 mins**

**Servings: 10**

### INGREDIENTS:

- ¼ cup canola oil
- 1½ tsp. vanilla
- 4 tbsp. honey
- 1 cup almond
- 6 cups old fashioned rolled oats
- 2 cups bran flakes
- ½ cup shredded unsweetened coconut
- 1 cups raisins
- ¾ cup chopped walnuts
- Cooking spray

### DIRECTIONS:

1. Set the oven to 325 °F-160°C and get it ready.
2. In a saucepan, heat the oil and vanilla over a low flame, stirring every so often for about 5 minutes.
3. Put everything except raisins into a large bowl and mix them all together.
4. Slowly stir in the honey and oil mixture, making sure that all of the grains are well coated.
5. Put parchment paper on the baking sheet or lightly grease it with cooking spray. Spread the cereal out evenly on the baking sheet. Bake for 25 minutes, stirring the mixture every so often to keep it from burning, or until it has a light brown color.
6. When it's done, take the cereal out and set it aside to cool.
7. Mix the raisins in well and slice it into bars.

### NUTRITIONAL VALUE PER SERVING:

Calories: 458 /kcal; Carbs: 62 g; Protein: 21 g; Fat: 12 g.

## CINNAMON SUGAR OATMEAL CASSEROLE

**Prep time:** 10 mins

**Cooking time:** 45 mins

**Total time:** 55 mins

**Servings:** 8

### INGREDIENTS:

- 2 cups quick-cooking oats
- ½ tsp. Baking powder
- 2 eggs
- 1 cup buttermilk
- 1/3 cup raisins
- ½ cup unsweetened applesauce
- 1½ tsp. cinnamon
- 2 tbsp. almonds (slivered)
- 1/3 cup Splenda
- 1 tsp. vanilla extract
- ½ tsp. salt

### DIRECTIONS:

1. Turn oven on to 325°F-160°C. Spray cooking spray on a pie plate.
2. Mix the oats, Splenda, cinnamon, salt and baking powder together in a large bowl. Blend well.
3. Beat the eggs, buttermilk, and applesauce together in a separate bowl. Pour into the bowl with the dry ingredients and mix together until everything is well blended. Almonds and raisins should be added at this point.
4. Pour the mixture into a pie dish. Bake for 40-45 minutes.
5. Cool down all the way before serving.

### NUTRITIONAL VALUE PER SERVING:

Calories: 121 /kcal; Carbs: 5 g; Protein: 6 g; Fat: 2 g.

## AMERICAN SCRAMBLE

**Prep time:** 5 mins

**Cooking time:** 5 mins

**Total time:** 10 mins

**Servings:** 1

### INGREDIENTS:

- ¼ cup liquid egg substitute
- 1 slice turkey bacon, crumbled
- 1 tbsp. reduced-fat shredded Cheddar cheese
- 1 tsp. light butter

### DIRECTIONS:

1. Melt the butter in an omelet pan over medium heat, rotating the pan to get an even coating.
2. Add the turkey bacon and cook it for 4 to 5 minutes, until it softens and just starts to turn brown.
3. Add the egg substitute and stir gently but continuously with a rubber spatula to keep it moving and prevent it from browning.
4. Turn off the heat and add the cheese. With the spatula, fold the cheese in a gentle way. Put the scramble on a plate when the cheese is soft but not completely melted.

### NUTRITIONAL VALUE PER SERVING:

Calories: 118 /kcal; Carbs: 0.5 g; Protein: 11 g; Fat: 8 g.

## CHEESE-FILLED ACORN SQUASH

**Prep time:** 10 mins

**Cooking time:** 50 mins

**Total time:** 1 hour

**Servings:** 2

### INGREDIENTS:

- 1 lb. tofu, firm
- 1 pinch black pepper, freshly ground
- 1 tsp. basil
- 1 tsp. garlic powder
- 1 tsp. onion, chopped finely
- 2 pieces acorn squash, halved, seeded
- 1 cup cheddar cheese, reduced fat, shredded
- 1 cup fresh mushrooms, sliced
- 1 cup celery, diced
- 1/8 tsp. salt
- 1 tsp. oregano
- 8 oz. tomato sauce

### DIRECTIONS:

1. Preheat the oven by setting it to 350 °F-180°C.
2. Put the cut sides of the acorn squash pieces down in the bottom of a glass dish.
3. Put it in the oven and cook it for about 20 minutes or until it's soft. Set aside.
4. Put the tofu in a pan that doesn't stick and heat it on medium (sliced into cubes). Cook until the tofu is browned, then add celery and onion. Cook the onion for two minutes, or until it is clear.
5. Add in the mushrooms. Mix everything together and cook for another two to three minutes. Pour the tomato sauce and dry spices into the pan.
6. Mix everything well, and then put equal amounts of the mixture into each piece of acorn squash.
7. Cover it and put it in the oven for about 15 minutes. Remove the cover and put the cheese on top before putting it back in the oven. Cook for another five minutes, or until the cheese is bubbling and melted.

### NUTRITIONAL VALUE PER SERVING:

Calories: 328 /kcal; Carbs: 47 g; Protein: 17 g; Fat: 10 g.

## CHEESY SPINACH BAKE

**Prep time: 5 mins**

**Cooking time: 35 mins**

**Total time: 40 mins**

**Servings: 3**

### INGREDIENTS:

- 2 Eggs, whole
- 2 cups Cottage cheese, fat-free
- ½ cup Parmesan cheese
- 10 oz. frozen Spinach, thawed and drained

### DIRECTIONS:

1. To get the oven ready, set it to 350 °F-180°C. In the meantime, put parchment paper on the bottom of an 8x8 baking pan.
2. Put everything into a large bowl. Stir in order to mix. Pour the spinach and cheese mixture into the bed pan. Put in the oven for 20–30 minutes, or until the cheese on surface is bubbling.
3. Take it out of the oven and let cool for 5 minutes.
4. Serve and enjoy.

### NUTRITIONAL VALUE PER SERVING:

Calories: 292 /kcal; Carbs: 4 g; Protein: 26 g; Fat: 19 g.

## GREEK YOGURT, GRANOLA, AND BERRY PARFAIT

**Prep time: 10 mins**

**Cooking time: 0 mins**

**Total time: 10 mins**

**Servings: 1**

### INGREDIENTS:

- 1 tsp. honey
- ½ cup nonfat plain Greek yogurt
- 1 tbsp. rolled oats
- ¼ cup fresh raspberries
- ¼ cup fresh blueberries
- 1 tbsp. chopped pecans
- 1 tbsp. chopped walnuts

### DIRECTIONS:

1. Put the yogurt in a glass.
2. Add oats, raspberries, blueberries, pecans and walnuts to the top. Pour the honey over the top. Enjoy right away.

### NUTRITIONAL VALUE PER SERVING:

Calories: 245 /kcal; Carbs: 25 g; Protein: 16 g; Fat: 11 g.

## EGGS FLORENTINE

**Prep time: 10 mins**

**Cooking time: 10 mins**

**Total time: 20 mins**

**Servings: 2**

### INGREDIENTS:

- 2 large eggs
- 5 tbsp. egg fast Alfredo sauce
- 1 tbsp. extra virgin olive oil
- 1 handful organic baby spinach
- 4 tbsp. parmesan cheese
- 1 pinch red pepper flakes

### DIRECTIONS:

1. Put the oven rack in the top notch that is closest to the broiler. Start up the broiler.
2. Put olive oil in a pan that doesn't stick and heat it over medium-high heat.
3. Fry eggs gently over a medium flame until the whites are solid but the yolks are still runny. It takes about 4 minutes. Do not flip over eggs.
4. Make a casserole while you wait. Put a little olive oil in two casserole dishes.
5. Spread half of the Alfredo sauce on the bottom of the casserole. Slide the half-cooked egg gently on top of the sauce.
6. Spread the eggs with the leftover Alfredo sauce and 2 tbsp. of the grated parmesan cheese.
7. Put the casserole underneath the broiler and broil for 2 to 3 minutes or until the eggs have firmed down and the top has bubbly yellow spots.
8. Take it out of the oven and top it with baby spinach leaves that have been thinly sliced, leftover parmesan cheese and a pinch of red pepper flakes.

### NUTRITIONAL VALUE PER SERVING:

Calories: 500 /kcal; Carbs: 3 g; Protein: 29 g; Fat: 3 g.

## MEXICAN SCRAMBLED EGGS

**Prep time: 10 mins**

**Cooking time: 5 mins**

**Total time: 15 mins**

**Servings: 3**

### INGREDIENTS:

- 6 eggs, lightly beaten
- 3 oz. cheese, shredded
- 1 tomato, diced
- 1 tbsp. butter
- 2 tbsp. chopped green onions
- Salt and pepper to taste

### DIRECTIONS:

- Put butter in a large pan over medium heat and

- let it melt.
- Cook the green onions and tomatoes while stirring until they smell good. it takes about 3 minutes
- Add the eggs and keep cooking, stirring for two minutes.
- Add cheese, season to your taste, and keep cooking until the cheese melts.

### NUTRITIONAL VALUE PER SERVING:
Calories: 239 /kcal; Carbs: 8 g; Protein: 22 g; Fat: 5 g.

## DENVER SCRAMBLE

**Prep time: 5 mins**

**Cooking time: 5 mins**

**Total time: 10 mins**

**Servings: 1**

### INGREDIENTS:
- 1 tsp. light butter
- 1½ tsp. chopped yellow onion
- 1½ tsp. chopped green bell pepper
- 1 slice ham, chopped
- 1½ tsp. chopped tomato
- 1 tbsp. shredded Cheddar cheese
- ¼ cup liquid egg substitute

### DIRECTIONS:
1. Melt the butter in an omelet pan over medium heat, swirling the pan to coat it evenly.
2. Add the onion, pepper, and tomato, and cook for 4 to 5 minutes, until they are soft. Add the ham and keep cooking.
3. Add the egg substitute and scrape the bottom of the pan with a rubber spatula while stirring gently.
4. Add the cheese and turn down the heat. With the spatula, fold the cheese into the scramble in a gentle way. Put the scramble on a plate when the cheese is soft but not completely melted.

### NUTRITIONAL VALUE PER SERVING:
Calories: 126 /kcal; Carbs: 3 g; Protein: 14 g; Fat: 6 g.

## GROUND BEEF AND SPINACH SCRAMBLE

**Prep time: 5 mins**

**Cooking time: 10 mins**

**Total time: 15 mins**

**Servings: 1**

### INGREDIENTS:
- 1 tsp. light butter
- 1/3 cup chopped fresh spinach leaves, stems removed
- 6 tsp. lean, browned ground beef
- 1 tbsp. shredded Parmesan cheese
- ¼ cup liquid egg substitute

### DIRECTIONS:
1. Melt the butter in a pan over medium heat, swirling the pan to coat it evenly. Add the ground beef and cook it for 4 to 5 minutes.
2. Add the spinach and keep cooking until all of the spinach has wilted. Add the egg substitute and scrape the bottom of the pan with a rubber spatula while stirring gently but constantly to keep the eggs from getting brown.
3. Add the cheese and turn the heat off when the eggs are almost done. With the rubber spatula, fold the cheese into the eggs in a gentle way. Put the scramble on a plate when the cheese is soft but not completely melted.

### NUTRITIONAL VALUE PER SERVING:
Calories: 141 /kcal; Carbs: 1 g; Protein: 18 g; Fat: 7 g.

## QUINOA BREAKFAST BOWL

**Prep time: 15 mins**

**Cooking time: 15 mins**

**Total time: 30 mins**

**Servings: 1**

### INGREDIENTS:
- ¼ cup quinoa, rinsed
- 1 small banana
- 2 tbsp. dried berries
- ¾ cup water, divided
- ¼ cup almond milk
- 1 tbsp. maple syrup
- 1/8 tsp. vanilla extract
- 1/8 tsp. ground cinnamon
- 1 tbsp. chopped walnuts
- ¼ cup blueberries
- 1 tbsp. pumpkin seeds
- 1 tbsp. slivered almonds

### DIRECTIONS:
1. Boil 1/2 cup of water in a small saucepan.
2. Toss in the quinoa. Reduce heat to low and cook, covered, for 12-15 minutes. In the meantime, soak the berries in the leftover water for 10 minutes before draining.
3. Half should be sliced, while the other half should be mashed.
4. Take the quinoa off the heat and fluff it with a fork.
5. In a large mixing bowl, combine the almond milk, mashed banana, maple syrup, cinnamon, and vanilla.
6. Add walnuts, blueberries, almonds, banana slices, pumpkin seeds, and goji berries to a separate bowl.
7. Serve with more maple syrup and almond milk if desired.

### NUTRITIONAL VALUE PER SERVING:
Calories: 200 /kcal; Carbs: 83 g; Protein: 13 g; Fat: 13 g.

## SCRAMBLED EGGS WITH AVOCADO ON TOAST

Prep time: 5 mins

Cooking time: 5 mins

Total time: 10 mins

Servings: 4

### INGREDIENTS:

- 4 eggs
- ¼ tsp. hot paprika
- ¼ tsp. chili powder
- 2 slices of sourdough bread
- ½ tsp. turmeric
- 1/3 cup nut milk
- ½ lemon, juice
- 1 ripe avocado
- pinch of dried red chili flakes
- 1 tbsp. extra virgin olive oil
- sea salt flakes, to taste
- 2 tsp. butter

### DIRECTIONS:

1. In a mixing dish, crack the eggs and whisk in the seasonings and milk.
2. Preheat the oven to broil.
3. Drizzle extra virgin olive oil over the sourdough pieces, and then season them with sea salt flakes and broil them in pre-heated oven. Meanwhile, remove the seed from the avocado and split it in half. Scrape out the flesh and smash it with a little salt and lemon juice.
4. In a nonstick pan, melt the butter over high heat and add in the eggs mixture with a generous sprinkle of salt. Allow to cook for a few seconds until the bottom begins to firm, and then carefully flip the eggs over and through one another.
5. Once the eggs mix is still slightly liquid, remove it from the heat.
6. Spread the mashed avocado over the toasted sourdough and top with scrambled eggs with a dash of chilli flakes.
7. Serve immediately and enjoy.

### NUTRITIONAL VALUE PER SERVING:

Calories: 234 /kcal; Carbs: 10 g; Protein: 22 g; Fat: 15 g.

## QUINOA-PEAR BREAKFAST BAKE

Prep time: 15 mins

Cooking time: 55 mins

Total time: 1 hour 10 mins

Servings: 2

### INGREDIENTS:

- ¼ cup quinoa, rinsed
- 1 tbsp. honey
- ¼ cup ripe pear, cubes
- 1 cup water
- dash of ground ginger
- ¼ tsp. vanilla extract
- ¼ tsp. ground cinnamon
- dash of ground nutmeg
- 1 tbsp. brown sugar
- ¼ cup sliced almonds
- plain Greek yogurt, optional
- 1 tbsp. butter, softened

### DIRECTIONS:

1. Preheat the oven to 350°F-180°C.
2. Mix the quinoa, honey, pear cubes, water, ground ginger, vanilla extract, ground cinnamon and nutmeg in a mixing bowl; transfer to a prepared 3-cup baking dish. Bake for 50 minutes with the lid on.
3. Combine brown sugar, almonds, and butter in a separate small dish; spread over the baked quinoa mixture.
4. Bake further for 5-10 minutes more, uncovered, until gently browned.
5. Allow 10 minutes to rest before serving. Serve with yogurt, if preferred.

### NUTRITIONAL VALUE PER SERVING:

Calories: 177 /kcal; Carbs: 35 g; Protein: 6 g; Fat: 13 g.

## CAULIFLOWER BREAKFAST CASSEROLE

Prep time: 30 mins

Cooking time: 40 mins

Total time: 1 hour 10 mins

Servings: 12

### INGREDIENTS:

- 4 cups riced cauliflower
- 9 large eggs, lightly beaten
- ½ red pepper, chopped
- 1 cup chopped sweet onion
- ½ green pepper, chopped
- 1 lb. bacon strips, chopped
- 1½ cups ricotta cheese
- ½ tsp. pepper
- 2 cups shredded cheddar cheese
- ¼ tsp. salt
- 1 cup shredded Swiss cheese

### DIRECTIONS:

1. Preheat the oven to 350°F-180°C.
2. Cook bacon in a large pan over medium heat, turning periodically, until crisp. Take it out on a plate.
3. To the drippings, add the onion and chopped peppers; cook and stir on medium-high heat until soft, about 6-8 minutes.
4. Whisk together the eggs and ricotta in a large mixing dish and then combine the riced cauliflower, bacon, shredded cheeses, onion, pepper, and salt.
5. Fill a greased 13x9-inch baking dish halfway with the batter.
6. Bake for 40-45 minutes, uncovered, till a skewer

inserted near the middle comes out clean.
7. Allow the casserole 10 minutes resting time before serving.

**NUTRITIONAL VALUE PER SERVING:**
Calories: 333 /kcal; Carbs: 7 g; Protein: 21 g; Fat: 22 g.

## OAT WAFFLES

**Prep time:** 5 mins

**Cooking time:** 5 mins

**Total time:** 10 mins

**Servings:** 6

**INGREDIENTS:**
- 1 cup oat flour
- ½ tsp. salt
- 4 tsp. baking powder
- 1 tbsp. sugar
- 1 cup all-purpose flour
- 2 tbsp. canola oil
- 1¾ cups fat-free milk
- 1 tsp. vanilla extract
- 2 large eggs, room temperature

**DIRECTIONS:**
1. Combine the dry ingredients in a large mixing dish.
2. In a separate bowl, whisk together the eggs, vanilla extract, oil, milk and mix into the dry ingredients till incorporated.
3. Pour 1/2 cup of batter onto a hot waffle iron and bake until golden brown.

**NUTRITIONAL VALUE PER SERVING:**
Calories: 234 /kcal; Carbs: 24 g; Protein: 7 g; Fat: 6 g.

## BREAKFAST PARFAITS

**Prep time:** 10 mins

**Cooking time:** 0 mins

**Total time:** 10 mins

**Servings:** 4

**INGREDIENTS:**
- ½ cup chopped raisins or dates
- 2 cups pineapple chunks
- 1 cup vanilla yogurt
- 1 cup sliced ripe banana
- 1 cup fresh or frozen raspberries
- ¼ cup sliced almonds

**DIRECTIONS:**
1. Layer the pineapple, yogurt, dates, raspberries, and banana in 4 parfait glasses. Almonds should be sprinkled on top.
2. Serve right away.

**NUTRITIONAL VALUE PER SERVING:**
Calories: 211 /kcal; Carbs: 60 g; Protein: 5 g; Fat: 4 g.

## HERB-BAKED EGGS

**Prep time:** 5 mins

**Cooking time:** 5 mins

**Total time:** 10 mins

**Servings:** 1

**INGREDIENTS:**
- 1 tsp. melted butter
- 1 tbsp. milk
- 2 eggs
- ¼ tsp. garlic powder,
- Pinch of dried oregano
- Pinch of dried parsley
- Pinch of dried dill
- Pinch of dried thyme

**DIRECTIONS:**
1. Preheat the oven to "Broil" on low.
2. Using the butter and milk, brush the base of a small baking dish. On top of the butter and milk mixture, break the eggs.
3. Sprinkle the garlic and dry herbs over top of eggs and bake it for 5 minutes, or until the eggs are fully cooked.

**NUTRITIONAL VALUE PER SERVING:**
Calories: 322 /kcal; Carbs: 3 g; Protein: 20 g; Fat: 17 g.

## YOGURT PARFAIT WITH RASPBERRIES AND CHIA SEEDS

**Prep time:** 10 mins

**Cooking time:** 0 mins

**Total time:** 10 mins

**Servings:** 4

**INGREDIENTS:**
- 16 oz. plain Greek yogurt
- ½ cup fresh raspberries
- 2 tbsp. chia seeds
- pinch of cinnamon
- ½ cup blackberries
- 1 tsp. maple syrup
- ½ cup strawberries

**DIRECTIONS:**
1. In a small mixing dish, place the raspberries, black berries and strawberries.
2. Mash the berries with the back of a fork until they have a jam-like consistency.
3. Add the honey, chia seeds, and cinnamon to the mixing dish.
4. Continue mashing till all the ingredients are completely combined. In the base of a medium

glass or jar, spread a layer of yogurt.
5. Add a layer of prepared berry chia mix on top. Finish with a layer of yogurt on top.
6. Top with a splash of maple syrup and serve.

**NUTRITIONAL VALUE PER SERVING:**
Calories: 125 /kcal; Carbs: 67 g; Protein: 11 g; Fat: 9 g.

## GRAIN BREAKFAST BOWLS

*Prep time:* 10 mins

*Cooking time:* 25 mins

*Total time:* 35 mins

*Servings:* 2

**INGREDIENTS:**
- 1 cup of grains
- 1 cinnamon stick
- 1 star anise pod
- 2½ cups coconut water
- 2 whole cloves
- ½ apple, chopped
- 2 tbsp. blackberries
- ½ pear, chopped
- 2 tbsp. maple syrup

**DIRECTIONS:**
1. To prepare the grain bowls, in a saucepan, bring the coconut water, grains, and seasonings to a boil.
2. Cover and decrease the heat to medium-low after the water has boiled. Cook till the grains are soft, about 20-25 minutes.
3. Take the pan off the heat and discard the spices.
4. Top with apples, pears, blackberries and maple syrup.
5. Serve and enjoy.

**NUTRITIONAL VALUE PER SERVING:**
Calories: 200 /kcal; Carbs: 60 g; Protein: 10 g; Fat: 7 g.

## QUINOA CHIA PORRIDGE

*Prep time:* 5 mins

*Cooking time:* 5 mins

*Total time:* 10 mins

*Servings:* 2

**INGREDIENTS:**
- 1 cup thick cashew milk
- ½ tsp. ground cinnamon
- 1 tbsp. chia seeds
- 2 cups cooked quinoa
- 1 cup fresh blueberries
- ¼ cup toasted walnuts
- 2 tsp. raw honey

**DIRECTIONS:**
1. Warm the cashew milk and quinoa and together in a saucepan over low heat.
2. Stir in the blueberries, cinnamon, and walnuts until everything is warmed through. Remove the pan from the heat and add the raw honey.
3. Chia seeds are sprinkled on top.
4. Serve and enjoy.

**NUTRITIONAL VALUE PER SERVING:**
Calories: 128 /kcal; Carbs: 27 g; Protein: 6 g; Fat: 7 g.

## MANGO, CHIA AND ALMOND BREAKFAST BOWL

*Prep time:* 10 mins

*Cooking time:* 0 mins

*Total time:* 10 mins

*Servings:* 2

**INGREDIENTS:**
- ¼ cup rolled oats
- 2 tbsp. Chia seeds
- ½ tsp ground cinnamon
- 1 mango, cubed
- 1 cup almond milk
- 1/3 cup plain Greek yogurt
- 2 tbsp. sliced almonds

**DIRECTIONS:**
1. In a mixing dish, combine the oats and chia seeds. Stir in the milk and cinnamon until everything is well combined. Wrap with cling film and store in the refrigerator overnight.
2. Separate the oat mixture into two bowls. Each one should be topped with yogurt, almonds and mango. Add a pinch of cinnamon on top.

**NUTRITIONAL VALUE PER SERVING:**
Calories: 233 /kcal; Carbs: 25 g; Protein: 15 g; Fat: 10 g.

## BLUEBERRY ALMOND OATS

*Prep time:* 5 mins + chilling time

*Cooking time:* 2 mins

*Total time:* 7 mins + chilling time

*Servings:* 4

**INGREDIENTS:**
- 1½ cups old-fashioned rolled oats
- 1 tsp. vanilla extract
- 2 tbsp. flaxseed meal
- 2 cups vanilla almond milk, unsweetened
- ¼ tsp. salt
- ¼ tsp. ground cinnamon
- 1 cup blueberries
- ½ cup low-fat, plain Greek yogurt
- ¼ cup sliced almonds, for topping

**DIRECTIONS:**

**DIRECTIONS:**

1. Mix the oats, vanilla, milk, flaxseed, cinnamon, and salt in a small bowl.
2. Divide the oat mixture between 4 serving cups or jars.
3. Add 2 tbsp. of Greek yogurt in each cup and cover it with a lid.
4. Put the blueberries in an oven-safe and heat it for 1 to 2 minutes or until the blueberries burst and make a sauce.
5. Add 2 oz. blueberries and sliced almonds on top of each yogurt cup.
6. Put in the fridge for at least 2 hours or overnight.
7. You can eat it cold or warm it up for 20 to 30 seconds in the microwave.

**NUTRITIONAL VALUE PER SERVING:**

Calories: 225 /kcal; Carbs: 30 g; Protein: 9 g; Fat: 8 g.

## PROTEIN PANCAKES

**Prep time:** 5 mins

**Cooking time:** 5 mins

**Total time:** 10 mins

**Servings:** 6

**INGREDIENTS:**

- 1 cup low-fat cottage cheese
- 3 large eggs
- 1/3 cup flour
- Nonstick cooking spray
- Low-fat Greek yogurt, low-sugar syrup, nut butter, or fresh berries for serving
- 1/8 tsp. baking powder

**DIRECTIONS:**

1. Mix the flour, cottage cheese, baking powder and eggs in a blender until everything is smooth.
2. Put a small pan over medium-low heat to warm up. Use cooking spray that doesn't stick.
3. Pour a quarter cup of the pancake batter into the pan. Flip the pancake when it starts to bubble.
4. Cook for about 2 to 3 minutes per side, or until both sides are golden brown.
5. Do the same thing with the rest of the pancake batter.
6. Serve with low-sugar syrup, fresh berries, Greek yogurt or nut butter.

**NUTRITIONAL VALUE PER SERVING:**

Calories: 89 /kcal; Carbs: 6 g; Protein: 8 g; Fat: 3 g.

## SHAKSHUKA EGG BAKE

**Prep time:** 10 mins

**Cooking time:** 30 mins

**Total time:** 40 mins

**Servings:** 4

**INGREDIENTS:**

- 1 tsp. extra-virgin olive oil
- 1 garlic clove, minced
- ½ onion, minced
- ½ tsp. ground cumin
- ½ tsp. smoked paprika
- 2 oz. feta cheese, crumbled
- 15 oz. diced tomatoes
- 4 large eggs

**DIRECTIONS:**

1. Set the oven temperature to 350°F180°C.
2. Heat the oil in a medium-sized pan over medium heat. Add the onions and garlic and cook for about 5 minutes, or until the onions are clear. Cook for one more minute after adding the paprika and cumin.
3. Mix in the tomatoes until everything is well mixed. Simmer for 5 to 10 minutes, until the mixture starts to thicken into a sauce.
4. Spread the sauce out evenly in 4 ramekins, and then do the same with the cheese, making sure it is spread out evenly.
5. Make wells in the tomato sauce with a spoon and crack an egg into each one, being careful not to break the yolk.
6. Bake the eggs in the ramekins for 15 minutes or longer if you like the yolks to be hard, and then serve.

**NUTRITIONAL VALUE PER SERVING:**

Calories: 144 /kcal; Carbs: 7 g; Protein: 9 g; Fat: 9 g.

## DENVER EGG MUFFINS

**Prep time:** 15 mins

**Cooking time:** 30 mins

**Total time:** 45 mins

**Servings:** 12

**INGREDIENTS:**

- Nonstick cooking spray
- 12 slices deli ham
- ½ onion, diced
- 1 tsp. extra-virgin olive oil
- 10 large eggs
- ½ green pepper, minced
- ½ cup Cheddar cheese
- ¼ cup low-fat milk

**DIRECTIONS:**

1. Set the oven temperature to 350°F-180°C.
2. Use cooking spray to grease a muffin tin.
3. Put a slice of ham in each cup and push it down so it fits tightly against the edge of each cup.
4. Heat the oil in a small pan over medium heat. Add the green pepper and onion and cook for 3 minutes, or until the onion and pepper are soft. Take the pan off the heat and pour out any liquid.
5. Whisk the milk and eggs together in a large

bowl. Mix again after adding the cheese and cooked vegetables.
6. Fill each cup with ¼ cup of the egg mixture. If there is any left over, put it in each cup equally.
7. Bake for 20 to 25 minutes, or until the eggs are no longer runny and firm. Serve.

### NUTRITIONAL VALUE PER SERVING:
Calories: 99 /kcal; Carbs: 6 g; Protein: 8 g; Fat: 1 g.

## CHEESY EGG CASSEROLE

**Prep time:** 15 mins

**Cooking time:** 4 hours

**Total time:** 4 hours 15 mins

**Servings:** 8

### INGREDIENTS:
- 1 lb. fresh Italian chicken sausage
- 30 oz. frozen hash browns
- Nonstick cooking spray
- ½ medium onion, diced
- 1 red bell pepper, seeded and diced
- 1½ cups low-fat shredded Cheddar cheese
- 12 large eggs
- 1 cup low-fat milk
- 4 oz. diced green chiles
- ½ tsp. freshly ground black pepper
- ½ tsp. salt

### DIRECTIONS:
1. Take the sausage casings off and throw them away.
2. Brown the meat in a large skillet over medium heat, breaking it up as it cooks into smaller pieces. This should take about 7 minutes, or until the meat is no longer pink.
3. Spray a 5-quart slow cooker with nonstick cooking spray, and then layer half of the frozen hash browns, pepper, cooked sausage, chiles, onion, and 1/2 cup of cheese. Repeat with the rest of the cheese, chiles, peppers, onions, sausage, and hash browns.
4. Whisk the milk, eggs, salt, and pepper together in a large bowl.
5. Pour the egg mixture over the layers of vegetables and sausage, and then sprinkle the last half cup of cheese on top.
6. Cook for 4 hours on high and then serve.

### NUTRITIONAL VALUE PER SERVING:
Calories: /kcal; Carbs: g; Protein: g; Fat: g.

## BREAKFAST BURRITOS

**Prep time:** 15 mins

**Cooking time:** 20 mins

**Total time:** 35 mins

**Servings:** 8

### INGREDIENTS:
- 12 large eggs
- 1 tsp. extra-virgin olive oil
- ¼ cup low-fat milk
- ½ yellow onion, diced
- 1 cup canned black beans, drained and rinsed
- 1 green bell pepper, seeded and diced
- ½ cup Cheddar cheese, shredded
- 8 whole wheat tortillas
- 8 oz. salsa

### DIRECTIONS:
1. Whisk the eggs and milk together in a large bowl.
2. Heat the oil in a large pan over medium heat. Add the bell pepper, onion, and black beans. Sauté the onion for about 5 minutes, until it turns clear, and then put it on a plate.
3. Pour the egg mixture into the pan and gently stir it until the eggs are firm and fluffy.
4. Spread the eggs and onions out evenly on the tortillas, and then add the cheese and salsa on top.
5. Tuck in both sides of tortilla and roll it tightly to close it. Do the same with the rest of the tortillas.
6. Serve right away and enjoy.

### NUTRITIONAL VALUE PER SERVING:
Calories: 264 /kcal; Carbs: 24 g; Protein: 21 g; Fat: 12 g.

## CHIA PUDDING

**Prep time:** 5 mins + chilling time

**Cooking time:** 0 mins

**Total time:** 5 mins + chilling time

**Servings:** 1

### INGREDIENTS:
- 3 tbsp. chia seeds
- 1 tsp. pure vanilla extract
- 1 tbsp. maple syrup
- ¾ cup almond milk

### DIRECTIONS:
1. In a mason jar with a tight-fitting lid, combine the milk, maple syrup, vanilla, and chia seeds.
2. Stir thoroughly with a fork or spoon, and then let aside for 1 minute before stirring twice more.
3. Then put it in the fridge for 2 hours to overnight.
4. When ready to consume, give it a good stir and top and enjoy.

**NUTRITIONAL VALUE PER SERVING:**
Calories: 112 /kcal; Carbs: 13 g; Protein: 12 g; Fat: 8 g.

## BREAKFAST PIZZA

**Prep time: 5 mins**

**Cooking time: 5 mins**

**Total time: 10 mins**

**Servings: 1**

**INGREDIENTS:**

- 4 large egg whites
- ½ tsp. Italian seasoning
- Nonstick cooking spray
- ¼ cup pizza sauce
- ¼ tsp. garlic powder
- 1 tbsp. chopped fresh basil
- ¼ cup mozzarella cheese, shredded

**DIRECTIONS:**

1. Whisk the egg whites together in a small bowl.
2. Spray an 8-inch pan with nonstick spray and place it over medium-low heat. Add the beaten egg whites in the pan.
3. Let the egg whites cook for a minute or two.
4. Lift the edges of the egg gently with a rubber spatula and tilt the pan to let the uncooked egg white run underneath and begin to cook. Repeat till no liquid remains.
5. Sprinkle the garlic powder and Italian seasoning. When the egg is almost done, put sauce and cheese on top. Cook for another minute, or until the cheese has started melting.
6. Transfer the pizza onto a plate and top it with fresh basil and serve right away.

**NUTRITIONAL VALUE PER SERVING:**
Calories: 189 /kcal; Carbs: 9 g; Protein: 23 g; Fat: 6 g.

## FARMER'S MARKET SCRAMBLE

**Prep time: 10 mins**

**Cooking time: 20 mins**

**Total time: 30 mins**

**Servings: 4**

**INGREDIENTS:**

- 8 large eggs
- ½ tsp. extra-virgin olive oil
- ½ cup mushrooms, sliced
- 4 oz. Cheddar cheese
- ½ lb. extra-lean turkey breakfast sausage
- 1 ripe tomato, seeded and diced
- ¼ cup low-fat milk
- 1 cup baby spinach

**DIRECTIONS:**

1. Whisk the milk, eggs and cheese together in a large bowl.
2. Heat the oil in a large pan over medium heat. Add the mushrooms and cook for two to three minutes, or until they are soft. Place on a plate.
3. To the pan, add the turkey sausage. Break the sausage into small chunks with a rubber spatula and cook for 5 to 8 minutes, until it is browned and no longer pink.
4. Turn the heat down to medium-low and add the egg mixture and sausage to the skillet. Move the eggs around the pan gently and let them cook for half the time before adding the tomato and spinach.
5. Keep cooking until the eggs have risen and the spinach has turned limp.
6. Put the mushrooms back in the pan and mix gently until everything is combined.
7. Divide between four plates, and serve.

**NUTRITIONAL VALUE PER SERVING:**
Calories: 386 /kcal; Carbs: 4 g; Protein: 35 g; Fat: 25 g.

## RASPBERRY LEMON MUFFINS

**Prep time: 15 mins**

**Cooking time: 25 mins**

**Total time: 40 mins**

**Servings: 12**

**INGREDIENTS:**

- 2 cups almond flour
- 3 large eggs
- ⅛ tsp. salt
- Zest of 1 lemon
- ½ tsp. baking powder
- 6 oz. low-fat, plain Greek yogurt
- 3 tbsp. raw honey
- ½ tsp. baking soda
- 1/3 cup freshly squeezed lemon juice
- 1 cup fresh raspberries
- 1 tsp. vanilla extract

**DIRECTIONS:**

1. Set the oven temperature to 350°F-180°C. Line a 12-cup muffin pan with paper liners.
2. Mix the baking soda, almond flour, salt and baking powder in a medium bowl.
3. Whisk the three eggs in a separate large bowl. Add the vanilla, lemon zest, honey, and lemon juice to the yogurt. Mix until it's smooth.
4. Mix the dry ingredients with care into the wet ones.
5. Try not to break the raspberries as you fold them into the dough.
6. Put the mixture into the muffin pan cups using a 1/3-cup measuring cup. The mixture should reach the top of the paper cups.
7. Bake the muffins for 20 to 25 minutes.
8. Carefully take the muffins out of the pan and let them cool on a wire rack. Store them in a bag that can be closed or a container that keeps air out.

**NUTRITIONAL VALUE PER SERVING:**

**MAINTENANCE DIET**

Calories: 160 /kcal; Carbs: 11 g; Protein: 7 g; Fat: 11 g.

## PROTEIN WAFFLES

**Prep time: 5 mins**

**Cooking time: 5 mins**

**Total time: 10 mins**

**Servings: 5**

Ingredients:
- 2 scoops vanilla protein powder
- ¼ cup almond milk
- 2/3 cup Greek yogurt
- 1 cup oat flour
- 4 eggs large

DIRECTIONS:
1. Waffle maker should be prepared.
2. Whisk together the yogurt, eggs, and milk in a mixing dish. Whisk together the protein powder and oat flour until thoroughly mixed.
3. Prepare waffles according to the directions on your waffle maker. Vary according to the size of your waffle maker; you'll need different amounts of batter.
4. Waffles should be cooked for 4-5 minutes, till nicely browned and crispy.

**NUTRITIONAL VALUE PER SERVING:**
Calories: 212 /kcal; Carbs: 19 g; Protein: 21 g; Fat: 7 g.

## PUMPKIN SPICE MUFFINS

**Prep time: 10 mins**

**Cooking time: 25 mins**

**Total time: 35 mins**

**Servings: 12**

**INGREDIENTS:**
- 1½ cups whole wheat flour
- 1 tsp. baking soda
- 2 tsp. pumpkin pie spice
- 4 tbsp. butter, softened
- ½ tsp. salt
- 1 tsp. vanilla extract
- 2 tbsp. maple syrup
- 2/3 cup erythritol
- 2 large eggs

**DIRECTIONS:**
1. Set the oven temperature to 350°F-180°C. Use muffin liners to line a muffin tin.
2. Mix the pumpkin pie spice, flour, salt and baking soda in a large bowl.
3. Using a hand mixer, blend the butter, maple syrup, erythritol, and vanilla in another large bowl until smooth. Add one egg at a time, beating until the mixture is smooth.
4. Add small amounts of the dry mixture to the wet ingredients and mix in between.
5. Put the same amount of batter in each of the 12 muffin cups.
6. Bake the muffins for about 25 minutes, or until a toothpick stuck in the middle comes out clean.
7. Cool the muffins completely on a wire rack then put them in a bag that can be closed or another airtight container.

**NUTRITIONAL VALUE PER SERVING:**
Calories: 107 /kcal; Carbs: 13 g; Protein: 3 g; Fat: 5 g.

## EGG WHITE PIZZA

**Prep time: 5 mins**

**Cooking time: 5 mins**

**Total time: 10 mins**

**Servings: 4**

**INGREDIENTS:**
- 1 tbsp. extra-virgin olive oil
- ½ tsp. Italian seasoning
- 12 large egg whites
- ¼ tsp. salt
- ½ tsp. garlic powder
- ½ cup shredded mozzarella cheese
- Nonstick cooking spray
- 1 cup sliced tomato

**DIRECTIONS:**
1. Heat the olive oil over medium heat in a large pan.
2. Mix the garlic powder, Italian seasoning, and salt with the egg whites in a large bowl.
3. Pour the mixture into the pan and put the lid on it. Cook until bubbles form in the egg whites around 1 to 2 minutes. Carefully lift the edges of the egg whites with a spatula to make sure they don't stick to the pan.
4. If they stick, turn down the heat, carefully lift the egg whites out of the pan, and spray them with cooking spray before putting them back in the pan.
5. Take off the lid and sprinkle the eggs with the mozzarella cheese.
6. On top, put the tomato slices. Cover the pan and heat it for another minute or two until the cheese melts.
7. Carefully take the pizza made with egg whites out of the pan. Cut into four pieces and serve hot.

**NUTRITIONAL VALUE PER SERVING:**
Calories: 180 /kcal; Carbs: 6 g; Protein: 19 g; Fat: 11 g.

## SOUTHWEST SCRAMBLE

Prep time: 5 mins

Cooking time: 10 mins

Total time: 15 mins

Servings: 4

### INGREDIENTS:

- 8 tsp. extra-virgin olive oil
- ½ cup diced red or yellow onion
- 8 large eggs
- ½ cup canned tomatoes
- Pinch of ground black pepper
- ¼ tsp. salt
- ½ cup diced bell pepper
- ½ cup sliced avocado

### DIRECTIONS:

1. Heat olive oil in a pan.
2. Whisk the eggs well for about a minute in a medium bowl. Set aside.
3. Add the pepper and onion and cook, stirring often, until the onion is translucent, for about 5 minutes.
4. Add the beaten egg and cook for another minute or two, stirring often, until the egg is done.
5. Add diced tomatoes and cook for another minute or two. Take off the heat.
6. Season the scrambled eggs with salt and pepper. Put slices of avocado on top of the scrambled eggs and serve.

### NUTRITIONAL VALUE PER SERVING:
Calories: 266 /kcal; Carbs: 6 g; Protein: 14 g; Fat: 21 g.

## ITALIAN STYLE SCRAMBLE

Prep time: 5 mins

Cooking time: 5 mins

Total time: 10 mins

Servings: 4

### INGREDIENTS:

- 1 cup diced tomatoes
- Nonstick cooking spray
- 8 large eggs
- 1 tsp. Italian seasoning
- 1 cup shredded mozzarella cheese
- ¼ tsp. salt
- 1 tsp. garlic powder

### DIRECTIONS:

1. Spray a large pan with cooking spray that doesn't stick, and heat it over medium heat.
2. Beat the eggs, mozzarella cheese, tomato, garlic powder, Italian seasoning, and salt together in a large bowl until everything is well mixed.
3. Pour the mixture into the pan and cook, stirring often, for 3 to 5 minutes, until the eggs are set.
4. Take it off the stove and serve.

### NUTRITIONAL VALUE PER SERVING:
Calories: 241 /kcal; Carbs: 6 g; Protein: 21 g; Fat: 16 g.

## CHEESEBURGER SCRAMBLE

Prep time: 5 mins

Cooking time: 10 mins

Total time: 15 mins

Servings: 4

### INGREDIENTS:

1. Nonstick cooking spray
2. 8 oz. lean ground beef
3. ½ cup tomatoes, diced
4. 4 large eggs
5. ¼ tsp. salt
6. ½ cup shredded Cheddar cheese

### DIRECTIONS:

1. Spray a pan with cooking spray and sauté the ground beef over medium heat stirring often, until it is fully browned, for about 3 minutes.
2. Take the beef off the heat. Spoon the beef into a bowl or jar and set it aside. Pour the fat into a jar or bowl and keep aside.
3. Put the pan back on medium heat and spray it with cooking spray once more. In a small bowl, break the eggs and beat them well. Pour the eggs into the skillet and cook for 2 to 3 minutes, stir the mixture often, until the eggs are set.
4. Bring down the heat. Add the Cheddar cheese, tomato, beef, and salt to the skillet and mix well. Heat the mixture for another minute or two, or until the cheese is melted.
5. Take it off the stove and serve.

### NUTRITIONAL VALUE PER SERVING:
Calories: 218 /kcal; Carbs: 2 g; Protein: 21 g; Fat: 13 g.

## TURKEY, ZUCCHINI AND TOMATO HASH

Prep time: 5 mins

Cooking time: 15 mins

Total time: 20 mins

Servings: 4

### INGREDIENTS:

- 1 tbsp. extra-virgin olive oil
- 2 cups zucchini, diced
- 8 oz. lean ground turkey
- ½ cup diced onion
- 1 cup diced tomatoes, drained
- ¼ tsp. salt

### DIRECTIONS:

MAINTENANCE DIET

1. Heat the olive oil over medium heat in a large pan. Put the ground turkey in the pan and cook it for about 5 minutes, stirring it often, until it is browned. Take the turkey out of the pan and put it in a small bowl. Set aside.
2. Put the zucchini, onion and tomato in a skillet and cook, stirring every so often, for 7 to 10 minutes, or until the onion is clear and the zucchini is soft. Mix well after adding the salt.
3. Turn off the heat. Mix the turkey and the vegetables together, and then serve.

### NUTRITIONAL VALUE PER SERVING:

Calories: 110 /kcal; Carbs: 6 g; Protein: 12 g; Fat: 4 g.

## SPINACH AND CHEDDAR QUICHE

**Prep time:** 5 mins

**Cooking time:** 25 mins

**Total time:** 30 mins

**Servings:** 4

### INGREDIENTS:

- Nonstick cooking spray
- 4 large eggs
- 1 cup chopped spinach
- ¼ tsp. salt
- ½ cup shredded Cheddar cheese

### DIRECTIONS:

1. Set the oven temperature to 350°F-180°C.
2. Put eight cupcake liners in a muffin tin and spray each one with cooking spray that won't stick.
3. Put a few inches of water in the bottom of a medium saucepan and put a steamer basket in it. Bring the water to a boil, then put the spinach in the basket and steam it for 3 minutes. Take the food off the heat and drain it well in a colander by pressing on it with the back of a spoon.
4. Mix the spinach, Cheddar cheese, eggs, and salt together in a medium bowl. Pour the mixture into the cups that have been lined.
5. Bake the quiche for 15 to 20 minutes, or until a toothpick stuck in the middle comes out clean.

### NUTRITIONAL VALUE PER SERVING:

Calories: 128 /kcal; Carbs: 1 g; Protein: 10 g; Fat: 9 g.

## TOFU SCRAMBLER

**Prep time:** 10 mins

**Cooking time:** 25 mins

**Total time:** 35 mins

**Servings:** 2

### INGREDIENTS:

- 1 tsp. olive oil
- ⅛ tsp. turmeric
- ¼ cup green pepper
- 1 tsp. onion powder
- ¼ cup red pepper
- 1 cup tofu
- 1 clove garlic
- ¼ tsp. garlic powder

### DIRECTIONS:

1. Sauté the bell peppers with garlic in a medium sized skillet.
2. Soak and rinse the tofu and then add it into skillet. Now add in the remaining ingredients and stir well.
3. Cook, stirring, until the tofu becomes a soft golden colour, about 20 minutes.
4. The water in the mixture would evaporate. Serve the tofu scrambler when it's still warm.

### NUTRITIONAL VALUE PER SERVING:

Calories: 210 /kcal; Carbs: 4 g; Protein: 15 g; Fat: 5 g.

## VEGAN BREAKFAST SCRAMBLE

**Prep time:** 10 mins

**Cooking time:** 25 mins

**Total time:** 35 mins

**Servings:** 6

### INGREDIENTS:

- 6 oz. firm tofu
- 3 tbsp. nutritional yeast
- 3 tbsp. avocado oil
- 1 onion
- 1½ tsp. turmeric
- 3 cloves garlic
- 1 medium head of cauliflower
- ½ tsp. black pepper
- ½ tsp. salt

### DIRECTIONS:

1. Heat avocado oil in a skillet over medium heat.
2. When the pan is hot, add the diced onion and cook for 5 minutes and then add the garlic and fry, stirring constantly, for another 1-2 minutes, until fragrant.
3. Stir in cauliflower florets and crumbled tofu, and fry for 5 minutes, or until cauliflower is tender.
4. Season it with nutritional yeast, turmeric, salt and black pepper.
5. Cook for another minute while stirring.
6. Serve and enjoy.

### NUTRITIONAL VALUE PER SERVING:

Calories: 134 /kcal; Carbs: 5 g; Protein: 9 g; Fat: 6 g.

## OAT AND BERRY ACAI BOWL

Prep time: 10 mins

Cooking time: 0 mins

Total time: 10 mins

Servings: 1

### INGREDIENTS:

- ½ cup milk
- 1/3 cup traditional oats
- ¼ cup frozen blueberries
- 1 tbsp. white chia seeds
- ¼ cup frozen raspberries
- ½ ripe banana
- 1 tsp acai powder
- 2 tsp. pomegranate seeds
- 100 g mixed berries
- 2 tbsp. Coles Dried Cranberries
- 1 tbsp. pistachios, chopped
- 1 tbsp. chia seeds

### DIRECTIONS:

1. Combine the oats, banana, milk, frozen berries, and acai powder in a blender until smooth. Allow to thicken for a few minutes.
2. Transfer the mixture to a serving dish. On top, arrange the berries, pistachios, and seeds and serve.

### NUTRITIONAL VALUE PER SERVING:

Calories: 250 /kcal; Carbs: 69 g; Protein: 18 g; Fat: 19 g.

## VANILLA CHIA PUDDING

Prep time: 10 mins

Cooking time: 0 mins

Total time: 10 mins

Servings: 2

### INGREDIENTS:

- 1 cup plain almond milk
- ¾ tsp. vanilla extract
- 1 tbsp. liquid stevia
- 3 tbsp. chia seeds
- 1 pinch salt
- ¼ tsp. vanilla bean paste
- ½ cup Chia Berry Jam
- ½ cup mixed fresh berries
- 2 fresh cherries

### DIRECTIONS:

1. In a medium mixing bowl, combine all of the ingredients.
2. Cover and chill for 2 hours.
3. Now take two 8-ounce glasses and put 3 tbsp. chia Berry Jam in each of them.
4. In two glasses, divide the chia pudding and put 1 tbsp. chia Berry Jam on top of each.
5. Finish with a sprinkling of fresh berries. Add a cherry on the top of each one. Enjoy.

### NUTRITIONAL VALUE PER SERVING:

Calories: 320 /kcal; Carbs: 40 g; Protein: 10 g; Fat: 0.7 g.

## EGG MUFFINS

Prep time: 5 mins

Cooking time: 15 mins

Total time: 20 mins

Servings: 12

### INGREDIENTS:

- 4 oz. green chilies
- ½ tsp. ground cumin
- cooking spray
- 3 cups cooked rice
- 2 eggs
- ½ cup skim milk
- 4 oz. cheddar cheese
- 2 oz. pimentos
- ½ tsp. black pepper

### DIRECTIONS:

1. Add rice, cream, eggs, 2 oz. cheese, chilies, pimentos, cumin, and pepper in a big mixing bowl. Spray nonstick cooking spray into muffin cups.
2. Divide the mixture equally among the 12 muffin cups.
3. The remaining 2 oz. of cheese should be sprinkled on top of each cup.
4. Bake the muffins for 15 minutes at 400° F-200°C.

### NUTRITIONAL VALUE PER SERVING:

Calories: 134 /kcal; Carbs: 8 g; Protein: 25 g; Fat: 7 g.

## TURKEY BURRITOS

Prep time: 15 mins

Cooking time: 25 mins

Total time: 40 mins

Servings: 8

### INGREDIENTS:

- 1 lb. ground turkey
- ¼ cup canola oil
- 2 tbsp. fresh scallions
- ½ tsp. paprika
- ½ tsp. chili powder
- 8 flour burrito shells
- ¼ cup onions
- 8 beaten eggs
- 2 tbsp. jalapeño peppers
- ¼ cup bell peppers
- 2 tbsp. fresh cilantro
- 1 cup low-fat cheese

### DIRECTIONS:

**MAINTENANCE DIET**

1. Use half of the oil to sauté the onions, peppers, meatloaf, scallions, and cilantro.
2. Stir in the spices, and then remove from the heat.
3. In a separate big sauté pan, heat the remaining oil and scramble eggs over medium-high heat.
4. Fill burrito shells with equal quantities of meat and vegetable blend, eggs and cheese and then fold and serve.

**NUTRITIONAL VALUE PER SERVING:**
Calories: 156 /kcal; Carbs: 6 g; Protein: 26 g; Fat: 10 g.

## MINI FRITTATAS

*Prep time:* 15 mins

*Cooking time:* 20 mins

*Total time:* 35 mins

*Servings:* 12

**INGREDIENTS:**

- 1/3 cup red bell pepper
- 12 eggs
- ¼ tsp. pepper
- 1/3 cup broccoli
- 1/3 cup zucchini
- 3 tbsp. fresh basil
- ¼ cup shredded cheese
- ½ tsp. salt free seasoning

**DIRECTIONS:**

1. Preheat the oven 350°F-180°C.
2. Use oil, to grease muffin tray or line them with muffin liners.
3. Combine the broccoli, zucchini, red bell pepper, and basil in a medium mixing dish. Whisk along eggs, pepper, salt free seasoning, and cheese in a big mixing cup.
4. Stir the egg mixture into the veggie mixture to blend.
5. Fill muffin cups with prepared mixture using a measuring cup.
6. Bake the muffins for 16 to 18 minutes or until the eggs are firm from the middle.

**NUTRITIONAL VALUE PER SERVING:**
Calories: /kcal; Carbs: g; Protein: g; Fat: g.

## PEANUT BUTTER PANCAKES

*Prep time:* 5 mins

*Cooking time:* 20 mins

*Total time:* 25 mins

*Servings:* 6

**INGREDIENTS:**

- 1 large egg
- avocado oil
- 1 large ripe banana
- ¼ cup peanut butter
- ½ cup almond milk
- 2 scoops protein powder
- ¼ cup quick oats
- 2 tsp. baking powder

**DIRECTIONS:**

1. Combine all ingredients in a food processor or blender and pulse until smooth.
2. Preheat a pan over low-medium heat and grease it with oil.
3. Divide the prepared batter into three pancakes and cook for 3-5 minutes, or until the tops are no longer jiggly, then turn and cook for the next 3-5 minutes.
4. Serve and enjoy.

**NUTRITIONAL VALUE PER SERVING:**
Calories: 225 /kcal; Carbs: 10 g; Protein: 13 g; Fat: 7 g.

## BROCCOLI AND CHEESE OMELET

*Prep time:* 15 mins

*Cooking time:* 25 mins

*Total time:* 40 mins

*Servings:* 8

**INGREDIENTS:**

- 4 cups broccoli florets
- ¼ cup grated parmesan cheese
- cooking spray
- 1 cup egg whites
- 4 whole eggs
- ¼ cup reduced fat cheddar
- 1 tbsp. olive oil
- fresh pepper to taste

**DIRECTIONS:**

1. Broccoli should be steamed with a little water; it will take around 5 minutes.
2. When the broccoli is done, mash it up.
3. Grease muffin pans and scoop broccoli mixture equally into each muffin cup.
4. In a medium mixing bowl, whisk together parmesan cheese egg whites, eggs, and pepper.
5. Fill the with egg mixture. Top with shredded cheddar and bake for 20 minutes, or until cheese is melted.
6. Serve right away.

**NUTRITIONAL VALUE PER SERVING:**
Calories: 230 /kcal; Carbs: 10 g; Protein: 25 g; Fat: 11 g.

## MUSHROOM FRITTATA

Prep time: 15 mins

Cooking time: 20 mins

Total time: 35 mins

Servings: 4

### INGREDIENTS:

- 1 tbsp. unsalted butter
- 1 tbsp. milk
- 5 egg whites
- ½ lb. mushrooms, finely chopped
- 4 shallots, finely chopped
- 2 tsp. fresh parsley, chopped
- Black pepper to taste
- 1 tsp. dried thyme
- 3 eggs
- ¼ cup parmesan cheese, grated

### DIRECTIONS:

1. In a pan melt butter over medium heat, then add shallots and mushrooms and cook for 5 minutes, or until golden.
2. Combine the chopped mushroom, thyme, parsley, and black pepper in a mixing bowl.
3. Whisk together the egg whites, milk, parmesan and eggs in a medium mixing dish.
4. Pour the egg mixture over the mushrooms in the skillet and transfer the skillet to the oven.
5. Bake it in oven for 15 minutes, or until the frittata is fully cooked.

### NUTRITIONAL VALUE PER SERVING:

Calories: 130 /kcal; Carbs: 6 g; Protein: 11 g; Fat: 9 g.

## BUTTERMILK PANCAKES

Prep time: 10 mins

Cooking time: 5 mins

Total time: 15 mins

Servings: 6

### INGREDIENTS:

- 2 cups all-purpose flour
- 2 cups buttermilk
- 1½ tsp. baking soda
- 1 tsp. tartar cream
- 2 tbsp. sugar
- 2 eggs
- ¼ cup canola oil

### DIRECTIONS:

1. In a big mixing bowl, combine the dry ingredients.
2. Mix the dry ingredients with the wet ingredients with a whisk or a spoon until they are fully moist.
3. Brush the pan with canola oil and put it on medium high heat.
4. Scoop the 1/3 cup of pancake batter into the pan with a measuring cup.
5. Cook each pancake for 2 minutes from each side.
6. Transfer to a serving plate and Serve.

### NUTRITIONAL VALUE PER SERVING:

Calories: 245 /kcal; Carbs: 12 g; Protein: 19 g; Fat: 12 g.

## VEGGIE EGGS

Prep time: 5 mins

Cooking time: 10 mins

Total time: 15 mins

Servings: 2

### INGREDIENTS:

- 3 cup fresh spinach
- 1 tbsp. oil
- 4 whole eggs
- 1 garlic clove
- 1 cup cauliflower
- ¼ cup bell pepper
- ¼ tsp. black pepper
- ¼ cup onion
- fresh parsley, for garnish
- salt, to taste

### DIRECTIONS:

1. Whisk eggs with black pepper and salt until fluffy and light.
2. In a big pan add the oil and put it over medium heat.
3. Sauté the onions and peppers for 3 minutes and then add the garlic, cauliflower and spinach.
4. When vegetables are sautéed, then reduce heat to medium-low and add the eggs and whisk to mix with the vegetables.
5. Garnish with fresh parsley and enjoy.

### NUTRITIONAL VALUE PER SERVING:

Calories: 230 /kcal; Carbs: 28 g; Protein: 25 g; Fat: 12 g.

# LUNCH RECIPES

## CUMIN MUSHROOM QUESADILLAS

**Prep time:** 10 mins

**Cooking time:** 12 mins

**Total time:** 22 mins

**Servings:** 4

### INGREDIENTS:

- ½ lb. white mushrooms
- 1 tbsp. olive oil
- 1 tbsp. low-fat butter
- 2 tsp. ground cumin
- 1 small clove garlic, minced
- ¼ tsp. paprika
- 1/8 tsp. cayenne pepper
- 2 tbsp. nonfat sour cream
- ½ tsp. kosher salt
- ¾ cup reduced-fat shredded Cheddar cheese
- 4 low-carb whole-wheat tortillas
- ¼ cup chopped fresh cilantro

### DIRECTIONS:

1. You can use a mushroom brush or paper towels to clean them. Cut off the end of the stems and throw them away. The mushrooms should be cut into thin pieces.
2. Over medium heat, melt the butter and oil in a medium nonstick pan. Add the garlic, mushrooms, cumin, salt, paprika, and pepper. For 8 minutes, stir them often, until the mushrooms are soft. Stir in the sour cream and keep cooking, stirring once or twice, for minutes. Take the pan off the stove.
3. Set the oven temperature to 375°F-190°C. Put the tortillas on a pan for baking. Put the mushrooms on half side of each tortilla in an even amount. Divide the cheese in half and spread it over the mushrooms.
4. Fold each tortilla's empty half over the mushroom half. For about a minute, until the cheese has melted, bake the quesadillas in the oven.

**NUTRITIONAL VALUE PER SERVING:**
Calories: 168 /kcal; Carbs: 16 g; Protein: 12 g; Fat: 9 g.

## CLASSIC TURKEY AND SWISS WRAP

**Prep time:** 15 mins

**Cooking time:** 0 mins

**Total time:** 15 mins

**Servings:** 8

### INGREDIENTS:

- 2 tbsp. non-fat mayonnaise
- 1/8 tsp. black pepper
- 2 tsp. prepared sweet mustard
- 4 whole lettuce leaves
- 4 low-carb tortillas
- 4 slices low-fat Swiss cheese
- 12 oz. thin sliced roasted turkey
- 8 thin red onion ring slices
- 2 Italian plum tomatoes, cored and sliced

### DIRECTIONS:

1. Mix the mustard, mayo, and pepper together in a small bowl. Spread the mixture on 4 tortillas in an even way. Next, put lettuce, Swiss cheese, turkey, tomato, and onion in layers.
2. Wrap the filling tightly in the tortillas, then wrap the whole thing in plastic wrap and put it in the fridge for at least an hour before serving. Cut each wrap in half to serve.

**NUTRITIONAL VALUE PER SERVING:**
Calories: 150 /kcal; Carbs: 11 g; Protein: 17 g; Fat: 6 g.

## SPINACH TURKEY WRAPS

**Prep time:** 10 mins

**Cooking time:** 0 mins

**Total time:** 10 mins

**Servings:** 4

### INGREDIENTS:

- 4 oz. nonfat cream cheese
- 1 tsp. Dijon mustard
- 2 tbsp. sliced green onions
- 1¼ cups fresh spinach, shredded
- 4 low-carb tortillas
- 1/4 cup reduced-fat shredded Cheddar cheese
- 6 oz. thinly sliced roasted turkey breast
- 2 tbsp. minced red bell pepper

### DIRECTIONS:

1. Mix the cream cheese, green onions, and the Dijon mustard together in a small bowl.
2. Spread the same amount of the mixture on each tortilla. Next, add spinach, cheese, turkey, and bell pepper in equal amounts. Wrap the filling tightly in the tortillas, and then wrap the rolls in plastic wrap.

**NUTRITIONAL VALUE PER SERVING:**

Calories: 184 /kcal; Carbs: 21 g; Protein: 23 g; Fat: 6 g.

## AVOCADO, CREAM CHEESE AND BACON SANDWICH

**Prep time:** 10 mins

**Cooking time:** 0 mins

**Total time:** 10 mins

**Servings:** 1

### INGREDIENTS:

- 1 oz. nonfat cream cheese
- 2 slices low-sodium, cooked turkey bacon
- 2 slices toasted diet wheat bread
- ¼ ripe avocado, thinly sliced

### DIRECTIONS:

1. Spread equal amounts of cream cheese on each piece of bread. Break or cut the strips of bacon in half, and then put each half on one slice. Next, put the avocado slices on top of the bacon and cover with the other slice of bread. Serve by cutting in the diagonal.

### NUTRITIONAL VALUE PER SERVING:

Calories: 223 /kcal; Carbs: 24 g; Protein: 13 g; Fat: 10 g.

## CHICKEN SALAD SANDWICH

**Prep time:** 15 mins

**Cooking time:** 0 mins

**Total time:** 15 mins

**Servings:** 2

### INGREDIENTS:

- 4 oz. cooked chicken breast, diced
- 1 tsp. minced onion
- 2 large pitted black olives, sliced
- 1 tsp. fresh finely chopped parsley
- 2 tsp. finely chopped tomato
- black pepper, to taste
- 2 tsp. non-fat mayonnaise
- ½ tsp. lemon juice
- ½ tsp. capers, chopped
- 2 sprigs fresh parsley
- 1 English muffin, halved

### DIRECTIONS:

1. Mix the chicken, onion, olives, tomato, pepper, chopped parsley, mayonnaise, capers, lemon juice, and lemon zest in a small bowl. Blend well. On top of each toasted half of an English muffin, put half of the chicken salad and a sprig of parsley.

### NUTRITIONAL VALUE PER SERVING:

Calories: 136 /kcal; Carbs: 13 g; Protein: 16 g; Fat: 2 g.

## CLASSIC TURKEY, CRANBERRY, AND CREAM CHEESE SANDWICH

**Prep time:** 10 mins

**Cooking time:** 0 mins

**Total time:** 10 mins

**Servings:** 1

### INGREDIENTS:

- 2 slices whole grain bread, toasted
- 2 tsp. reduced-fat cream cheese
- 1 tsp. nonfat mayonnaise
- 2 oz. sliced turkey meat
- 2 tbsp. cranberry sauce
- 1 leaf lettuce

### DIRECTIONS:

1. Spread the mayonnaise on one slice of bread and the cream cheese on the other. Spread the cranberry sauce on top of the cream cheese. Put the turkey on top of the cranberry sauce, and then put the lettuce on top of the turkey. Place the other slice of toast on top and cut it in half.

### NUTRITIONAL VALUE PER SERVING:

Calories: 214 /kcal; Carbs: 27 g; Protein: 17 g; Fat: 5 g.

## ULTIMATE VEGGIE SANDWICH

**Prep time:** 10 mins

**Cooking time:** 0 mins

**Total time:** 10 mins

**Servings:** 1

### INGREDIENTS:

- 2 slices whole grain bread, toasted
- 1 tsp. nonfat cream cheese
- ¼ ripe avocado
- small pinch of black pepper
- small pinch of salt
- 3 thinly sliced green bell pepper rings
- 2 thick slices of tomato
- 3 thinly sliced red onion rings
- 6 thinly sliced cucumber coins, peeled

### DIRECTIONS:

1. Spread the avocado on one slice of bread and the cream cheese on the other. Put the pepper, salt, onion, tomato, bell pepper, cucumber, sprouts, and onion on top of the avocado. Put the last slice of bread on top, stick toothpicks through it, cut it in half, and serve.

### NUTRITIONAL VALUE PER SERVING:

Calories: 209 /kcal; Carbs: 30 g; Protein: 8 g; Fat: 9 g.

## FRESH MOZZARELLA AND TOMATO SANDWICH

Prep time: 10 mins

Cooking time: 0 mins

Total time: 10 mins

Servings: 1

**INGREDIENTS:**

- 2 slices whole grain bread, toasted
- 1 tsp. olive tapenade
- 2 tsp. nonfat mayonnaise
- 2 thick slices tomato
- 2 slices fresh mozzarella cheese

**DIRECTIONS:**

1. Spread the same amount of mayonnaise on both pieces of bread. Spread the tapenade on one slice, and then add the mozzarella and the tomato. Place the other slice of bread on top. Cut the bread diagonally into fourths, and serve.

**NUTRITIONAL VALUE PER SERVING:**

Calories: 263 /kcal; Carbs: 24 g; Protein: 14 g; Fat: 13 g.

## BAKED HAM AND CHEESE SANDWICH

Prep time: 10 mins

Cooking time: 5 mins

Total time: 15 mins

Servings: 1

**INGREDIENTS:**

- 2 slices whole-grain bread
- ½ tsp. Dijon mustard
- 2 tsp. nonfat mayonnaise
- 2 thick slices tomato
- 2 oz. sliced ham
- 1 slice reduced-fat Swiss cheese

**DIRECTIONS:**

1. Set the oven temperature to 350°F-180°C. Spread the mayonnaise on one slice of bread and the mustard on the other.
2. On one slice, put the ham, then the tomato slices, and finally the cheese. Place on a sheet pan and top with the other slice of bread.
3. Toast the sandwich for about 5 minutes, or until the cheese is melted and the bread is nicely toasted. Half it and serve it hot.

**NUTRITIONAL VALUE PER SERVING:**

Calories: 266 /kcal; Carbs: 26 g; Protein: 24 g; Fat: 8 g.

## SALMON SANDWICH

Prep time: 10 mins

Cooking time: 0 mins

Total time: 10 mins

Servings: 2

**INGREDIENTS:**

- 6 oz. canned salmon
- 2 English muffin halves, toasted
- 1 tbsp. nonfat mayonnaise
- 2 thick tomato slices

**DIRECTIONS:**

1. Mix the salmon and mayonnaise together in a small bowl. On each muffin half, put a slice of tomato and then the salmon mixture.

**NUTRITIONAL VALUE PER SERVING:**

Calories: 220 /kcal; Carbs: 24 g; Protein: 24 g; Fat: 4 g.

## TURKEY SANDWICH

Prep time: 10 mins

Cooking time: 0 mins

Total time: 10 mins

Servings: 1

**INGREDIENTS:**

- ¼ tsp. chopped fresh tarragon
- 2 oz. non-fat cream cheese
- ¼ tsp. chopped fresh chives
- 2 slices whole-grain bread, toasted
- ¼ tsp. chopped fresh parsley
- 2 oz. sliced turkey breast
- 6 thinly sliced cucumber, coins

**DIRECTIONS:**

1. Mix the cream cheese, tarragon, chives, and parsley together in a small bowl. On each piece of bread, spread half of the mixture.
2. Place the cucumbers evenly on top of the cream cheese mixture, and then place the turkey on top of the cucumbers. Add the other slice of bread on top, and serve.

**NUTRITIONAL VALUE PER SERVING:**

Calories: 221 /kcal; Carbs: 24 g; Protein: 24 g; Fat: 4 g.

## EGG SALAD SANDWICH

Prep time: 10 mins

Cooking time: 0 mins

Total time: 10 mins

Servings: 2

### INGREDIENTS:

- 2 whole hard-boiled eggs
- 2 tsp. nonfat mayonnaise
- 2 hard-boiled eggs, whites only
- 1 tsp. finely chopped chives
- ¼ tsp. Dijon mustard
- 2 whole-grain English muffin halves, toasted
- ¼ tsp. celery seed

### DIRECTIONS:

1. Crush the hard-boiled eggs and egg whites with a fork in a small bowl. Mix together the mustard, mayonnaise, chives, and celery seed. Put half of the egg salad on top of each muffin half, and serve.

### NUTRITIONAL VALUE PER SERVING:

Calories: 164 /kcal; Carbs: 14 g; Protein: 13 g; Fat: 6 g.

## BACON, LETTUCE, TOMATO, AND CREAM CHEESE SANDWICH

Prep time: 10 mins

Cooking time: 0 mins

Total time: 10 mins

Servings: 1

### INGREDIENTS:

- 2 whole grain bread, toasted
- 2 strips low-sodium, turkey bacon
- 1 oz. nonfat cream cheese
- 2 lettuce leaves
- 2 thick slices tomato

### DIRECTIONS:

1. Spread equal amounts of cream cheese on each bread slice. Put the bacon strips on one slice in the shape of a cross from corner to corner.
2. Stack the tomato, pepper, and lettuce leaves, then put the last slice of bread on top. Stick a toothpick through each half of the sandwich, cut it in half, and serve.

### NUTRITIONAL VALUE PER SERVING:

Calories: 186 /kcal; Carbs: 23 g; Protein: 12 g; Fat: 7 g.

## PITA PIZZA

Prep time: 10 mins

Cooking time: 15 mins

Total time: 25 mins

Servings: 4

### INGREDIENTS

- 4 small whole wheat pita breads
- 1 tsp. dried oregano
- 2½ oz. low-sodium tomato paste
- 1 tsp. dried thyme
- 1 tsp. dried basil
- 1 cup cooked chicken breast, cubed
- ½ cup sliced fresh mushrooms
- 4 tbsp. grated Parmesan cheese
- 2½ oz. sliced olives, drained
- ¾ cup shredded mozzarella cheese

### DIRECTIONS:

1. Set the oven temperature to 375°F-190°C. Spray some cooking spray on a sheet pan. Put the pitas on the baking sheet.
2. Spread 1 tablespoon of tomato paste on each pita bread in an even layer. Spread the oregano, thyme, basil, Parmesan, mushrooms, olives, chicken and mozzarella out evenly on the pizzas.
3. Bake the pizzas for about 15 minutes, or until the cheese starts to brown and bubble.

### NUTRITIONAL VALUE PER SERVING:

Calories: 284 /kcal; Carbs: 24 g; Protein: 25 g; Fat: 9 g.

## SIMPLE SLOPPY JOE

Prep time: 10 mins

Cooking time: 20 mins

Total time: 30 mins

Servings: 4

### INGREDIENTS:

- 1 cup chopped onion
- 1 clove fresh garlic, chopped
- 1/3 cup diced red bell pepper
- ½ tsp. ground basil
- ½ tsp. ground oregano
- ½ tsp. cayenne pepper
- ½ tsp. paprika
- 1 cup low-carb ketchup
- 3/4 cup soy crumbles
- 1 cup tomato sauce, no added salt

### DIRECTIONS:

1. Spray cooking spray on a large skillet and heat it over medium-high heat.
2. Put in the red pepper, onion, garlic, oregano, paprika, basil, and cayenne pepper. Keep cooking for another 5 minutes, or until the pepper and onion start to get soft.
3. Add the soy crumbles and keep cooking, stirring often, for another 5 minutes. Add the ketchup and tomato sauce and keep cooking, stirring every now and then, for another 8 to 10 minutes.

### NUTRITIONAL VALUE PER SERVING:

Calories: 208 /kcal; Carbs: 18 g; Protein: 20 g; Fat: 3 g.

## MEDITERRANEAN CHICKEN

**Prep time:** 10 mins

**Cooking time:** 25 mins

**Total time:** 35 mins

**Servings:** 4

### INGREDIENTS:

- 2 tsp. olive oil, divided
- 2 garlic cloves minced
- 1/3 cup feta cheese
- 1 cup fresh spinach, chopped
- ¼ cup sun dried tomatoes, sliced
- salt and pepper, to taste
- 1 tsp. crushed oregano
- ¼ cup chopped onions
- 4 chicken thighs
- 6 small mushrooms sliced
- 1/3 cup Italian cheese, grated

### DIRECTIONS:

1. In an oven-safe skillet, heat 1 tsp. olive oil.
2. Season the chicken thighs with pepper, salt, and oregano. Then brown the chicken on each side in a hot skillet and keep it aside.
3. Cook the garlic, onions and mushrooms until tender in another tsp. of olive oil in the skillet. Sun-dried tomatoes, spinach, feta, and browned chicken are then added to the pan.
4. Now sprinkle the cheeses on top and bake skillet for 20-30 minutes in preheated oven at 350°F-180°C. Allow 5 minutes for flavors to meld before serving.

### NUTRITIONAL VALUE PER SERVING:
Calories: 360 /kcal; Carbs: 8 g; Protein: 26 g; Fat: 20 g.

## MEXICAN STYLE STUFFED SUMMER SQUASH

**Prep time:** 5 mins

**Cooking time:** 23 mins

**Total time:** 28 mins

**Servings:** 2

### INGREDIENTS:

- ½ cup refried black beans
- 1 tomato, diced
- ½ cup cooked quinoa
- 2 scallions, chopped
- 2 tbsp. black olives, sliced
- Non-stick spray
- 1 cup shredded Colby jack cheese

### DIRECTIONS:

1. Set the oven temperature to 400°F-200°C.
2. Remove the insides of the summer squash before putting it in a baking dish. Poke it with a fork before baking. Bake it for three and four minutes.
3. Mix the rest of the ingredients, then put the mixture in the summer squash.
4. Put the cheese on top and put it in the oven for 20 minutes.
5. When it's done, dish it out and top it with the chopped scallions.
6. Your food is now ready to eat.

### NUTRITIONAL VALUE PER SERVING:
Calories: 232 /kcal; Carbs: 12 g; Protein: 22 g; Fat: 5 g.

## BARLEY AND MUSHROOM RISOTTO

**Prep time:** 5 mins

**Cooking time:** 35 mins

**Total time:** 40 mins

**Servings:** 6

### INGREDIENTS:

- 1 tsp. garlic, minced
- 1 tbsp. extra virgin olive oil
- 2 leaks, diced
- 3 cups fresh spinach leaves
- 4 cups sliced mushrooms
- 1 cup chicken broth
- ½ cup barley
- ½ cup white wine
- 2 tsp. thyme

**INDIRECTIONS** Put the garlic and olive oil in a large, deep pan. Add the mushrooms and leeks after a few seconds.

1. Cook for a few minutes after adding the thyme and barley.
2. Add the wine and make sure it is well mixed.
3. Add the broth and let it cook over low heat for 30 minutes.
4. Now add the spinach and stir it around until it starts to wilt.
5. Your dish is done and ready to eat.

### NUTRITIONAL VALUE PER SERVING:
Calories: 198 /kcal; Carbs: 11 g; Protein: 13 g; Fat: 5 g.

## COCONUT AND TOFU CURRY

**Prep time:** 10 mins

**Cooking time:** 15 mins

**Total time:** 25 mins

**Servings:** 6

### INGREDIENTS

- 1 tbsp. minced garlic
- 1 tbsp. grated ginger
- ½ tsp. turmeric
- ¼ tsp. cinnamon

- ½ tsp. ground cumin
- 2 tsp. curry powder
- 14 oz. extra firm tofu
- 3 tbsp. coconut oil
- 1 cup tomato puree
- 2 cups unsweetened coconut milk
- 2 stems bok choi
- 2 carrots, diced
- ½ cup fresh cilantro
- 2 cups chicken broth

**INDIRECTIONS** Saute the tofu cubes in the coconut oil for 3–4 minutes, or until a firm layer forms on top of the cubes.

1. Take the tofu out of the pan before adding the rest of the ingredients.
2. Blend in the coconut milk. Now add the tofu and Bok choi to the mixture and cook it for a few minutes.
3. Serve it with rice and add fresh cilantro to the top.

**NUTRITIONAL VALUE PER SERVING:**
Calories: 167 /kcal; Carbs: 12 g; Protein: 17 g; Fat: 7 g.

## EGGPLANT ROLLATINI

*Prep time:* 20 mins

*Cooking time:* 55 mins

*Total time:* 1 hour 15 mins

*Servings:* 6

**INGREDIENTS:**

- 1 large eggplant
- 1 tsp. extra virgin olive oil
- 1 tbsp. salt
- ½ cup mozzarella cheese
- 10 cups fresh spinach
- 1 egg
- 1 cup marinara sauce
- ½ cup ricotta cheese
- 1 tsp. minced garlic
- 1 cup Parmigiano Reggiano cheese

**INDIRECTIONS** Cut the eggplant in half and sprinkle the salt on each half. Let it rest for 10 minutes.

1. Now wash the salt off the eggplant and put it in an oven that has already been heated for 10 minutes.
2. Add the garlic, olive oil, and spinach to a large pan and cook until the spinach is soft.
3. Now, layer the eggplant, marinara sauce, and spinach in a baking dish.
4. Put cheese on top, wrap it in aluminum foil, and bake it for 30 minutes.
5. Take off the foil and bake it for 10 minutes longer.
6. Your dish is done and ready to eat.

**NUTRITIONAL VALUE PER SERVING:**
Calories: 234 /kcal; Carbs: 20 g; Protein: 33 g; Fat: 17 g.

## CHICKEN RICOTTA

*Prep time:* 15 mins

*Cooking time:* 15 mins

*Total time:* 30 mins

*Servings:* 4

**INGREDIENTS:**

- 1 lb. chicken tenders
- 1 cup cherry tomatoes, roasted
- 1 tsp. oregano, crushed
- 1 tbsp. olive oil
- ½ cup parmesan cheese
- 1 cup ricotta cheese
- Spiralized yellow squash, lightly sautéed
- olives, garnish optional

**DIRECTIONS:**

1. Sauté chicken tenders with olive oil in a skillet.
2. Parmesan, Ricotta, and oregano should be combined together in a small bowl.
3. Spirals of yellow squash should be combined with olive oil and season with salt and pepper to taste.
4. To assemble, spread ricotta cheese mixture over chicken tenders and top with roasted tomatoes.
5. Place under the broiler to roast for 5 minutes and serve with Squash spirals.

**NUTRITIONAL VALUE PER SERVING:**
Calories: 270 /kcal; Carbs: 5 g; Protein: 36 g; Fat: 11 g.

## EGGPLANT, CHICKPEA, AND QUINOA CURRY

*Prep time:* 15 mins

*Cooking time:* 25 mins

*Total time:* 40 mins

*Servings:* 6

**INGREDIENTS:**

- 1 large eggplant, cut into chunks
- 3 tomatoes, diced
- 1 large summer squash, cut into chunks
- 1 tsp. extra virgin olive oil
- 1 tbsp. ground cumin
- 1 bell pepper, chopped
- 1 onion, chopped
- ½ cup water
- 1 cup vegetable broth
- 1 tsp. turmeric
- 4 tsp. minced garlic
- ½ tsp. smoked paprika
- ½ tsp. cayenne pepper
- ½ cup quinoa, cooked
- 1 cup chickpeas, cooked

**DIRECTIONS:**

1. Put the onions and garlic in a large pan and

cook them.
2. Now, add the vegetables and tomatoes and cook for a few minutes.
3. Add the water, chickpeas, vegetable broth, and spices.
4. Simmer it on a low heat for about 10–15 minutes.
5. They should be served on top of the quinoa.
6. Your dish is done and ready to eat.

**NUTRITIONAL VALUE PER SERVING:**
Calories: 231 /kcal; Carbs: 14 g; Protein: 25 g; Fat: 14 g.

## CAULIFLOWER AND CHEESE CASSEROLE

**Prep time:** 10 mins

**Cooking time:** 45 mins

**Total time:** 55 mins

**Servings:** 6

**INGREDIENTS:**
- 1 cup low fat Greek yogurt
- 1 tbsp. Dijon mustard
- 2 cup cauliflower florets, partially cooked
- 1 cup shredded cheddar cheese
- 1 tbsp. garlic powder
- ½ cup shredded mozzarella cheese

**DIRECTIONS:**
1. Set the oven temperature to about 400°F-200°C.
2. Combine the cauliflower, Dijon mustard, garlic powder, and yogurt in a baking dish.
3. Put cheese on top and wrap it in aluminum foil. Put it in the oven for 35 minutes.
4. Take off the aluminum foil and broil for 10 minutes
5. Your dish is done and ready to eat.

**NUTRITIONAL VALUE PER SERVING:**
Calories: 236 /kcal; Carbs: 20 g; Protein: 25 g; Fat: 10 g.

## ROASTED CHICKEN WITH VEGETABLES

**Prep time:** 20 mins

**Cooking time:** 45 mins

**Total time:** 1 hour 5 mins

**Servings:** 6

**INGREDIENTS:**
- 6 bone-in chicken thighs
- 6 medium red potatoes, cubed
- 3 garlic cloves, minced
- ¾ tsp. pepper, divided
- 2 tbsp. olive oil
- 1 large onion, chopped
- ½ tsp. paprika
- 1¼ tsp. salt, divided
- 1 tsp. dried rosemary, divided
- 6 cups baby spinach

**DIRECTIONS:**
1. Preheat the oven to 425°F-220°C.
2. Toss onion, 3/4 tsp. salt, potatoes, oil, 1/2 tsp. rosemary, garlic, and 1/2 tsp. pepper in a large mixing bowl to coat. Place the coated vegetables in a baking pan that has been sprayed with cooking spray.
3. Combine paprika, the remaining rosemary, salt, and pepper in a small bowl and coat the chicken with the paprika mixture and place it on top of the vegetables.
4. Roast the chicken and vegetables for 35-40 minutes, or until a thermometer placed in the chicken registers 170°-175°F (80°C) and the veggies are just tender.
5. Transfer the chicken to a serving plate and set aside to keep warm.
6. Add spinach to the veggies as a garnish and roast for another 8-10 minutes. Toss the vegetables together and serve with the chicken.

**NUTRITIONAL VALUE PER SERVING:**
Calories: 350/kcal; Carbs: 28 g; Protein: 28 g; Fat: 14 g.

## BASIL AND GARLIC GRILLED CHICKEN

**Prep time:** 10 mins

**Cooking time:** 15 mins

**Total time:** 25 mins

**Servings:** 2

**INGREDIENTS:**
- 1 cup low fat Greek yogurt
- 1 tbsp. Dijon mustard
- 2 lb. chicken breast
- 1 tsp. dried basil
- 1 tbsp. garlic powder
- 2 tbsp. olive oil
- salt to taste

**DIRECTIONS:**
1. Combine all of the ingredients together in a large bowl.
2. Now put the chicken pieces on a grill that has olive oil on it. Grill it from each side for total of 15 minutes.
3. Cut the grilled chicken into pieces and end up serving with grilled vegetables of your choice.

**NUTRITIONAL VALUE PER SERVING:**
Calories: 245 /kcal; Carbs: 17 g; Protein: 30 g; Fat: 10 g.

## BLACK BEAN AND BUTTERNUT SQUASH ENCHILADAS

**Prep time:** 15 mins

**Cooking time:** 40 mins

**Total time:** 55 mins

Servings: 8

INGREDIENTS:

- 1 tsp. garlic, minced
- 1 bell pepper, diced
- 1 butternut squash, diced
- 1 tsp. low sodium taco seasoning
- 1 jalapeno pepper, diced
- 1 onion, diced
- 2 tbsp. extra virgin olive oil
- 1 cup enchilada sauce
- 2 cups black beans, cooked
- 2 tomatoes, diced
- 8 whole wheat tortilla
- scallions, chopped for garnishing
- ½ cup black olives, sliced
- 1 cup cheddar cheese, shredded

DIRECTIONS:

1. Set the oven temperature to 400°F-200°C.
2. Now add the garlic, onions, and olive oil. Cook for 3-4 minutes.
3. Cook the mixture for further 5 minutes after adding the vegetables.
4. Now put the enchilada sauce in a baking dish and line it with tortillas. Put the cooked mixture on top along with the cheddar cheese, and bake for 30 minutes.
5. Add the scallions to the top as a garnish.
6. Your dish is done and ready to eat.

NUTRITIONAL VALUE PER SERVING:

Calories: 212 /kcal; Carbs: 17 g; Protein: 21 g; Fat: 8 g.

## TUNA CASSEROLE

Prep time: 10 mins

Cooking time: 45 mins

Total time: 55 mins

Servings: 6

INGREDIENTS:

- 1 cup low fat Greek yogurt
- 1 tbsp. Dijon mustard
- 2 cups partially cooked tuna, cut into chunks
- 1 cup shredded aged cheddar cheese
- 1 tbsp. garlic powder
- ½ cup shredded mozzarella cheese

DIRECTIONS:

1. Set the oven temperature to about 400°F-200°C.
2. Combine the tuna, Dijon mustard, garlic powder, and yogurt in a baking dish.
3. Put cheese on top and wrap it in aluminum foil. Put it in the oven for 35 minutes.
4. Take off the aluminum foil and broil for 10 minutes.
5. Your dish is done and ready to eat.

NUTRITIONAL VALUE PER SERVING:

Calories: 232 /kcal; Carbs: 23 g; Protein: 33 g; Fat: 8 g.

## GREEK YOGURT CHICKEN

Prep time: 1 hour

Cooking time: 1 hour

Total time: 2 hours

Servings: 4

INGREDIENTS:

- 2 lb. chicken pieces
- ¼ tsp. cinnamon
- ½ tsp. curry powder
- Pinch of salt and pepper
- 1 tbsp. olive oil
- ½ cup plain Greek yogurt
- ½ tsp. minced garlic
- ½ tbsp. lemon juice
- 3 tbsp. Butter

DIRECTIONS:

1. Place the chicken pieces in a big plastic Ziploc bag.
2. Combine oil, curry powder, garlic, salt, yogurt, lemon juice, cinnamon, and pepper in a small bowl. Place the ingredients in a plastic bag with the chicken and marinate for at least 1 hour.
3. Preheat the oven to 375°F-190°C.
4. Heat 3 tsp. butter in a medium iron or oven-proof skillet over medium heat until butter melts. Brown a couple pieces of chicken in a skillet for about 4-5 minutes each side. As the chicken browns, remove it to a dish and add more pieces to the skillet until all of the chicken is browned.
5. Put all chicken pieces to the oven and roast for 40-50 minutes, or until thoroughly done.

NUTRITIONAL VALUE PER SERVING:

Calories: 237 /kcal; Carbs: 2 g; Protein: 20 g; Fat: 16 g.

## HERB ROASTED SALMON

Prep time: 10 mins

Cooking time: 25 mins

Total time: 35 mins

Servings: 2

INGREDIENTS:

- 1 cup low fat Greek yogurt
- 1 tbsp. Dijon mustard
- 2 lb. salmon
- 1 tsp. dried basil
- 1 tbsp. garlic powder
- 2 tsp. oregano
- 2 leaves of thyme
- 2 tbsp. olive oil
- salt to taste

DIRECTIONS:

1. Combine all of the ingredients together in a

large bowl.
2. Now put the salmon pieces on the greased baking sheet.
3. Bake it at 375°F-190°C in an oven that has already been heated.
4. Cut the grilled salmon into pieces and end up serving with grilled vegetables of your choice.

### NUTRITIONAL VALUE PER SERVING:
Calories: 110 /kcal; Carbs: 11 g; Protein: 21 g; Fat: 5 g.

## ROASTED PESTO SALMON

**Prep time:** 5 mins

**Cooking time:** 20 mins

**Total time:** 25 mins

**Servings:** 2

### INGREDIENTS:
- 2 lb. Salmon fillet
- 2 tbsp. Basil pesto
- 1 tbsp. Extra virgin olive oil

### DIRECTIONS:
1. Set the oven temperature to 375°F-190°C.
2. Mix all the ingredients together, cover with aluminum foil, and bake for 15-20 minutes.
3. Serve it with rice or roasted vegetables.

### NUTRITIONAL VALUE PER SERVING:
Calories: 235 /kcal; Carbs: 9 g; Protein: 16 g; Fat: 9 g.

## BAKED HALIBUT

**Prep time:** 5 mins

**Cooking time:** 20 mins

**Total time:** 25 mins

**Servings:** 2

### INGREDIENTS:
- 1 tsp. dried oregano
- 3 tbsp. extra virgin olive oil
- 2 lb. halibut fillet, deboned
- 1 tbsp. minced garlic
- 3 tbsp. chopped capers
- pepper to taste
- 1 cup white wine
- salt to taste

### DIRECTIONS:
1. Set the oven temperature to 375°F-190°C.
2. Mix all the ingredients together, cover with aluminum foil, and bake for 15-20 minutes.
3. Serve it with rice or roasted vegetables.

### NUTRITIONAL VALUE PER SERVING:
Calories: 199 /kcal; Carbs: 12 g; Protein: 30 g; Fat: 10 g.

## FRIED COD FILLETS

**Prep time:** 10 mins

**Cooking time:** 10 mins

**Total time:** 20 mins

**Servings:** 2

### INGREDIENTS:
- 1 tsp. dried oregano
- 3 tbsp. extra virgin olive oil
- 2 lb. cod fillet, deboned
- 1 tbsp. minced garlic
- 3 tbsp. capers
- 1 cup white wine
- salt to taste
- ½ cup flour
- pepper to taste

### DIRECTIONS:
1. Combine all the ingredients together except for the flour in a mixing bowl and marinate cod fillets in it.
2. Now, deep fry the cod fillets after coating them in flour.
3. Your dish is ready to eat with any dip you want.

### NUTRITIONAL VALUE PER SERVING:
Calories: 390/kcal; Carbs: 21 g; Protein: 19 g; Fat: 19 g.

## BAKED SALMON

**Prep time:** 10 mins

**Cooking time:** 20 mins

**Total time:** 30 mins

**Servings:** 2

### INGREDIENTS:
- 1 tsp. dried oregano
- 3 tbsp. extra virgin olive oil
- 2 lb. salmon fillet, deboned
- 1 tbsp. minced garlic
- 3 tbsp. orange juice
- 1 cup white wine
- ½ cup Kalamata olives, pitted
- 1 fennel bulb
- salt to taste
- pepper to taste
- 2 bay leaves

### DIRECTIONS:
1. Set the oven temperature to 375°F-190°C.
2. Mix all the ingredients together, cover with aluminum foil, and bake for 15-20 minutes.
3. After baking, take the dish out of the oven and put the olives on top.
4. Serve it with rice or roasted vegetables.

### NUTRITIONAL VALUE PER SERVING:

Calories: 210 /kcal; Carbs: 22 g; Protein: 32 g; Fat: 15 g.

## LEMON AND PARSLEY CRAB BALLS

**Prep time:** 15 mins

**Cooking time:** 10 mins

**Total time:** 25 mins

**Servings:** 4

### INGREDIENTS:

- ½ tsp. Dijon mustard
- Nonstick spray
- 1 tbsp. lemon juice
- 12 oz. crab meat
- 3 tbsp. whole wheat bread crumbs
- 1 egg
- 3 tbsp. parsley, chopped
- 2 tbsp. low fat mayonnaise
- 1 tsp. cayenne pepper

### DIRECTIONS:

1. Mix the crab meat, cayenne pepper, Dijon mustard, low-fat mayonnaise, lemon juice, and parsley well in a large bowl.
2. Now, roll the dough into small balls and dip them in the egg and bread crumbs
3. Fry these balls, then put fresh parsley on top.
4. Your dish is done and ready to eat.

### NUTRITIONAL VALUE PER SERVING:

Calories: 321 /kcal; Carbs: 19 g; Protein: 21 g; Fat: 16 g.

## CABBAGE AND MEAT CURRY

**Prep time:** 10 mins

**Cooking time:** 20 mins

**Total time:** 30 mins

**Servings:** 6

### INGREDIENTS:

- 1 tsp. olive oil
- ¼ tsp. cinnamon
- 8 oz. low carb marinara
- 1 clove garlic, minced
- 1 small onion, chopped
- 3 cups chopped cabbage
- 14.5 oz. can diced tomatoes
- 1 lb. lean ground beef
- ¼ tsp. salt

### DIRECTIONS:

1. Heat the oil in a big pan, then add the onions and cook for 2-3 minutes after that add garlic and ground meat.
2. Brown the ground beef in a skillet, then drain the fat before adding the marinara, tomatoes, and spices. Stir in the cabbage until everything is well combined.
3. Bring to a low boil, and then reduce to a low heat and cover. Cook it for 15-20 minutes, or until the cabbage is tender.

### NUTRITIONAL VALUE PER SERVING:

Calories: 280 /kcal; Carbs: 16 g; Protein: 26 g; Fat: 12 g.

## GRILLED CHICKEN WINGS

**Prep time:** 15 mins

**Cooking time:** 20 mins

**Total time:** 35 mins

**Servings:** 8

### INGREDIENTS:

- 1 cup buffalo wing sauce
- ½ tsp. garlic, minced
- 2 lb. frozen chicken wings
- black pepper to taste
- 3 tbsp. extra virgin olive oil
- salt to taste

### DIRECTIONS:

1. Mix everything together, and then marinate them for 10 minutes.
2. Now, put some olive oil on a grill and put the wings that have been marinated on top.
3. Grill until both sides are brown and crispy.
4. Your dish is done and ready to eat.

### NUTRITIONAL VALUE PER SERVING:

Calories: 199 /kcal; Carbs: 22 g; Protein: 32 g; Fat: 9 g.

## STUFFED CHICKEN BREAST

**Prep time:** 5 mins

**Cooking time:** 20 mins

**Total time:** 25 mins

**Servings:** 1

### INGREDIENTS:

- 1 chicken breast
- 1 artichoke heart
- pinch of pepper
- ¼ tsp. curry powder
- 1 oz. low-fat mozzarella
- 5 large basil leaves
- 1 tsp. sundried tomato, chopped
- 1 clove garlic
- ¼ tsp. paprika
- toothpicks

### DIRECTIONS:

1. Preheat the oven to 365°F-285°C.
2. Cut a slit from the center of the chicken breast to form a pocket for the stuffing.
3. Cut the artichoke, mozzarella, tomato, basil, and garlic into small pieces.
4. To combine, mix everything together. Stuff the

prepared mixture into the pocket made in the chicken breast and seal the chicken breast all around filling with toothpicks.
5. Season the top of chicken breast with curry powder, pepper, and paprika and place it on a baking sheet or foil.
6. Bake it in oven for around 20 minutes. Once done remove the toothpicks and serve.

**NUTRITIONAL VALUE PER SERVING:**

Calories: 262 /kcal; Carbs: 8 g; Protein: 46 g; Fat: 4 g.

## SWEET AND SOUR SALMON

**Prep time: 15 mins**

**Cooking time: 20 mins**

**Total time: 35 mins**

**Servings: 4**

**INGREDIENTS:**

- 4 salmon fillets
- 1/8 tsp. salt
- 1 tbsp. olive oil
- 1 tbsp. butter
- 2 tbsp. Dijon mustard
- 2 tbsp. low-sodium soy sauce
- ½ tsp. pepper
- 1 lb. fresh green beans, trimmed

**DIRECTIONS:**

1. Preheat the oven to 425°F-220°C.
2. Fill a 15x10-inch baking pan with fillets and spray with cooking spray.
3. Melt butter in a small pan, and then add soy sauce, oil, mustard, pepper, and salt.
4. Half of the sauce should be brushed over the fish. Toss green beans in a large mixing dish with the remaining sauce to coat. Arrange green beans in a circle around the fillets.
5. Roast for 14-16 minutes, or until green beans are crisp-tender and fish flakes easily with a fork.

**NUTRITIONAL VALUE PER SERVING:**

Calories: 390 /kcal; Carbs: 17 g; Protein: 31 g; Fat: 22 g.

## TUNA AND MANGO KABABS

**Prep time: 15 mins**

**Cooking time: 10 mins**

**Total time: 25 mins**

**Servings: 4**

**INGREDIENTS:**

- 2 sweet red peppers, cubes
- 1 tsp. coarsely ground pepper
- 1 medium mango, cubes
- 1 lb. tuna steaks, cubes

**DIRECTIONS:**

1. Season the tuna with pepper.
2. Thread mango tuna, and red peppers alternately moistened wooden skewers.
3. Cook the skewers on grill over medium heat, stirring periodically, for 10 minutes, or until tuna is barely pink in the middle and peppers are soft.

**NUTRITIONAL VALUE PER SERVING:**

Calories: 205 /kcal; Carbs: 20 g; Protein: 29 g; Fat: 2 g.

## BEEF AND VEGETABLE CHILI DRY

**Prep time: 10 mins**

**Cooking time: 40 mins**

**Total time: 50 mins**

**Servings: 6**

**INGREDIENTS:**

- ½ lb. lean ground beef
- 1 carrot, chopped
- ½ tsp. salt
- 1 tsp. olive oil
- 1 clove garlic, minced
- 1 small onion, chopped
- 2 stalks celery, chopped
- 1 small bell pepper, chopped
- 14.5 oz. can diced tomatoes, with liquid
- ¾ cup mild rotel
- sour cream, optional
- salt and pepper to taste
- ¼ tsp. cinnamon
- 2/3 cup chicken broth, low- sodium
- ½ tbsp. chili powder
- ½ tbsp. cumin
- 15 oz. can kidney beans, rinsed
- grated cheese, optional

**DIRECTIONS:**

1. In a medium soup pot, heat the oil, and then add the onion, celery, carrot, beef, garlic, and bell pepper.
2. Over medium heat, cook and stir until the meat is browned. Stir with the remaining ingredients. Seasonings can be adjusted as needed.
3. Simmer for 30 minutes on low heat. If desired, top with sour cream and shredded cheese.

**NUTRITIONAL VALUE PER SERVING:**

Calories: 113 /kcal; Carbs: 20 g; Protein: 23 g; Fat: 5 g.

## VEGETABLE CURRY

Prep time: 10 mins

Cooking time: 35 mins

Total time: 45 mins

Servings: 5

### INGREDIENTS:

- 1 tbsp. olive oil
- 14 oz. can tomato, diced
- 1½ cups water
- 10 oz. frozen mixed vegetables
- 2 cloves crushed garlic
- 1 onion, chopped
- 2 tbsp. tomato paste
- 2 tbsp. chopped fresh cilantro
- 2½ tbsp. curry powder
- 1 cube vegetable bouillon
- salt and pepper to taste

### DIRECTIONS:

1. Heat the oil in a big saucepan over medium-high heat and cook the onion and garlic until golden and aromatic.
2. Cook for further 2 to 3 minutes after adding the tomato paste and curry powder.
3. Now toss in the mixed veggies, water, vegetable bouillon cube, tomatoes, and season to taste with salt and pepper.
4. Cook the curry for 30 minutes, or until veggies are tender and soft. Before serving, garnish with fresh cilantro.

### NUTRITIONAL VALUE PER SERVING:

Calories: 103 /kcal; Carbs: 15 g; Protein: 13 g; Fat: 3 g.

## SPICY CHICKEN BREASTS

Prep time: 15 mins

Cooking time: 15 mins

Total time: 30 mins

Servings: 4

### INGREDIENTS:

- 1 tbsp. salt
- 1 tbsp. ground cayenne pepper
- 2 tbsp. garlic powder
- 1 tbsp. dried thyme
- 1 tbsp. onion powder
- 1 tbsp. ground black pepper
- 4 skinless, chicken breast halves

### DIRECTIONS:

1. Combine the thyme, garlic powder, paprika, onion powder, salt, cayenne pepper, and ground black pepper in a medium mixing bowl.
2. 3 tbsp. of the spice combination should be used for the chicken marination and the rest should be stored in an airtight container for later use.
3. Preheat the grill to medium-high. On both sides of the chicken breasts, rub the prepared spice mixture.
4. Grease the grill grate lightly. Grill the chicken for 6 to 8 minutes per side, or until the juices run clear.

### NUTRITIONAL VALUE PER SERVING:

Calories: 173 /kcal; Carbs: 9 g; Protein: 29 g; Fat: 3 g.

## MEDITERRANEAN PORK

Prep time: 10 mins

Cooking time: 35 mins

Total time: 45 mins

Servings: 4

### INGREDIENTS:

- 4 boneless pork loin chops
- 1 tbsp. fresh rosemary, finely snipped
- ¼ tsp. black pepper
- ¼ tsp. salt
- 3 cloves garlic, minced

### DIRECTIONS:

1. Preheat the oven to 425°F-220°C.
2. Wrap a shallow roasting pan using aluminium foil.
3. Season the chops using salt, pepper, garlic and rosemary.
4. In the prepared roasting pan, arrange the chops on a rack.
5. Chops should be roasted for 10 minutes and then reduce the oven temperature to 350°F-180°C and continue roasting for another 25 minutes, or until no pink remains and the juices flow clear.

### NUTRITIONAL VALUE PER SERVING:

Calories: 160 /kcal; Carbs: 1 g; Protein: 25 g; Fat: 5 g.

## MEDITERRANEAN MEATBALLS

Prep time: 10 mins

Cooking time: 20 mins

Total time: 30 mins

Servings: 8

### INGREDIENTS:

- 12 oz. roasted red peppers
- 2 lb. lean ground beef
- 2 eggs lightly beaten
- 1½ cups whole-wheat bread crumbs
- ½ cup fresh basil, snipped
- 1/3 cup tomato sauce
- ½ tsp. salt
- ¼ tsp. ground black pepper
- ¼ cup fresh flat-leaf parsley, snipped

### DIRECTIONS:
1. Combine basil, tomato sauce, parsley, bread crumbs, roasted red peppers, beaten eggs, salt, and pepper in a large mixing bowl. Mix in the ground beef well.
2. Make 48 meatballs out of the meat mixture.
3. Place meatballs in a baking tray lined with foil. Preheat oven to 350°F-180°C and bake for 20 minutes, or until done.

### NUTRITIONAL VALUE PER SERVING:
Calories: 95 /kcal; Carbs: 2 g; Protein: 13 g; Fat: 3 g.

## ROASTED PORK

**Prep time:** 10 mins

**Cooking time:** 30 mins

**Total time:** 40 mins

**Servings:** 4

### INGREDIENTS:
- 2 cloves garlic, minced
- 3 tbsp. barbecue sauce
- 1 tbsp. dry sherry
- 2 whole pork tenderloins
- 1 tbsp. low-sodium soy sauce
- ½ tsp. crushed peppercorns

### DIRECTIONS:
1. Preheat the oven to 350°F-180°C.
2. In a small bowl, combine the sherry, soy sauce, garlic, barbecue sauce and peppercorns.
3. Mixture should be applied equally to the pork tenderloins.
4. Place the roasts on a rack in a shallow roasting pan coated with foil. Bake for 15 minutes on one side, then flip and brush with the remaining barbecue sauce mixture. Roast for around 30 minutes.
5. Place the roast on a chopping board and cover it with foil. Allow 10 to 15 minutes to rest before cutting.
6. Slice diagonally and serve warm with rice.

### NUTRITIONAL VALUE PER SERVING:
Calories: 200 /kcal; Carbs: 3 g; Protein: 32 g; Fat: 5 g.

## ASIAN BEEF KABABS

**Prep time:** 10 mins

**Cooking time:** 12 mins

**Total time:** 22 mins

**Servings:** 8

### INGREDIENTS:
- 1 lb. beef Sirloin Steak Boneless, cubes
- 6 green onions, sliced diagonally
- 2 tbsp. dry sherry
- ¼ cup hoisin sauce
- 1 tsp. dark sesame oil

### DIRECTIONS:
1. Whisk together the hoisin sauce, sherry and sesame oil. Trim any excess fat from the beef steak.
2. Cut the meat into 1/4-inch-thick pieces crosswise. Thread meat and green onion slices onto skewers alternately, weaving back and forth.
3. Place the kabobs on the rack in the broiler pan, 3 to 4 inches away from the heat. Half of the hoisin mixture should be brushed on.
4. Broil the kababs for 9 to 12 minutes, flipping once and basting with the remaining hoisin mixture before serving.

### NUTRITIONAL VALUE PER SERVING:
Calories: 53 /kcal; Carbs: 2 g; Protein: 7 g; Fat: 2 g.

## BEEF PEPPER STEAK

**Prep time:** 30 mins

**Cooking time:** 12 mins

**Total time:** 42 mins

**Servings:** 4

### INGREDIENTS:
- 1/3 cup Dijon-style mustard
- 1 tbsp. fresh cilantro, minced
- 4 beef steaks, cut 3/4 inch thick
- 2 tsp. ground cumin
- 2 tbsp. mixed peppercorns, coarsely ground
- 1 tsp. garlic, minced
- ¼ cup butter, softened
- 2 mild green chili peppers

### DIRECTIONS:
1. In a small bowl, combine cumin, peppercorns and mustard.
2. Remove half and set aside for brushing. The leftover mustard mixture should be spread on both sides of the steaks.
3. Marinate the steaks for 30 minutes after covering.
4. In a small bowl, combine the butter, cilantro, and garlic.
5. Grill the steaks and peppers in a grill pan for 12 minutes until steaks are medium rare and peppers are blackened, rotating periodically, and brushing steaks with conserved mustard mixture.
6. Remove the charred peppers from the pan, cover, and set aside for 5 minutes. Skin, stems, and seeds should all be removed.
7. Chop the peppers and add half of them to the butter mixture.
8. Pour 1 tsp. butter mixture on top of each steak and add the remaining chopped peppers on top and serve.

### NUTRITIONAL VALUE PER SERVING:

Calories: 270 /kcal; Carbs: 9 g; Protein: 37 g; Fat: 1 g.

## MUSTARD ROAST BEEF

_Prep time:_  10 mins

_Cooking time:_  40 mins

_Total time:_  50 mins

_Servings: 8_

### INGREDIENTS:

- ¼ cup apricot preserves
- 2 tbsp. spicy brown mustard
- 2 lb. boneless beef sirloin tip roast, fat trimmed
- 3 tsp. reduced-sodium Worcestershire sauce
- 1 tsp. caraway seeds, crushed
- 1 tbsp. prepared horseradish
- 1 tsp. crushed black peppercorns
- ¼ tsp. ground allspice

### DIRECTIONS:

1. In a medium mixing dish, combine all ingredients except the beef. Apply the marinade to the meat's surfaces.
2. In a roasting pan, place the meat on a rack. Roast for 40 minutes in oven at 350°F-180°C. Serve and enjoy.

### NUTRITIONAL VALUE PER SERVING:

Calories: 170 /kcal; Carbs: 9 g; Protein: 20 g; Fat: 5 g.

## PEANUT BUTTER SALMON

_Prep time:_  10 mins

_Cooking time:_  20 mins

_Total time:_  30 mins

_Servings: 3_

### INGREDIENTS:

- 1 lb. salmon
- ¼ cup orange juice
- 2 tsp. chili garlic sauce
- freshly ground pepper, to taste
- ¼ cup peanut butter
- 1 tsp. olive oil

### DIRECTIONS:

1. Preheat the oven to 400°F-200°C and line a baking sheet with aluminum foil.
2. Place the salmon on a baking sheet, massage it with olive oil, and season to taste with pepper.
3. Bake the salmon for 15-20 minutes, or until cooked through.
4. Whisk together orange juice, peanut butter and chili garlic sauce in a small sauce pot over medium-low heat until heated.
5. Pour the peanut butter sauce over the salmon and serve.

### NUTRITIONAL VALUE PER SERVING:

Calories: 300 /kcal; Carbs: 5 g; Protein: 27 g; Fat: 3 g.

## CHIPOTLE LIME GRILLED CHICKEN

_Prep time:_  1 hour

_Cooking time:_  10 mins

_Total time:_  1 hour 10 mins

_Servings: 6_

### INGREDIENTS:

- 6 chicken breasts, boneless
- 1 tsp. chipotle pepper powder
- ¼ cup olive oil, extra virgin
- 1/3 cup lime juice
- 1 tbsp. garlic, minced
- 2 tbsp. cilantro, chopped
- 1 tsp. salt
- 1 tsp. chili powder
- ½ tsp. ground cumin

### DIRECTIONS:

1. Combine all ingredients in a gallon Ziploc bag and marinate the chicken breasts for one hour.
2. Cook the steaks on a grill pan on medium-high until the chicken is thoroughly cooked through.
3. This should take around 10 minutes after that Serve right away and enjoy.

### NUTRITIONAL VALUE PER SERVING:

Calories: 300 /kcal; Carbs: 2 g; Protein: 48 g; Fat: 15 g.

## EASY CHICKEN CURRY

_Prep time:_  10 mins

_Cooking time:_  30 mins

_Total time:_  40 mins

_Servings: 4_

### INGREDIENTS:

- 2 lb. chicken breasts, strips
- ½ tsp. cayenne pepper
- ¼ tsp. pepper
- 3 tbsp. tomato paste
- 1 tbsp. curry powder
- 2 tbsp. olive oil, extra virgin
- 1 onion, diced
- 1½ tsp. garlic, minced
- 1 cup coconut milk, unsweetened
- 1 cup chicken stock
- ½ tsp. salt
- Green onions, for garnish

### DIRECTIONS:

1. In a large pan over medium heat, heat olive oil. Add chopped onion and minced garlic and cook until the onion is transparent.
2. In the skillet, add the chicken strips and increase the heat to medium high and fry the chicken from both sides.

3. Once the outside of chicken strips no longer seems raw, you're ready to proceed.
4. Combine the remaining ingredients in the pan. Gently mix and cook on low heat for 25-30 minutes.
5. As the sauce simmers, it will thicken.
6. Serve with cauliflower rice, steamed vegetables, or regular rice. Garnish with finely sliced green onion.

### NUTRITIONAL VALUE PER SERVING:
Calories: 280 /kcal; Carbs: 10 g; Protein: 52 g; Fat: 25 g.

## CHICKEN AND MUSHROOM GRAVY

**Prep time:** 5 mins

**Cooking time:** 20 mins

**Total time:** 25 mins

**Servings:** 4

### INGREDIENTS:
- 2 tbsp. olive oil
- 1 tbsp. garlic, minced
- 1 tbsp. arrowroot flour
- 8 oz. sliced mushrooms
- 1½ lb. chicken breasts, sliced
- ¾ tsp. black pepper
- ¼ tsp. paprika
- 1 tsp. salt
- 2 cups chicken stock
- 1 tbsp. fresh parsley, chopped
- ½ tsp. dried thyme
- 3 tbsp. balsamic vinegar
- ½ tbsp. onion powder
- ½ tsp. dried rosemary
- 1 tbsp. cold water

### DIRECTIONS:
1. In a big skillet over medium-high heat, heat 2 tbsp. of oil. Add mushrooms and chicken after the oil is heated. Season the mushrooms and chicken with sea salt and freshly ground pepper.
2. Sauté them for 7 to 10 minutes, turning periodically, or until chicken is browned and mushrooms are soft. Now add the garlic and sauté for approximately one minute or until garlic is golden and aromatic.
3. Combine the thyme, onion powder, balsamic vinegar, chicken stock, rosemary, and paprika in a medium mixing bowl and add this sauce in the chicken and mushrooms gravy.
4. Cover and simmer for 4 to 5 minutes, or until gravy is well heated.
5. Add fresh parsley and turn off heat.
6. In a small bowl combine arrowroot flour and water and shake. Pour the mixture into the gravy and whisk until well combined.
7. Serve with side of your choice and enjoy.

### NUTRITIONAL VALUE PER SERVING:
Calories: 300 /kcal; Carbs: 12 g; Protein: 41 g; Fat: 13 g.

## GRILLED BALSAMIC CHICKEN

**Prep time:** 5 mins

**Cooking time:** 20 mins

**Total time:** 25 mins

**Servings:** 4

### INGREDIENTS:
- 1 lb. boneless skinless chicken breasts
- 1/2 cup balsamic vinegar
- 1 tsp. poultry seasoning

### DIRECTIONS:
1. Heat grill to 350°F-180°C.
2. Remove any parts that you don't want from the chicken breasts and coat them on all sides with poultry seasoning. Set aside while the grill gets hot.
3. About 5–6 minutes on each side is enough time to grill a chicken breast.
4. While the chicken is cooking or resting, put vinegar in a small skillet and heat it over medium-low heat. Let it simmer slowly and stir it constantly until it starts to thicken. It could take up to ten minutes for the glaze to shrink by about half.
5. Take the vinegar off the heat and pour it over the chicken that has been grilled.

### NUTRITIONAL VALUE PER SERVING:
Calories: 160 /kcal; Carbs: 6 g; Protein: 24 g; Fat: 3 g.

## LASAGNA STEW

**Prep time:** 15 mins

**Cooking time:** 25 mins

**Total time:** 40 mins

**Servings:** 8

### INGREDIENTS:
- 1 lb. lean ground beef
- 2 cloves garlic, minced
- 1 small onion yellow, diced
- 1 tbsp. Italian seasoning
- 8 oz. spinach fresh, roughly chopped
- 1/2 tsp. salt
- 1/2 tsp. pepper
- 12 oz. marinara
- 1 zucchini diced
- 28 oz. crushed tomatoes
- shredded mozzarella for topping
- 1 cup chicken broth

### DIRECTIONS:
1. Bring a big stock pot to a medium-high temperature. Garlic and onion are used to brown the meat. Drain. Salt and Italian seasoning, then cook for another minute.
2. Add the remaining ingredients and lower down the heat and let it cook for 20 minutes.

**MAINTENANCE DIET**

**NUTRITIONAL VALUE PER SERVING:**
Calories: 137 /kcal; Carbs: 13 g; Protein: 16 g; Fat: 3 g.

## CHICKEN AND VEGETABLE STEW

*Prep time:* 15 mins

*Cooking time:* 30 mins

*Total time:* 45 mins

*Servings:* 4

### INGREDIENTS:

- 4 tsp. olive oil
- 1 green bell pepper diced
- ½ large white onion diced
- 2 carrots peeled, diced
- 1 cup white mushrooms diced
- 2 tsp. chili powder
- 2 tsp. cumin
- 1½ cups vegetable broth
- 1/2 tsp. oregano
- 2 tbsp. cilantro fresh, minced
- 1 lb. chicken boneless, skinless

### DIRECTIONS:

1. Set pressure cooker to sauté mode and add pepper, garlic, oil, onion, mushrooms, carrots, and seasonings.
2. Cook until the vegetables are soft, then add broth and scrape the pot's bottom. Turn off the stove. Push the chicken into the broth. Put the lid back on and turn the valve to the seal position. 15 minutes, then let the pressure come down for 10 minutes.
3. Open the lid and put the chicken on a cutting board when the pressure is gone. Shred the chicken and put it back in the pan. Mix in chopped cilantro.

**NUTRITIONAL VALUE PER SERVING:**
Calories: 185 /kcal; Carbs: 4 g; Protein: 28 g; Fat: 9 g.

## TACO CHICKEN

*Prep time:* 5 mins

*Cooking time:* 15 mins

*Total time:* 20 mins

*Servings:* 4

### INGREDIENTS:

- 1 lb. boneless, skinless chicken breast
- 1/4 tsp. pepper
- 1 cup chicken broth
- 1/4 tsp. salt
- 1 cup salsa of choice

### DIRECTIONS:

1. In the bottom of the pressure cooker, pour chicken broth. Season chicken breast using salt and pepper.
2. Add chicken to the pot and pour half cup of salsa over top. Close the valve so that it is sealed. If the chicken is fresh, choose high pressure for 4 minutes. If the chicken is frozen, choose high pressure for 10 minutes.
3. Allow pressure releasing for 10 minutes. Then turn the valve to the open position, being careful to let steam out if necessary. Open the lid and make sure the chicken is cooked.
4. Remove from pot. Shred the meat and put the last half cup of salsa on top. Add any other toppings you want and serve.

**NUTRITIONAL VALUE PER SERVING:**
Calories: 145 /kcal; Carbs: 4 g; Protein: 23 g; Fat: 3 g.

## QUESO CHICKEN CHILI

*Prep time:* 10 mins

*Cooking time:* 4 hours

*Total time:* 4 hour 10 mins

*Servings:* 6

### INGREDIENTS:

- 1 lb. chicken breast boneless, skinless
- 3 wedges spreadable cheese
- 14.5 oz. chicken broth
- 2 tsp. cumin
- 15 oz. white beans
- 2 tsp. chili powder
- 14 oz. diced tomatoes
- 4 oz. diced green chilies
- 2 oz. shredded cheese

### DIRECTIONS:

1. Put chicken in the slow cooker's bottom.
2. Drain and rinse the beans, then put them in the slow cooker. Add cheese wedges that can be spread, and mix until a slurry forms. Add to chicken.
3. Add the cumin, tomatoes, chili powder, green chilies, and broth. Cook for 4-6 hours on low with the lid on.
4. When the chicken is done cooking, put it on a cutting board and shred or chop it. Put it back to crock pot. Stir in the cheese and serve.

**NUTRITIONAL VALUE PER SERVING:**
Calories: 242 /kcal; Carbs: 22 g; Protein: 28 g; Fat: 5 g.

## INSIDE OUT EGG ROLLS

*Prep time:* 20 mins

*Cooking time:* 10 mins

*Total time:* 30 mins

*Servings:* 6

### INGREDIENTS:

- 2 tbsp. sesame oil
- 1 medium onion, diced
- 6 cloves garlic, crushed
- 1 tsp. fresh ginger minced
- 2 lb. ground pork
- 2 tbsp. garlic chili paste
- ¼ cup soy sauce
- 2 tbsp. rice wine vinegar
- 28 oz. coleslaw mix
- 8 whole green onions chopped

### DIRECTIONS:

1. In a large stir fry pan, heat the oil. Cook the onion, garlic, and ginger for a few minutes, until they are clear and smell good.
2. Add the meat, rice wine vinegar, chili paste, soy sauce, and stir until the meat is cooked.
3. Add the coleslaw mix and stir it for a few more minutes, until it has become soft.
4. Add the green onions and stir.
5. Serve as a complete meal or with brown rice or cauliflower rice, if you like.

### NUTRITIONAL VALUE PER SERVING:

Calories: 221 /kcal; Carbs: 6 g; Protein: 21 g; Fat: 8 g.

## SPICY THAI CHICKEN SLAW

**Prep time:** 15 mins

**Cooking time:** 0 mins

**Total time:** 15 mins

**Servings:** 8

### INGREDIENTS:

- 1 0 oz. shredded, matchstick carrots
- 4 cups cooked, shredded chicken
- ½ head red cabbage, shredded
- ½ head green cabbage, shredded
- 1/3 cup peanut butter
- ¾ cup unsalted peanuts
- 1 tbsp. fish sauce
- 3 tbsp. coconut aminos
- 2 tbsp. sesame oil
- 2 tbsp. rice vinegar
- 2 tbsp. fresh, minced garlic
- 1 tbsp. maple syrup
- 1 tsp. red pepper flakes
- 1 tbsp. lime juice

### DIRECTIONS:

1. In a large bowl, mix together shredded carrots, unsalted peanuts, shredded cabbage, and shredded chicken. Set mixture aside
2. Put the remaining ingredients into a blender. Mix until everything is smooth and well mixed. Pour the prepared peanut sauce over the veggies and stir it up. Put the meat in the fridge and let it sit for 30 minutes. Serve cold.

### NUTRITIONAL VALUE PER SERVING:

Calories: 167 /kcal; Carbs: 7 g; Protein: 18 g; Fat: 5 g.

DINNER
RECIPES

## INSTANT POT TURKEY CHILI

Prep time: 10 mins

Cooking time: 15 mins

Total time: 25 mins

Servings: 6

### INGREDIENTS:

- 2 tbsp. olive oil
- 1½ tbsp. chili powder
- 1½ tsp. cumin
- 1 lb. lean ground turkey
- 1 cup chicken broth
- 1 can kidney beans, rinsed and drained
- 1 onion, chopped
- 28 oz. crushed tomato
- Salt and pepper to taste

### DIRECTIONS:

1. On the Instant Pot's sauté setting, heat the oil and onion. Cook until softened.
2. Add turkey and spices. Saute the turkey until it turns brown.
3. Add broth and crushed tomatoes and stir. Close the lid and cook for 10 minutes on high.
4. Once done, open the valve. Stir in kidney beans and Serve.

### NUTRITIONAL VALUE PER SERVING:

Calories: 212 /kcal; Carbs: 23 g; Protein: 25 g; Fat: 6 g.

## GARLIC SHRIMP STIR FRY

Prep time: 5 mins

Cooking time: 15 mins

Total time: 20 mins

Servings: 4

### INGREDIENTS:

- 1½ tbsp. olive oil
- 1/3 cup coconut aminos
- 1 tbsp. garlic, minced
- ¼ + ¼ tsp. salt
- 1 bell pepper, thinly sliced
- 12 oz. green beans
- ¼ tsp. ground ginger
- ¼ tsp. garlic powder
- ¼ tsp. black pepper
- 1 tsp. sesame oil
- 1 lb. shrimp, peeled and deveined
- Parsley chopped, for garnish

### DIRECTIONS:

1. In a large skillet over medium-high heat, heat the olive oil.
2. Add the green beans and sliced bell pepper to the heated oil and cook for 5–7 minutes, tossing regularly, until green beans begin to brown but remain crisp.
3. Add the minced garlic and sauté for 1 minute, or until the garlic becomes golden.
4. Season the shrimps with pepper, salt, and garlic powder while vegetables are sautéing.
5. Combine sesame oil, 1/4 tsp. salt, ground ginger and coconut aminos in a pan along with the vegetables. Stir.
6. Add the shrimp that have been seasoned. Cook, covered, for 3–4 minutes, or until shrimps are pink.
7. Garnish with fresh parsley, and serve.

### NUTRITIONAL VALUE PER SERVING:

Calories: 230 /kcal; Carbs: 13 g; Protein: 25 g; Fat: 8 g.

## BUFFALO LETTUCE WRAPS

Prep time: 10 mins

Cooking time: 10 mins

Total time: 20 mins

Servings: 6

### INGREDIENTS:

- 2 tbsp. olive oil
- ¼ cup diced celery
- 1/3 cup Buffalo sauce
- 1 cup shredded rotisserie chicken
- 1 cup diced onion
- 6 romaine leaves

### DIRECTIONS:

1. Add olive oil, buffalo sauce, and chopped celery and onion to a pan over medium heat.
2. When the onions and celery are soft and cooked all the way through, add the chicken and stir.
3. Serve the prepared mixture on romaine leaves and top it with condiments of your choice.

### NUTRITIONAL VALUE PER SERVING:

Calories: 101 /kcal; Carbs: 3 g; Protein: 17 g; Fat: 3 g.

## LEMON CAPER CHICKEN

Prep time: 5 mins

Cooking time: 15 mins

Total time: 20 mins

Servings: 2

### INGREDIENTS:

- 1 large chicken breast
- 2 tbsp. olive oil
- pinch of salt
- 1 tbsp. lemon juice
- 1 tbsp. capers
- ¼ cup almond flour
- 2 tbsp. fresh parsley
- ½ cup chicken stock

### DIRECTIONS:

1. In a mixing bowl, combine almond flour and salt. Dip the chicken breasts in flour gently to coat them.
2. Heat 1 tbsp. oil in a large pan over medium-high heat Add the chicken to the heated oil and cook for around 5 minutes on each side, or until brown and cooked through. Remove the chicken from the pan and set aside.
3. Add the remaining olive oil, lemon juice, capers, and chicken stock to the pan. Gently crush a few of the capers with a fork. Heat the liquid to a boil, and then lower to a low heat to keep it warm. Allow for 3-4 minutes of cooking time.
4. Return the chicken to the pan, stir in the parsley, and twist the breasts to coat them in the juices.
5. Season the sauce to taste with additional salt and pepper if necessary and serve.

### NUTRITIONAL VALUE PER SERVING:
Calories: 206 /kcal; Carbs: 4 g; Protein: 24 g; Fat: 14 g.

## SHRIMP AND BROCCOLI

**Prep time:** 5 mins

**Cooking time:** 20 mins

**Total time:** 25 mins

**Servings:** 4

### INGREDIENTS:
- 16 oz. fresh broccoli florets
- ½ + ¼ tsp. salt
- 1 lb. shrimp, peeled and deveined
- ½ tsp. dried oregano
- ¼ + ¼ tsp. garlic powder
- 1½ + 1 tbsp. olive oil
- ½ tsp. dried basil
- 1 tbsp. lemon juice
- ¼ tsp. garlic powder
- ¼ tsp. onion powder

### DIRECTIONS:

1. Preheat oven to 425°F-220°C.
2. On a baking sheet, spread broccoli florets in a layer.
3. Season the broccoli with ½ tsp. salt, ¼ tsp. garlic powder and drizzle 1 1/2 tbsp. olive oil all over the broccoli.
4. Roast it for 15 minutes in the oven.
5. Meanwhile, combine shrimp, oregano, lemon juice, 1 tbsp. olive oil, ¼ tsp. garlic powder, basil, onion powder, and ¼ tsp. salt in a mixing bowl.
6. After 15 minutes, take broccoli from oven and place shrimp in the baking tray along with broccoli and bake for another 5–7 minutes in the oven.

### NUTRITIONAL VALUE PER SERVING:
Calories: 230 /kcal; Carbs: 8 g; Protein: 26 g; Fat: 11 g.

## TOMATO AND COCONUT CHICKEN CURRY

**Prep time:** 5 mins

**Cooking time:** 20 mins

**Total time:** 25 mins

**Servings:** 4

### INGREDIENTS:
- 1 tbsp. coconut oil
- 1 tbsp. cumin
- 2 tbsp. tomato paste
- 3 cups spinach
- ¾ tsp. salt
- 1 tbsp. water
- 1 cup chicken stock
- 1 tbsp. minced garlic
- ½ onion
- 1 tbsp. garam masala
- 2 tsp. minced ginger
- 1 cup coconut milk
- 1½ lb. chicken breasts
- fresh cilantro, for garnish

### DIRECTIONS:

1. In a big heavy skillet, heat the oil over medium heat. Add and cook onions until they are golden brown.
2. Cook, stirring constantly, for another minute after adding the garlic and ginger.
3. Now add the tomato paste, cumin, garam masala and salt in the pan along with the chicken stock and coconut cream the pan and simmer for 5-7 minutes on low heat, or until the mixture thickens. Cook for another 10-15 minutes, or until the chicken is cooked through.
4. In the last minute of cooking, add the spinach to wilt it. Garnish with fresh cilantro and serve with cauliflower rice.

### NUTRITIONAL VALUE PER SERVING:
Calories: 212 /kcal; Carbs: 11 g; Protein: 36 g; Fat: 19 g.

## BEEF ENCHILADA CASSEROLE

**Prep time:** 5 mins

**Cooking time:** 4 hours

**Total time:** 4 hour 5 mins

**Servings:** 8

### INGREDIENTS:
- 1 cup red enchilada sauce
- 1 cup tri-bean blend, drained and rinsed
- ¼ cup frozen corn
- ½ lb. lean ground beef
- ¼ cup quinoa, uncooked
- ½ cup shredded cheese
- ¼ cup onion, chopped

### DIRECTIONS:
1. Mix the onion, corn, enchilada sauce, quinoa, beans, and 1/3 cup water in the bowl of a slow cooker. Stir to combine.
2. Crumble the beef on top, stir it around to coat it, and then spread it out in an even layer. Add cheese on top.
3. Cook covered for 4-5 hours on high.
4. Serve and enjoy.

### NUTRITIONAL VALUE PER SERVING:
Calories: 125 /kcal; Carbs: 10 g; Protein: 12 g; Fat: 4 g.

## CURRY SHRIMP AND VEGETABLES

**Prep time:** 5 mins

**Cooking time:** 4 hour 20 mins

**Total time:** 4 hour 25 mins

**Servings:** 6

### INGREDIENTS:
- 2 tbsp. green curry paste
- ½ cup low sodium chicken broth
- 1 cup light coconut milk
- ¼ cup bell pepper, large diced
- ¼ cup carrots, chopped
- 1 cup cauliflower florets
- 1 cup spinach, chopped
- 12 oz. shrimp, peeled and deveined

### DIRECTIONS:
1. Mix coconut milk, curry paste, and broth together in the bowl of a slow cooker.
2. Cauliflower, bell pepper and carrots should be added. Stir to combine.
3. Cover and cook on high for 3–4 hours.
4. Put in the shrimp and spinach. Cover and cook on high for another 20 minutes, or until the shrimp are done.

### NUTRITIONAL VALUE PER SERVING:
Calories: 98 /kcal; Carbs: 5 g; Protein: 15 g; Fat: 2 g.

## LEMON AND FENNEL CHICKEN THIGHS

**Prep time:** 10 mins

**Cooking time:** 50 mins

**Total time:** 1 hour

**Servings:** 6

### INGREDIENTS:
- 2 tbsp. olive oil
- ¼ cup chicken stock
- 1 tbsp. dried fennel seed
- ½ tsp. kosher salt
- 2 lbs. chicken thighs
- 1 cup baby red potatoes
- 3 cloves garlic
- 2 fennel bulb
- 1 tsp. Dijon mustard
- 1 tsp. paprika
- ground black pepper, to taste
- 1 lemon slices

### DIRECTIONS:
1. Preheat the oven to 350°F-180°C. A baking tray or roasting pan should be lightly oiled.
2. Toss garlic, baby potatoes, mustard, fennel bulb, garlic, and fennel seeds into the roasting dish and season the potatoes.
3. Prepare your chicken thighs by seasoning them with paprika, salt and pepper when the potatoes are cooking.
4. In a big skillet/frying pan over medium heat, heat one tablespoon olive oil. When the oil is heated, place the skin-side down seasoned chicken in the pan. Allow for around 5 minutes of cooking time, or until the skin begins to turn crispy, before turning and frying for the next 3-4 minutes on the other side. Remove the chicken from the heat once it's done.
5. Remove the roasting dish once the potato mixture has cooked for 15 minutes in the oven. Toss the chicken thighs with the lemon slices in the mixture to coat. Reduce the heat to 400°F-200°C and place the dish on the centre rack of the oven to roast for 25-30 minutes, or when the chicken is cooked completely.
6. Broil for the final -2 minutes to crunch up the skin. Serve right away and enjoy.

### NUTRITIONAL VALUE PER SERVING:
Calories: 210 /kcal; Carbs: 3 g; Protein: 25 g; Fat: 7 g.

## CHIPOTLE LIME SALMON

**Prep time:** 5 mins

**Cooking time:** 9 mins

**Total time:** 14 mins

**Servings:** 4

### INGREDIENTS:
- 4 salmon fillets
- ½ tsp. salt
- 2 tbsp. lime juice
- ¼ cup butter
- ¾ tsp. chipotle chile pepper
- 1 tbsp. olive oil
- ½ tsp. black pepper
- 2 tsp. garlic, minced
- 1 tbsp. fresh parsley, chopped

### DIRECTIONS:
1. In a large pan over medium-high heat, heat the olive oil.
2. Season the top of the salmon with salt, chipotle chilli pepper and black pepper.
3. When the oil is heated, put the salmon in the skillet skin side up and sauté for 4–5 minutes.
4. Flip the salmon carefully so that the skin side is now facing down.

5. In a pan, add lime juice, butter and chopped garlic and continue sautéing for an additional 3 to 4 minutes or until salmon is opaque.
6. When ready to serve, garnish parsley over the salmon and enjoy.

**NUTRITIONAL VALUE PER SERVING:**

Calories: 370 /kcal; Carbs: 1 g; Protein: 34 g; Fat: 20 g.

## SHRIMP OVER ZUCCHINI NOODLES

**Prep time:** 10 mins

**Cooking time:** 5 mins

**Total time:** 15 mins

**Servings:** 4

**INGREDIENTS:**

- 1 tsp. olive oil
- 1 lemon juiced
- 12 oz. shrimp, peeled and deveined
- 1 clove garlic, minced
- ½ tsp. tahini
- 2 tbsp. parsley, chopped
- 2 cups zucchini noodles

**DIRECTIONS:**

- Heat half of the olive oil in a pan over medium heat.
- Add the shrimp and cook for 2 minutes, or until they turn pink. Take out and put away.
- Mix the tahini and lemon juice together in a small bowl with a whisk.
- Heat the rest of the olive oil in the pan you used for the shrimp.
- Add the garlic and cook for 30 seconds, until it smells good. Mix tahini with water and add zucchini noodles. Cook the noodles for 3-4 minutes, until zucchini is just tender. Put the shrimp back in the pan and toss them to coat. Cook for another minute or two, or until the shrimp is done.
- Add parsley as a garnish and serve.

**NUTRITIONAL VALUE PER SERVING:**

Calories: 153 /kcal; Carbs: 4 g; Protein: 20 g; Fat: 6 g.

## CHILI LIME BURGERS

**Prep time:** 5 mins

**Cooking time:** 10 mins

**Total time:** 15 mins

**Servings:** 4

**INGREDIENTS:**

- 1 lb. lean ground turkey
- 1 tsp. chili powder
- ¼ cup red bell peppers, minced
- 2 tbsp. cilantro, chopped
- 1 lime, juiced and zested
- ¼ cup low fat plain Greek yogurt
- 1 tbsp. olive oil

**DIRECTIONS:**

1. Mix the chicken, chili powder, red bell peppers, lime zest, and 1 tablespoon of cilantro together in a bowl. Shape the mixture into 4 small patties.
2. Over medium-high heat, heat the olive oil in a pan. Add the patties and cook for 4-5 minutes per side, or until they are cooked all the way through.
3. In a small bowl, mix together the Greek yogurt, the rest of the cilantro, and the lime juice.
4. Serve burgers with a drizzle of cilantro cream on top.

**NUTRITIONAL VALUE PER SERVING:**

Calories: 144 /kcal; Carbs: 1 g; Protein: 25 g; Fat: 4 g.

## LEMON BUTTER SHRIMP

**Prep time:** 5 mins

**Cooking time:** 5 mins

**Total time:** 10 mins

**Servings:** 4

**INGREDIENTS:**

- 2 tsp. parsley, chopped
- ¼ cup butter
- 1 lb. shrimp
- 2 tbsp. lemon juice
- ½ tsp. salt
- ¼ tsp. pepper
- 1 tbsp. garlic

**DIRECTIONS:**

1. Season the shrimps with salt and freshly ground pepper.
2. On a medium heat, melt butter in a skillet. Add seasoned shrimps to the skillet after the butter has melted.
3. Cook for 3–5 minutes, stirring periodically, or until shrimps are pink.
4. Combine lemon juice and minced garlic in a small bowl and add it in shrimps and stir for 1 minute at a low heat.
5. Garnish with parsley and serve immediately.

**NUTRITIONAL VALUE PER SERVING:**

Calories: 217 /kcal; Carbs: 1 g; Protein: 23 g; Fat: 13 g.

## ITALIAN CHICKEN

**Prep time: 5 mins**

**Cooking time: 25 mins**

**Total time: 30 mins**

**Servings: 2**

### INGREDIENTS:

- 2 chicken breasts
- ¼ cup black olives
- 1 tbsp. garlic, minced
- ½ tsp. black pepper
- ½ tsp. salt
- 3 tbsp. olive oil
- 2 cups cherry tomatoes
- 1 tbsp. lemon juice
- 1 tbsp. dried oregano
- 1 tsp. dried thyme
- fresh basil, for garnish

### DIRECTIONS:

1. Preheat the oven to 350°F-180°C and gently oil a large, covered baking sheet.
2. In a large mixing dish, combine all the remaining ingredients and make sure the tomatoes and chicken are uniformly coated in all of the seasonings.
3. Take the chicken from the mixing dish and place it on the baking sheet that has been prepared and roast it for 15 minutes.
4. Take out the chicken from oven and place it in the dish with the leftover tomatoes, olives, and sauces.
5. Return the baking pan to the oven and roast for another 10 minutes, or until the internal temperature of the chicken reaches 165°F-75°C.
6. Serve with fresh basil on top of the chicken and tomatoes.

### NUTRITIONAL VALUE PER SERVING:
Calories: 167 /kcal; Carbs: 6 g; Protein: 20 g; Fat: 13 g.

## HONEY MUSTARD SALMON

**Prep time: 5 mins**

**Cooking time: 18 mins**

**Total time: 23 mins**

**Servings: 4**

### INGREDIENTS:

- 3 tbsp. white vinegar
- ½ cup breadcrumbs
- 3 tbsp. canola oil
- 1½ tsp. dry mustard
- 4 salmon fillets
- 3 tbsp. mustard paste
- 1 tbsp. sugar
- ½ tsp. black pepper
- 1 tsp. dried thyme

### DIRECTIONS:

1. Combine the mustard paste, vinegar, sugar, and dry mustard in a mixing bowl. Slowly drizzle in the oil and combine to make a sauce.
2. Preheat the oven to 350°F-180°C.
3. Season the salmon using thyme and black pepper and spread 1 tbsp. prepared mustard sauce on each slice of salmon.
4. Place breadcrumbs on top of the fish.
5. Place the salmon on a baking sheet and bake it for about 18 minutes until the salmon is crispy and golden brown.
6. On the side, serve the leftover mustard sauce.

### NUTRITIONAL VALUE PER SERVING:
Calories: 157 /kcal; Carbs: 12 g; Protein: 25 g; Fat: 9 g.

## SEAFOOD PARCELS

**Prep time: 15 mins**

**Cooking time: 20 mins**

**Total time: 35 mins**

**Servings: 2**

### INGREDIENTS:

- 2 cups broccoli florets
- 100g Pollock, cut into 2 chunks
- ½ cup parsley
- 1 tbsp. lemon juice
- 4 salmon fillets, cubed
- 3 lb. prawns
- 1 red pepper, cut into strips
- 6 spring onions, sliced 2 tbsp. water
- black pepper, to taste
- Lemon wedges, to serve
- 2 tsp. olive oil

### DIRECTIONS:

1. Preheat the oven to 400°F-200°C and blanch the broccoli in boiling water for 3–4 minutes before draining.
2. Divide the fish, shrimps and vegetables evenly between four squares of foil.
3. Add the parsley and a generous dash of pepper to taste. Add the olive oil and water after squeezing the lemon over each.
4. To form a parcel, fold the foil into the centre, then place on a baking pan and bake for 15 minutes.
5. Each parcel should be served with a lemon slice.

### NUTRITIONAL VALUE PER SERVING:
Calories: 250 /kcal; Carbs: 8 g; Protein: 27 g; Fat: 12 g.

## SQUID AND PRAWN SKEWERS

Prep time: 15 mins

Cooking time: 5 mins

Total time: 20 mins

Servings: 6

### INGREDIENTS:
- 4 lb. raw squid rings
- 1 lemon juice + zest
- 1 small red chilli, finely chopped
- 1 clove garlic, crushed
- 2 lb. raw peeled jumbo king prawns
- 1 tsp. rapeseed oil

### DIRECTIONS:
1. Combine the prawns and squid with the chilli, garlic, lemon juice, and zest, leaving a small amount of the zest for garnish.
2. On each skewer, thread a squid ring, a prawn, then another squid ring.
3. In a large nonstick frying pan, heat the oil and cook the skewers, flipping once, until the prawns are thoroughly cooked.

### NUTRITIONAL VALUE PER SERVING:
Calories: 42 /kcal; Carbs: 0.1 g; Protein: 7 g; Fat: 1 g.

## SCALLOPS WITH CHILLI AND LIME BUTTER

Prep time: 10 mins

Cooking time: 5 mins

Total time: 15 mins

Servings: 2

### INGREDIENTS:
- 1 tbsp. olive oil
- 1 red chilli, finely chopped
- 12 scallops, cleaned
- 2 tbsp. butter, softened
- 1 lime juice and grated rind
- ½ tsp. black pepper

### DIRECTIONS:
1. In a small mixing bowl, combine the chilli, oil, butter, lime rind, and juice.
2. Heat the butter mixture in a nonstick frying pan until it bubbles. Cook scallops for 1 minute on each side after adding them to the pan.
3. Remove scallops from the pan and top with a sprig of rocket and a drizzle of pan juices.

### NUTRITIONAL VALUE PER SERVING:
Calories: 150/kcal; Carbs: 0.1 g; Protein: 21 g; Fat: 7 g.

## CHICKEN AND BROCCOLI RICE BOWL

Prep time: 10 mins

Cooking time: 12 mins

Total time: 22 mins

Servings: 3

### INGREDIENTS:
- 3 cups broccoli florets, small sized
- 1 tbsp. olive oil
- ¼ tsp. black pepper
- ½ cup light processed cheese, 1-inch pieces
- ½ cup green onions, chopped
- 1 cup skinless, boneless chicken breasts
- 1 pack precooked brown rice
- ¼ tsp. kosher salt
- 2 tbsp. sliced almonds, toasted

### DIRECTIONS:
1. Steam the broccoli for around 5 minutes.
2. Heat rice, following the instructions.
3. Heat oil over medium-high heat in a large non-stick skillet. Add chicken and salt and pepper to taste. Cook, stirring regularly, for 4 minutes. Stir in the cheese and onions and stir until the cheese starts to melt.
4. Incorporate the rice; fold in the broccoli. Cook until fully heated or 1 minute.
5. Garnish it with some almonds.

### NUTRITIONAL VALUE PER SERVING:
Calories: 189 /kcal; Carbs: 3 g; Protein: 25 g; Fat: 7 g.

## STEAMED TROUT

Prep time: 10 mins

Cooking time: 8 mins

Total time: 18 mins

Servings: 2

### INGREDIENTS:
- 4 rainbow trout fillets
- 1 lime grated rind and juice
- ¼ inch piece ginger, grated
- 1 tbsp. low-sodium soy sauce
- 1 tbsp. sesame oil
- 2 cloves garlic, sliced
- 1 bunch spring onions, sliced

### DIRECTIONS:
1. Place the fish on top of a piece of baking parchment in a big steamer.
2. Combine the other ingredients in a bowl and pour the sauce over the fish.
3. Steam the fish for 6-8 minutes, or until the fish is done.
4. Serve with stir-fried vegetables.

### NUTRITIONAL VALUE PER SERVING:

Calories: 320 /kcal; Carbs: 4 g; Protein: 40 g; Fat: 16 g.

## TROUT WITH CITRUS AND BASIL SAUCE

Prep time: 10 mins

Cooking time: 10 mins

Total time: 20 mins

Servings: 2

### INGREDIENTS:

- 2 boneless, skinless trout fillets
- ¼ tsp. black pepper
- 2 tbsp. fresh basil, torn
- 1 orange juice and zest
- 2 tbsp. low-fat cream

### DIRECTIONS:

1. In a nonstick frying pan, place the fish fillets on medium heat.
2. Pour in the orange juice and zest, cover, and cook until the fish is done. It will take about 5–6 minutes.
3. Add the cream and basil to the fish and stir gently.
4. Season the sauce with salt and pepper to taste. Serve and enjoy.

### NUTRITIONAL VALUE PER SERVING:

Calories: 160 /kcal; Carbs: 4 g; Protein: 20 g; Fat: 8 g.

## CAPRESE STEAK

Prep time: 20 mins

Cooking time: 10 mins

Total time: 30 mins

Servings: 4

### INGREDIENTS:

- 4 beef sirloin steak
- ¾ cup balsamic vinegar
- 3 cloves garlic
- 1 tbsp. oregano
- 2 tbsp. honey
- 2 tbsp. olive oil
- 1 tbsp. thyme
- Salt to taste
- 2 tomatoes, sliced
- Fresh basil leaves, for garnish

### DIRECTIONS:

1. Combine together the garlic, olive oil, honey, balsamic vinegar, dried oregano, and dried thyme in a small bowl. Pour this mixture over steaks and set aside for 20 minutes to marinate.
2. Season the tomato slices with some salt and pepper to taste. Preheat the grill to high. Grill steak for 4 to 5 minutes each side and put tomatoes on top.
3. Serve with some fresh basil.

### NUTRITIONAL VALUE PER SERVING:

Calories: 187 /kcal; Carbs: 2 g; Protein: 27 g; Fat: 13 g.

## GREEN FISH CURRY

Prep time: 15 mins

Cooking time: 12 mins

Total time: 27 mins

Servings: 2

### INGREDIENTS:

- Handful fresh coriander, chopped
- ¼ cup parsley, chopped
- 1 red pepper, thinly sliced
- 10 fresh mint, roughly chopped
- ¾ cup water
- 1 lime juice
- 2 tsp. rapeseed oil
- 1 onion, finely chopped
- 2 cod fillets, large chunks
- ¼ inch ginger, finely chopped
- 1 chilli, finely chopped
- 2 tsp. mild curry powder
- 2 cloves garlic, crushed
- 1 salmon fillet, large chunks

### DIRECTIONS:

1. Blend the mint, parsley, coriander, lime juice and water and form a paste.
2. In a pan, heat the oil, and then add red pepper and onion. Cook the onions and pepper for 3–4 minutes, or until softened.
3. Stir in the ginger, chilli, and garlic and cook for 1–2 minutes. Mix thoroughly for another minute after adding the curry powder.
4. Place the cod and salmon chunks and cover it in all of the spices, being careful not to break up the pieces of fish.
5. Pour in the prepared green paste, bring to a mild boil, then reduce to a low heat and simmer for 3–4 minutes, turning periodically, until the fish is cooked through.
6. Serve with lime wedges and coriander sprigs.

### NUTRITIONAL VALUE PER SERVING:

Calories: 250 /kcal; Carbs: 12 g; Protein: 22 g; Fat: 12 g.

## ASIAN SALMON

Prep time: 10 mins

Cooking time: 8 mins

Total time: 18 mins

Servings: 6

### INGREDIENTS:

- 6 pieces salmon fillet
- pinch of chilli flakes
- Fresh coriander, for garnish
- 2 tsp. sesame oil

- 1 tbsp. low-salt soy sauce
- 1 tsp. fresh ginger, grated
- 2 tsp. runny honey
- 4 spring onions, chopped

### DIRECTIONS:

1. In a large mixing bowl, combine all of the marinade ingredients except fish and whisk thoroughly.
2. Add the salmon fillets, toss them in the marinade, and leave them aside to absorb the flavors.
3. Cook for 3–4 minutes over medium heat, then flip over and cook for another 3–4 minutes on the other side.
4. Serve with stir-fried vegetables of your choice.

### NUTRITIONAL VALUE PER SERVING:
Calories: 290 /kcal; Carbs: 3 g; Protein: 26 g; Fat: 20 g.

## CRISPY CHICKEN TENDERS

**Prep time: 20 mins**

**Cooking time: 10 mins**

**Total time: 30 mins**

**Servings: 4**

### INGREDIENTS:

- ½ tsp. garlic, minced
- 3 tbsp. extra virgin olive oil
- 1 tsp. dried parsley
- Black pepper to taste.
- 2 lb. frozen chicken tender pieces
- 1 egg
- ½ tsp. dried dill powder
- ½ tsp. dried basil
- ½ cup whole wheat bread crumbs
- salt to taste
- ½ tsp. dried onion powder

### DIRECTIONS:

1. Put the dried dill, chicken tenders, dried basil, pepper, dried onion powder, salt, and parsley in a large bowl and mix well.
2. Now, marinate it for 10 minutes.
3. After 10 minutes, coat each tender piece in the egg followed by the whole wheat bread crumbs.
4. Deep fry the chicken tenders in extra virgin olive oil and garnish with fresh parsley.

### NUTRITIONAL VALUE PER SERVING:
Calories: 213 /kcal; Carbs: 23 g; Protein: 30 g; Fat: 12 g.

## CHICKEN NACHOS AND SWEET BELL PEPPERS

**Prep time: 10 mins**

**Cooking time: 25 mins**

**Total time: 35 mins**

**Servings: 6**

### INGREDIENTS:

- ½ tsp. garlic powder
- 3 tbsp. extra virgin olive oil
- 1 tomato, diced
- 2 cups shredded chicken breast
- black pepper to taste
- nonstick cooking spray
- 1 cup shredded cheese
- ½ tsp. cumin powder
- ½ tsp. paprika
- 1 lb. mini bell peppers
- salt to taste
- ½ onion, minced
- jalapeno peppers, for garnish
- chopped scallions, for garnishing
- ½ cup black olives, sliced

### DIRECTIONS:

1. Roast the bell peppers for 10 minutes at 400°F-200°C in an oven that has already been heated.
2. In the meantime, put onions, olive oil, chicken, garlic, cumin powder, tomatoes, pepper, paprika, and salt in a pan and cook it for 10 minutes.
3. Add the mixture to the mini bell peppers, top with a few olives, jalapeno peppers and cheese, and bake for another ten minutes.
4. Add a few chopped scallions on top.
5. Your dish is done and ready to eat.

### NUTRITIONAL VALUE PER SERVING:
Calories: 320 /kcal; Carbs: 15 g; Protein: 21 g; Fat: 13 g.

## CREAMY BEEF STROGANOFF AND MUSHROOMS

**Prep time: 10 mins**

**Cooking time: 20 mins**

**Total time: mins**

**Servings: 2**

### INGREDIENTS:

- ½ cup low fat Greek yogurt
- 3 tbsp. extra virgin olive oil
- 1 tomato, diced
- 1 lb. beef steaks, extra lean
- nonstick cooking spray
- 1 cup water
- ½ tsp. dried dill
- 2 tbsp. whole wheat flour
- 1 cup beef broth
- ½ onion, minced
- ½ tsp. dried thyme
- ½ cup mushrooms, sliced
- salt to taste
- ½ cup parsley, finely chopped
- 1 tsp. Worcestershire sauce

### DIRECTIONS:

1. In a pan, cook the beef steaks until they are light brown.

2. Now, put olive oil and onions in another pan and cook the onions for two to three minutes
3. After a while, add the mushrooms and cook for a while before adding the Worcestershire sauce.
4. Add the broth, water, salt, dried thyme, dried dill, whole wheat flour, and tomatoes. Simmer for ten minutes.
5. Now add the yogurt and keep stirring until it's dissolved.
6. Put the beef strips and parsley in it
7. Your dish is done and ready to eat.

### NUTRITIONAL VALUE PER SERVING:
Calories: 333 /kcal; Carbs: 22 g; Protein: 33 g; Fat: 14 g.

## SLOPPY JOES

**Prep time:** 10 mins

**Cooking time:** 20 mins

**Total time:** 30 mins

**Servings:** 2

### INGREDIENTS:
- ½ cup chopped celery
- 3 tbsp. extra virgin olive oil
- nonstick cooking spray
- 1 lb. beef steaks, extra lean
- 2 tbsp. Dijon mustard
- ½ onion, minced
- salt to taste
- 1 tomato, diced
- ½ cup parsley, finely chopped
- 1 tsp. Worcestershire sauce

### DIRECTIONS:
1. In a pan, cook the beef steaks until they are light brown.
2. Now, put olive oil and onions in another pan and cook for 2-3 minutes.
3. After a while, add the tomatoes and cook for a while before adding the Worcestershire sauce.
4. Add the chopped celery and then cook for a few minutes
5. Put the beef steaks and parsley in it.
6. Your dish is done and ready to eat.

### NUTRITIONAL VALUE PER SERVING:
Calories: 231 /kcal; Carbs: 22 g; Protein: 25 g; Fat: 9 g.

## ITALIAN BEEF SANDWICHES

**Prep time:** 10 mins

**Cooking time:** 7 hours

**Total time:** 7 hour 10 mins

**Servings:** 4

### INGREDIENTS:
- 1 tbsp. balsamic vinegar
- 1 tsp. onion powder
- 1 tsp. garlic powder
- 1 lb. beef, extra lean
- 1 tsp. dried oregano
- 1 onion, chopped
- 1 tsp. dried basil
- 1 tsp. ground pepper
- 1 tsp. dried thyme
- 8 whole wheat bread slices
- salt to taste
- 1 red bell pepper, sliced

### DIRECTIONS:
1. In a slow cooker, put the onion, beef, and bell pepper.
2. Put the spices and herbs and the water into the slow cooker.
3. Cook on low heat for 7 hours.
4. Cut the pieces of beef into thin slices and put them in the slightly toasted bread.

### NUTRITIONAL VALUE PER SERVING:
Calories: 321 /kcal; Carbs: 21 g; Protein: 25 g; Fat: 9 g.

## ITALIAN CHICKEN SANDWICHES

**Prep time:** 10 mins

**Cooking time:** 4 hours

**Total time:** 4 hour 10 mins

**Servings:** 4

### INGREDIENTS:
- 1 tbsp. balsamic vinegar
- 1 tsp. onion powder
- 1 lb. chicken breast, extra lean
- 1 tsp. garlic powder
- 1 tsp. dried oregano
- 1 onion, chopped
- 1 tsp. dried basil
- 1 tsp. ground pepper
- 1 tsp. dried thyme
- 8 whole wheat bread slices
- salt to taste
- 1 red bell pepper, sliced

### DIRECTIONS:
1. In a slow cooker, put the onion, chicken and bell pepper.
2. Put the spices and herbs and the water into the slow cooker.
3. Cook on low heat for 4 hours.
4. Cut the chicken into pieces and put them on the bread that has been lightly toasted.
5. You can also put any sauce you want in it.
6. Your sandwich is done and ready to eat.

### NUTRITIONAL VALUE PER SERVING:
Calories: 212 /kcal; Carbs: 21 g; Protein: 15 g; Fat: 11 g.

## BAKED BEEF WITH FENNEL AND ASPARAGUS

Prep time: 15 mins

Cooking time: 20 mins

Total time: 35 mins

Servings: 2

### INGREDIENTS:

- 1 tsp. dried oregano
- 3 tbsp. extra virgin olive oil
- 2 lb. beef, deboned
- 1 tbsp. minced garlic
- 3 tbsp. orange juice
- 1 fennel bulb
- pepper to taste
- 1 cup white wine
- ½ cup asparagus
- salt to taste
- 2 bay leaves

### DIRECTIONS:

1. Set the oven temperature to 375°F-190°C.
2. Mix all the ingredients together, cover with aluminum foil, and bake for 15-20 minutes.
3. After baking, put it on a plate and top it with the roasted asparagus.
4. Serve it with rice or roasted vegetables.

### NUTRITIONAL VALUE PER SERVING:

Calories: 333 /kcal; Carbs: 22 g; Protein: 19 g; Fat: 15 g.

## BROCCOLI AND CHEESE CASSEROLE

Prep time: 10 mins

Cooking time: 45 mins

Total time: 55 mins

Servings: 6

### INGREDIENTS:

- 1 cup low fat Greek yogurt
- 1 tbsp. Dijon mustard
- 2 cup broccoli, partially cooked
- 1 cup shredded cheddar cheese
- 1 tbsp. garlic powder
- ½ cup shredded mozzarella cheese

### DIRECTIONS:

1. Set the oven temperature to about 400°F-200°C.
2. Put the broccoli, garlic powder, yogurt, and Dijon mustard in a baking dish.
3. Put cheese on top and wrap it in aluminum foil. Put it in the oven for 35 minutes.
4. Take off the aluminum foil and broil for 10 minutes.
5. Your dish is done and ready to eat.

### NUTRITIONAL VALUE PER SERVING:

Calories: 321 /kcal; Carbs: 18 g; Protein: 22 g; Fat: 10 g.

## FRIED CHICKEN FILLETS

Prep time: 10 mins

Cooking time: 10 mins

Total time: 20 mins

Servings: 2

### INGREDIENTS:

- 1 tsp. dried oregano
- 3 tbsp. extra virgin olive oil
- 2 lb. chicken fillet
- 1 tbsp. minced garlic
- 3 tbsp. capers
- pepper to taste
- 1 cup white wine
- ½ cup flour
- salt to taste

### DIRECTIONS:

1. Mix all of the ingredients together and then add them to the chicken fillets.
2. Now, coat the cod fillets by dipping them in flour and fry them in olive oil.
3. Your dish is ready to eat with any dip you want.

### NUTRITIONAL VALUE PER SERVING:

Calories: 223 /kcal; Carbs: 18 g; Protein: 18 g; Fat: 9 g.

## CHICKEN CASSEROLE

Prep time: 20 mins

Cooking time: 45 mins

Total time: 1 hour 5 mins

Servings: 6

### INGREDIENTS:

- 1 cup low fat Greek yogurt
- ½ cup shredded mozzarella cheese
- 1 tbsp. garlic powder
- 1 tbsp. chicken, partially cooked
- 1 cup shredded cheddar cheese

### DIRECTIONS:

1. Set the oven temperature to about 400°F-200°C.
2. Mix the chicken with the yogurt, Dijon mustard, garlic powder, and then put it in a baking dish.
3. Put cheese on top and wrap it in aluminum foil. Put it in the oven for 35 minutes.
4. Take off the aluminum foil and broil for 10 minutes.
5. Serve and enjoy.

### NUTRITIONAL VALUE PER SERVING:

Calories: 231 /kcal; Carbs: 23 g; Protein: 22 g; Fat: 12 g.

## BEEF AND BEAN CASSEROLE

Prep time: 20 mins

Cooking time: 45 mins

Total time: 1 hour 5 mins

Servings: 6

### INGREDIENTS:

- 1 cup low fat Greek yogurt
- 1 cup kidney beans, partially boiled
- 2 cups beef, partially boiled
- 1 tbsp. Dijon mustard
- ½ cup shredded mozzarella cheese
- 1 cup shredded cheddar cheese
- 1 tbsp. garlic powder

### DIRECTIONS:

1. Set the oven temperature to about 400°F-200°C.
2. Mix the boiled beef, kidney beans, Dijon mustard, and yogurt together and put it in a baking dish.
3. Put cheese on top and wrap it in aluminum foil. Put it in the oven for 35 minutes
4. Take off the aluminum foil and broil for 10 minutes.
5. Your dish is done and ready to eat.

### NUTRITIONAL VALUE PER SERVING:

Calories: 223 /kcal; Carbs: 21 g; Protein: 24 g; Fat: 12 g.

## MINCED BEEF BALLS

Prep time: 15 mins

Cooking time: 20 mins

Total time: 35 mins

Servings: 2

### Ingredients:

- ½ tsp. Dijon mustard
- Nonstick spray
- 1 tbsp. lemon juice
- 12 oz. minced beef meat
- 3 tbsp. whole wheat bread crumbs
- 1 Egg
- 3 tbsp. parsley, chopped
- 2 tbsp. low fat mayonnaise
- 1 tsp. cayenne pepper

### DIRECTIONS:

1. Mix the Dijon mustard, minced beef, lemon juice, cayenne pepper, low-fat mayonnaise, and parsley well in a large bowl.
2. Now, roll the dough into small balls and dip them in the egg and bread crumbs.
3. Fry these balls, then put fresh parsley on top
4. Your dish is done and ready to eat.

### NUTRITIONAL VALUE PER SERVING:

Calories: 321 /kcal; Carbs: 20 g; Protein: 23 g; Fat: 8 g.

## BAKED CHICKEN WITH MIX VEGETABLES

Prep time: 15 mins

Cooking time: 20 mins

Total time: 35 mins

Servings: 4

### INGREDIENTS:

- 1 tsp. dried oregano
- 3 tbsp. extra virgin olive oil
- 2 lb. chicken breast
- 1 tbsp. minced garlic
- 3 tbsp. orange juice
- 1 cup white wine
- 1 fennel bulb
- salt to taste
- ½ cup asparagus
- pepper to taste
- ½ cup potatoes
- ½ cup carrots
- 2 bay leaves

### DIRECTIONS:

1. Set the oven temperature to 375°F-190°C.
2. Mix all the ingredients together, cover with aluminum foil, and bake for 15-20 minutes.
3. When the chicken is baked, take it out of the oven and put the roasted potatoes, carrots, and asparagus on top.
4. Serve and enjoy.

### NUTRITIONAL VALUE PER SERVING:

Calories: 221/kcal; Carbs: 21 g; Protein: 25 g; Fat: 18 g.

## CHICKEN AND MUSHROOM RISOTTO

Prep time: 20 mins

Cooking time: 45 mins

Total time: 1 hour 5 mins

Servings: 6

### INGREDIENTS:

- 1 tsp. garlic, minced
- 1 tbsp. extra virgin olive oil
- 2 leeks, diced
- 3 cups fresh spinach leaves
- 4 cups sliced mushrooms
- 1 cup chicken broth
- ½ cup white wine
- 1 tsp. thyme
- 1 cup chicken pieces

### DIRECTIONS:

1. Put the olive oil and garlic in a large, deep pan.

MAINTENANCE DIET

Add the mushrooms and leeks after a few seconds.
2. Cook for a few minutes after adding the barley and thyme.
3. Add the wine and make sure it is well mixed.
4. Add the broth and let it cook over low heat for 30 minutes.
5. Now add the spinach and stir it around until it starts to wilt.
6. Your dish is done and ready to eat.

### NUTRITIONAL VALUE PER SERVING:

Calories: 256 /kcal; Carbs: 23 g; Protein: 25 g; Fat: 21 g.

## MINCED BEEF AND SPAGHETTI SQUASH CASSEROLE

*Prep time: 20 mins*

*Cooking time: 45 mins*

*Total time: 1 hour 5 mins*

*Servings: 8*

### INGREDIENTS:

- 1 cup Low fat Greek yogurt
- 1 tbsp. Dijon mustard
- 2 cups Minced beef
- 1 cup Shredded cheddar cheese
- 3 lb. Spaghetti squash
- 1 tbsp. Garlic powder
- ½ cup Shredded mozzarella cheese

### DIRECTIONS:

1. Set the oven temperature to about 400°F-200°C.
2. Roast the spaghetti squash for 10 minutes, then use a fork to scrape out the spaghetti-like insides and throw away the skin
3. Mix the spaghetti squash, garlic powder, minced beef and Dijon mustard together in a baking dish.
4. Put cheese on top and wrap it in aluminum foil. Put it in the oven for 25 minutes.
5. Take off the aluminum foil and broil for 10 minutes.
6. Your dish is done and ready to eat.

### NUTRITIONAL VALUE PER SERVING:

Calories: 234 /kcal; Carbs: 25 g; Protein: 24 g; Fat: 21 g.

## COCONUT AND CHICKEN CURRY

*Prep time: 15 mins*

*Cooking time: 25 mins*

*Total time: 40 mins*

*Servings: 6*

### INGREDIENTS:

- 1 tbsp. grated ginger
- ¼ tsp. cinnamon
- 1 tbsp. minced garlic
- 2 tsp. curry powder
- ½ tsp. turmeric
- 3 tbsp. coconut oil
- ½ tsp. ground cumin
- 2 cups unsweetened coconut milk
- 14 oz. chicken pieces
- 2 carrots, diced
- 1 cup tomato puree
- 2 cups chicken broth
- 2 stems bok choi
- ½ cup fresh cilantro

### DIRECTIONS:

1. Saute the chicken cubes in the oil for 3–4 minutes, or until a firm layer forms on top of them.
2. Take the chicken out of the pan before adding the rest of the ingredients.
3. Blend in the coconut milk. Now add the cooked chicken and Bok choi to the mixture and simmer it for a few minutes.

### NUTRITIONAL VALUE PER SERVING:

Calories: 321 /kcal; Carbs: 23 g; Protein: 25 g; Fat: 18 g.

## GARLIC AND HERB GRILLED BEEF

*Prep time: 10 mins*

*Cooking time: 25 mins*

*Total time: 35 mins*

*Servings: 2*

### INGREDIENTS:

1. 1 cup low-fat greek yogurt
2. 1 tbsp. Dijon mustard
3. 2 lb. beef steak
4. 1 tbsp. garlic powder
5. 1 tsp. dried thyme
6. 1 tsp. dried basil
7. 1 tsp. dried oregano
8. 1 tsp. dried dill
9. 2 tbsp. olive oil
10. salt to taste

### DIRECTIONS:

1. Combine all of the ingredients together in a large bowl and marinate the beef.
2. Now put the beef steaks on a grill with the olive oil.
3. On each side, cook.
4. Cut the meat into pieces and serve with roasted vegetables of your choice.

### NUTRITIONAL VALUE PER SERVING:

Calories: 231 /kcal; Carbs: 28 g; Protein: 22 g; Fat: 15 g.

## CINNAMON CHICKEN

**Prep time: 10 mins**

**Cooking time: 30 mins**

**Total time: 40 mins**

**Servings: 4**

### INGREDIENTS:

- 4 skinless, chicken breast halves
- 1 tsp. ground black pepper
- 2 tbsp. Italian-style seasoning
- 1 tsp. ground cinnamon
- 3 tsp. salt
- 1½ tsp. garlic powder

### DIRECTIONS:

1. Preheat the oven to 350°F-180°C.
2. Place the chicken in a 9x13 inch baking dish that has been greased with oil.
3. Season the chicken breasts with salt, garlic powder, Italian seasoning, ground cinnamon, and pepper, and mix well.
4. Bake the chicken for 30 minutes at 350°F-180°C or until it is baked through and juices flow clear.

### NUTRITIONAL VALUE PER SERVING:
Calories: 140 /kcal; Carbs: 3 g; Protein: 27 g; Fat: 2 g.

## CHICKEN TENDERS

**Prep time: 5 mins**

**Cooking time: 10 mins**

**Total time: 15 mins**

**Servings: 4**

### INGREDIENTS:

- 1 lb. chicken tenders
- 2 tsp. olive oil
- salt, to taste

### DIRECTIONS:

1. Preheat your air fryer to 375°F-190°C.
2. Season the chicken tenders generously with salt after tossing them in oil.
3. Air-fry them 8-10 minutes. Serve and enjoy.

### NUTRITIONAL VALUE PER SERVING:
Calories: 147 /kcal; Carbs: 0 g; Protein: 25 g; Fat: 5 g.

## BASIL-LIME SCALLOPS

**Prep time: 15 mins**

**Cooking time: 5 mins**

**Total time: 20 mins**

**Servings: 4**

### INGREDIENTS:

- 2 tbsp. chopped fresh basil
- 1/8 tsp. red pepper flakes
- Mixed baby greens, for garnish
- 1 tsp. low-sodium soy sauce
- 1 lime juice
- 1 clove garlic, minced
- 1 tsp. vegetable oil
- 8 jumbo sea scallops
- Lime wedges, for garnish

### DIRECTIONS:

1. In a shallow bowl, whisk soy sauce, garlic, lime juice, basil, oil, and red pepper flakes until smooth and thoroughly combined. Add the scallops and flip them to evenly coat them.
2. Over medium-high heat, heat a large nonstick skillet. Cook scallops for 3 minutes each side, or until done.
3. Serve with mixed greens and lime wedges as a garnish.

### NUTRITIONAL VALUE PER SERVING:
Calories: 92 /kcal; Carbs: 5 g; Protein: 14 g; Fat: 2 g.

## SHRIMP AND PINEAPPLE KABOBS

**Prep time: 10 mins**

**Cooking time: 5 mins**

**Total time: 15 mins**

**Servings: 4**

### INGREDIENTS:

- ¼ tsp. garlic powder
- ½ cup pineapple juice
- 1 green bell pepper, 1-inch pieces
- 12 chunks canned pineapple
- ½ lb. medium raw shrimp, peeled and deveined
- ¼ cup prepared chili sauce

### DIRECTIONS:

1. In a medium mixing dish, combine the garlic powder, shrimp and lemon juice; toss to coat.
2. Drain the shrimp and discard the marinade.
3. Thread pepper, pineapple, and shrimp alternately onto 4 skewers.
4. Now brush the chili sauce on skewers Chili sauce and grill them for 5 minutes, or until shrimp are opaque.

### NUTRITIONAL VALUE PER SERVING:
Calories: 100 /kcal; Carbs: 10 g; Protein: 14 g; Fat: 1 g.

## SAUTÉED SHRIMP

*Prep time: 10 mins*

*Cooking time: 5 mins*

*Total time: 15 mins*

*Servings: 2*

### INGREDIENTS:

- 4 sun-dried tomato halves
- ¼ tsp. black pepper
- 1 tbsp. olive oil
- ¼ cup hot boiling water
- 1 cup baby spinach leaves
- ½ lb. cooked and peeled shrimp
- 1 tsp. dried basil

### DIRECTIONS:

1. In a small dish, add the sun-dried tomato halves and boiling hot water Set aside for 10 minutes, turning regularly.
2. Remove the tomatoes from the water after 10 minutes, keeping the water for later use. Set aside chopped tomatoes.
3. Heat olive oil in a big sauté pan and sauté the cooked shrimp. Cook for a few minutes after adding the spinach and chopped tomato, then add the 1/4 cup of boiling water that was set aside.
4. Stir in the black pepper and dried basil until well blended, then serve right away.

### NUTRITIONAL VALUE PER SERVING:
Calories: 180 /kcal; Carbs: 5 g; Protein: 25 g; Fat: 8 g.

## ORANGE CHICKEN

*Prep time: 10 mins*

*Cooking time: 10 mins*

*Total time: 20 mins*

*Servings: 4*

### INGREDIENTS:

- 2 tbsp. frozen orange juice concentrate
- 2 tbsp. chopped fresh parsley
- 1 tsp. Dijon mustard
- 1 tbsp. orange marmalade, no-sugar-added
- 4 skinless chicken breast halves
- ¼ tsp. salt
- ½ cup fresh orange sections

### DIRECTIONS:

1. In an 8-inch shallow microwavable dish, mix the juice concentrate, salt and mustard, marmalade until the juice concentrate has thawed. Add the chicken and cover it in the sauce on both sides.
2. Arrange chicken around the dish's edge, not overlapping it. Cover with plastic wrap that has been ventilated and Microwave on high for 3 minutes, and then flip the chicken. Microwave on high for further 4 minutes or until chicken is no more pinkish in the center.
3. Place the chicken on a serving platter. Microwave the sauce for 2 to 3 minutes on high, or until slightly thickened.
4. Pour sauce over chicken and garnish with parsley and orange slices.

### NUTRITIONAL VALUE PER SERVING:
Calories: 150 /kcal; Carbs: 8 g; Protein: 26 g; Fat: 2 g.

## LEMON CAPER TILAPIA

*Prep time: 5 mins*

*Cooking time: 10 mins*

*Total time: 15 mins*

*Servings: 2*

### INGREDIENTS:

- Cooking spray
- 1 tbsp. capers
- 2 tilapia fillets
- 2 tsp. reduced-fat margarine
- ½ tsp. lemon zest
- 1 tsp. fresh-squeezed lemon juice
- 1 tbsp. white wine

### DIRECTIONS:

1. Grease a nonstick skillet over medium heat with cooking spray.
2. In a pan, melt the margarine, and then add the tilapia fillets.
3. Cook the fish for 2–3 mins on each side, or until a fork pierced the fish readily flakes.
4. Cover and keep the fish warm in a serving dish.
5. Now in the same skillet add the lemon juice, lemon zest, wine, and capers and mix to blend. Cook for 1 minute and then pour the sauce on fish and serve.

### NUTRITIONAL VALUE PER SERVING:
Calories: 115 /kcal; Carbs: 2 g; Protein: 21 g; Fat: 3 g.

## HERB MARINATED CHICKEN

*Prep time: 20 mins*

*Cooking time: 30 mins*

*Total time: 50 mins*

*Servings: 6*

### INGREDIENTS:

- 1½ lb. boneless, skinless chicken breasts
- 1 tsp. dry thyme
- ½ cup balsamic vinegar
- ¼ cup olive oil
- ½ tsp. dry parsley
- 3 cloves garlic, minced
- ¾ tsp. dry sage
- 1 tsp. dry rosemary

- 1 tsp. salt
- ½ tsp. coarse ground pepper

**DIRECTIONS:**

1. Place the chicken in a Ziploc bag.
2. Whisk together the other ingredients in a small dish and pour the marinade over the chicken. Close the bag firmly and gently shake it to thoroughly coat the chicken. Allow chicken to marinate for 25 minutes in the refrigerator, shaking bag lightly twice during this time to recoat chicken.
3. Remove the chicken from the marinade and discard the leftover marinade.
4. Preheat the grill to medium-high heat and grill the marinated chicken for 8–10 minutes from each side or until the chicken is no more pinkish and the juices are opaque.

**NUTRITIONAL VALUE PER SERVING:**

Calories: 145 /kcal; Carbs: 2 g; Protein: 26 g; Fat: 4 g.

## TOMATO SALMON

**Prep time:** 5 mins + marination time

**Cooking time:** 20 mins

**Total time:** 25 mins + marination time

**Servings:** 2

**INGREDIENTS:**

- Cooking spray
- ¼ cup sun-dried tomato vinaigrette
- 2 salmon fillets

**DIRECTIONS:**

1. Put salmon fillets in a Ziploc bag and drizzle with vinaigrette. To coat, seal the bag and gently shake it.
2. Refrigerate for 30 minutes after marinating.
3. Preheat the oven to 450°F-230°C. Using cooking spray, coat a baking dish. Place the salmon skin side down in the baking dish and pour the marinade on the top.
4. Bake uncovered for 20 minutes or until fish flakes. Remove the skin from each fillet and cut it in half.

**NUTRITIONAL VALUE PER SERVING:**

Calories: 150/kcal; Carbs: 1 g; Protein: 23 g; Fat: 6 g.

## LEMON PEPPER GRILLED SALMON

**Prep time:** 5 mins

**Cooking time:** 12 mins

**Total time:** 17 mins

**Servings:** 1

**INGREDIENTS:**

- Pinch of salt
- Wedge of lemon
- 1 salmon fillet
- Pinch of salt
- Wedge of lemon
- 1 salmon fillet
- ¼ tsp. olive oil
- Pinch of lemon pepper

**DIRECTIONS:**

1. Preheat the grill to medium.
2. Rub olive oil all over the salmon, making sure it's uniformly coated. Now season the salmon with salt and lemon pepper and to taste.
3. Grill the salmon for 6 minutes on each side over medium heat, or until it flakes gently when pricked with a fork.
4. Serve with a squeeze of fresh lemon juice on top.

**NUTRITIONAL VALUE PER SERVING:**

Calories: 140 /kcal; Carbs: 1 g; Protein: 23 g; Fat: 5 g.

## PEPPER STEAK WITH MUSTARD SAUCE

**Prep time:** 10 mins

**Cooking time:** 15 mins

**Total time:** 25 mins

**Servings:** 4

**INGREDIENTS:**

- 4 beef tenderloin steaks
- 1/3 cup low-salt beef broth
- cooking spray
- 2 tsp. coarsely ground black pepper
- 1/3 cup dry red wine
- 2 garlic cloves, minced
- 1 tbsp. Dijon mustard

**DIRECTIONS:**

1. Season the steaks with pepper.
2. Grease a medium nonstick skillet and place the steaks in a single layer in the pan and sear for about 1 minute, or until browned.
3. Cook for another 8 minutes, or until desired doneness is reached, flipping once.
4. Boil the wine and broth in a pan and stir in the mustard with a wire whisk until the sauce is fully combined. Serve the sauce on top of the steaks.

**NUTRITIONAL VALUE PER SERVING:**

Calories: 200 /kcal; Carbs: 0 g; Protein: 23 g; Fat: 9 g.

## CHICKEN MEATBALLS

**Prep time:** 5 mins

**Cooking time:** 30 mins

**Total time:** 35 mins

**Servings:** 4

**INGREDIENTS:**

### INGREDIENTS:

- 1½ lb. ground chicken
- 1 tsp. Italian season
- 1 tbsp. olive oil
- 1 tsp. flax seed powder
- ½ tsp. salt
- ½ tsp. garlic powder
- black pepper to taste
- ½ tsp. onion powder
- ¼ cup grated Parmesan
- 1 egg

### DIRECTIONS:

1. Preheat the oven to 400°F-200°C and line a baking pan with silicone baking sheets or tin foil.
2. Grease the tray and leave it aside.
3. In a large mixing dish, combine all of the ingredients until fully incorporated, then set aside for 5 minutes to rest.
4. Roll the mixture into 12 meatballs and place them on the baking pan and bake the meatballs for 30 minutes, or until slightly browned and cooked through.

### NUTRITIONAL VALUE PER SERVING:

Calories: 340 /kcal; Carbs: 1 g; Protein: 34 g; Fat: 23 g.

## YOGURT CHICKEN BREAST

**Prep time:** 10 mins

**Cooking time:** 40 mins

**Total time:** 50 mins

**Servings:** 4

### INGREDIENTS:

- 4 skinless chicken breasts
- 1 tsp. paprika
- 1 tbsp. lemon juice
- ½ tsp. chili powder
- Fresh parsley, for garnish
- 2 tbsp. garlic, minced
- 1½ cups Greek yogurt
- 1 tsp. black pepper
- 1 tsp. sea salt
- 1½ tsp. ground cumin
- ½ cup fresh herbs, chopped
- Lemon wedges, for serving

### DIRECTIONS:

1. Combine the garlic, fresh herbs, yogurt, spices and lemon juice in a large mixing bowl. Place the chicken breasts in a baking dish that is large enough to hold them tightly and pour the prepared marinade mixture all over the chicken. Grill the chicken breasts for 35–40 minutes over high heat, rotating once, until cooked through.
2. Remove the grilled chicken from the heat and serve with lemon wedges and finely chopped parsley.

### NUTRITIONAL VALUE PER SERVING:

Calories: 190 /kcal; Carbs: 4 g; Protein: 40 g; Fat: 2 g.

## BEEF STEW

**Prep time:** 30 mins

**Cooking time:** 1 hour 30 mins

**Total time:** 2 hours

**Servings:** 4

### INGREDIENTS:

- 1 lb. lean stewing beef, diced
- 1½ oz. plain flour
- 1 onion, chopped
- 2 cups beef stock
- 1 tbsp. vegetable oil
- 5 medium carrots, chopped
- salt and pepper, to taste

### DIRECTIONS:

1. In a frying pan, fry the meat on both sides until it is cooked through. Now add the chopped carrots and onions and cook them in frying pan. Remove the vegetables and meat from pan and add them to a pot.
2. Add the flour into the same frying pan and add the stock and seasonings. Give it a good mix.
3. Add this to vegetables and meat pot and simmer for 1 to 1½ hours, or until the meat is cooked, over a low heat.

### NUTRITIONAL VALUE PER SERVING:

Calories: 201 /kcal; Carbs: 14 g; Protein: 40 g; Fat: 8 g.

## CALIFORNIA GRILLED CHICKEN

**Prep time:** 20 mins

**Cooking time:** 20 mins

**Total time:** 40 mins

**Servings:** 4

### INGREDIENTS:

- 4 chicken breasts
- Pinch of ground pepper
- 4 slice of mozzarella cheese
- 2 tsp. Italian seasoning
- 2 tbsp. honey
- ¾ cup vinegar
- 2 tbsp. olive oil
- Salt to taste
- 4 slices tomato
- 4 slices avocado
- 2 tbsp. fresh basil
- 1 tsp. garlic powder

### DIRECTIONS:

1. Whisk together the Italian seasoning, honey, balsamic vinegar, oil, and garlic powder, in a small bowl.
2. Season it with some pepper and salt. Marinate the chicken for 20 minutes.
3. Once you're ready to grill, preheat the grill pan

on medium-high heat.
4. Grill chicken till crispy and cooked completely, 8 minutes from each side.
5. Top the chicken with the tomato, mozzarella, and avocado and cook for about 2 minutes, or till the cheese melts.
6. Garnish with basil, serve and enjoy.

**NUTRITIONAL VALUE PER SERVING:**
Calories: 200 /kcal; Carbs: 26 g; Protein: 41 g; Fat: 18 g.

## COCONUT BAKED CHICKEN

**Prep time:  15 mins**

**Cooking time:  20 mins**

**Total time:  35 mins**

**Servings: 6**

**INGREDIENTS:**
- 2 lb. chicken thighs
- Salt to taste
- ½ cup cilantro leaves
- 3 inch ginger
- 1 cup coconut milk
- ¼ cup lime juice
- 5 garlic cloves
- ¼ cup hot chili paste
- 2 tbsp. vegetable oil
- Lime wedges for serving

**DIRECTIONS:**
1. In a medium mixing dish, finely grind the ginger and garlic. Whisk in the salt, lime juice, chili paste, coconut milk, and 2 tbsp. oil. Toss in the chicken to coat.
2. Remove the chicken from the marinade, allowing the excess to drip back into the cup, and place it on a rimmed baking sheet.
3. Bake the chicken for 20 minutes in a preheated oven at 375°F-190°C.
4. Garnish with cilantro and enjoy.

**NUTRITIONAL VALUE PER SERVING:**
Calories: 212 /kcal; Carbs: 5 g; Protein: 14 g; Fat: 10 g.

## SALMON CAKES

**Prep time:  10 mins**

**Cooking time:  30 mins**

**Total time:  40 mins**

**Servings: 4**

Ingredients:
- 3 potatoes, boiled and mashed
- 1 bunch parsley, chopped
- 4 tbsp. flour
- 1 cup breadcrumbs
- Salt and pepper, to taste
- 1 cup cooked salmon
- 2 tbsp. fresh grated parmesan
- 1 tbsp. olive oil
- 1 egg, lightly beaten

DIRECTIONS:
- Combine the mashed potatoes, salmon, a pinch of salt and pepper, and half of the parsley in a mixing bowl.
- Form into round cakes with a mold or by hand. Add parmesan, breadcrumbs, and the remaining parsley in another bowl.
- Before rolling the fish cakes in the breadcrumb mixture, coat them in flour and then in beaten egg.
- In a frying pan, heat the olive oil and gently cook the fish cakes for 4 minutes from each side, or until golden brown.

**NUTRITIONAL VALUE PER SERVING:**
Calories: 230 /kcal; Carbs: 6 g; Protein: 10 g; Fat: 4 g.

## GRILLED CAJUN SALMON

**Prep time:  10 mins**

**Cooking time:  10 mins**

**Total time:  20 mins**

**Servings: 4**

**INGREDIENTS:**
- 4 salmon fillets
- 1 tsp. olive oil
- 1 tbsp. Cajun spice mix

**DIRECTIONS:**
1. Apply a thin layer of olive oil to each salmon fillet. Then season the fish with Cajun spice and marinate for 5 minutes in the fridge.
2. Cook the fish for 8 to 10 minutes on grill pan over medium high heat rotating once or twice.
3. Serve and enjoy.

**NUTRITIONAL VALUE PER SERVING:**
Calories: 145 /kcal; Carbs: 8 g; Protein: 15 g; Fat: 5 g.

## LEMON BASIL HALIBUT

**Prep time:  5 mins**

**Cooking time:  10 mins**

**Total time:  15 mins**

**Servings: 2**

**INGREDIENTS:**
- 2 halibut fillets
- ½ tsp. dried basil
- 1 tsp. dried parsley
- ¼ tsp. black pepper
- 1 tbsp. olive oil

- 1 clove minced garlic
- 2 tbsp. fresh lemon juice
- 1/8 tsp. salt
- 1/8 tsp. red pepper flakes

### DIRECTIONS:

1. Combine parsley, pepper, olive oil, garlic, lemon juice, salt, basil, and red pepper flakes in a mixing bowl.
2. Spread the marinade evenly over the halibut in a zip-top plastic bag and marinate it.
3. Place the grill pan on medium-high heat and cook for 4–6 minutes per side, or until the fish flakes readily when pierced with a fork.

### NUTRITIONAL VALUE PER SERVING:

Calories: 160 /kcal; Carbs: 2 g; Protein: 10 g; Fat: 9 g.

# DESSERT RECIPES

## RICE PUDDING

*Prep time:* 5 mins

*Cooking time:* 2 hour 30 mins

*Total time:* 2 hour 35 mins

*Servings:* 3

### INGREDIENTS:

- 1 cup of cooked brown rice
- 2 cups of almond milk
- 1 tsp. of vanilla extract
- ¼ cup of cranberries
- Raw honey, to taste

### DIRECTIONS:

1. Combine the rice, vanilla, and almond milk in the slow cooker and mix well.
2. Make sure the slow cooker is set to HIGH for 2 hour and 30 minutes.
3. The final step is to add some honey and cranberries before serving.

### NUTRITIONAL VALUE PER SERVING:

Calories: 106 /kcal; Carbs: 20 g; Protein: 2 g; Fat: 2 g.

## STRAWBERRY PUDDING

*Prep time:* 10 mins + chilling time

*Cooking time:* 0 mins

*Total time:* 10 mins + chilling time

*Servings:* 2

### INGREDIENTS:

- 16 oz. fresh strawberries
- 1 tsp. vanilla extract
- 2 cups almond milk
- ½ cup chia seeds
- ¼ cup honey

### DIRECTIONS:

1. Put the strawberries and almond milk in a blender and mix until smooth. Mix the butter, chia seeds, and vanilla into the strawberry purée.
2. Wrap the bowl in plastic and place it in the freezer for at least 4 hours, or until it has hardened.

### NUTRITIONAL VALUE PER SERVING:

Calories: 209 /kcal; Carbs: 37 g; Protein: 3 g; Fat: 6 g.

## BLUEBERRY MUFFINS

*Prep time:* 7 mins

*Cooking time:* 18 mins

*Total time:* 25 mins

*Servings:* 12

Ingredients:

- 1¾ cups whole flour
- ¾ cup milk
- ½ tsp. salt
- 1 egg, lightly beaten
- 2½ tsp. baking powder
- 1/3 cup stevia
- 1 cup blueberries, fresh or frozen
- 1/3 cup butter, softened

### DIRECTIONS:

1. Preheat the oven to 400°F-200°C.
2. Put the salt, flour, stevia and baking powder in a medium bowl and set it aside.
3. Cream the butter and stevia in a large bowl, then whisk in the milk with egg.
4. Fold in the blueberries after adding the flour mixture and stirring until the dry ingredients are just moistened.
5. Drop batter by rounded tablespoonful into 12 prepared muffin cups and bake for 18 minutes, or until a toothpick inserted in the middle comes out clean.

### NUTRITIONAL VALUE PER SERVING:

Calories: 160/kcal; Carbs: 11 g; Protein: 7 g; Fat: 3 g.

## CHOCO FROSTY

*Prep time:* 5 mins + chilling time

*Cooking time:* 0 mins

*Total time:* 5 mins + chilling time

*Servings:* 2

### INGREDIENTS:

- 1 tsp. vanilla
- 2 tbsp. unsweetened cocoa powder
- 8 drops liquid stevia
- 1 cup heavy cream
- 1 tbsp. almond butter

### DIRECTIONS:

1. Mix all the ingredients together in a bowl using an immersion blender until soft peaks form.
2. Put in the freezer for a total of 30 minutes.
3. Put the chilled mixture in a piping bag and then pipe it into the serving glasses.

### NUTRITIONAL VALUE PER SERVING:

Calories: 240 /kcal; Carbs: 4 g; Protein: 3 g; Fat: 25 g.

## CHEESECAKE BOMBS

*Prep time:* 10 mins + chilling time

*Cooking time:* 0 mins

**Total time:** 10 mins + chilling time

**Servings:** 2

### INGREDIENTS:

- 8 oz. cream cheese
- 2 tbsp. erythritol
- 1 ½ tsp. vanilla
- 4 oz. heavy cream
- 4 oz. coconut oil

### DIRECTIONS:

1. Put everything in a mixing dish and use an immersion blender to whip it until smooth.
2. Fill the small cupcake liners and chill the batter in the fridge for a few hours.
3. Serve.

### NUTRITIONAL VALUE PER SERVING:
Calories: 90 /kcal; Carbs: 1 g; Protein: 1 g; Fat: 9 g.

## MATCHA ICE CREAM

**Prep time:** 10 mins + chilling time

**Cooking time:** 0 mins

**Total time:** 10 mins + chilling time

**Servings:** 2

### INGREDIENTS:

- ½ tsp. vanilla
- 1 tsp. matcha powder
- 2 tbsp. stevia
- 1 cup heavy whipping cream

### DIRECTIONS:

1. Put all of the ingredients into the container.
2. Put the lid on the jar and shake it for four to five minutes to make the mixture expand.
3. Put in the fridge for 3 to 4 hours.
4. Serve cold and enjoy.

### NUTRITIONAL VALUE PER SERVING:
Calories: 215 /kcal; Carbs: 3 g; Protein: 2 g; Fat: 22 g.

## MIX BERRY SORBET

**Prep time:** 10 mins + chilling time

**Cooking time:** 0 mins

**Total time:** 10 mins + chilling time

**Servings:** 2

### INGREDIENTS:

- ½ cup raspberries, frozen
- 1 tsp. liquid stevia
- ½ cup blackberries, frozen
- 6 tbsp. water

### DIRECTIONS:

1. Put everything in a blender and blitz until completely smooth.
2. After blending all the ingredients together, transfer the liquid to the container.
3. Serve cold and enjoy.

### NUTRITIONAL VALUE PER SERVING:
Calories: 63 /kcal; Carbs: 14 g; Protein: 2 g; Fat: 1 g.

## FAT-FREE CHEESECAKE

**Prep time:** 15 mins

**Cooking time:** 1 hour 15 mins

**Total time:** mins

**Servings:** 16

### INGREDIENTS:

- 1¾ cups fat free cookies, crumbs
- 16 oz. fat-free or low-fat cream cheese
- ¼ cup butter, melted
- 8 oz. low-fat ricotta
- 1 cup fat-free sour cream
- 2 cups stevia
- 2 tsp. lemon zest
- ¾ cup egg substitute
- 2 tbsp. lemon juice

### DIRECTIONS:

1. Turn the oven temperature up to 325°F-165°C. Prepare a 9-inch cheesecake pan with nonstick spray.
2. Make a cookie crust by mixing cookie crumbs and butter in a bowl and press into pan's inside. Cool crust once it has been in the oven for 10 minutes.
3. Cream the sour cream, cream cheese, and ricotta until light and creamy; gradually whip in the Splenda and egg, scraping the bowl as necessary.
4. Mix in the juice and zest, then pour the mixture into the crust and bake for 65 minutes, until the top is golden brown and the center is somewhat jiggly but firm. Try not to overcook.
5. After it has cooled fully, run a knife around the outside, divide it into 16 pieces, and top each with a few fresh berries.

### NUTRITIONAL VALUE PER SERVING:
Calories: 130 /kcal; Carbs: 16 g; Protein: 8 g; Fat: 4 g.

## FAT-FREE GRANOLA

**Prep time:** 10 mins

**Cooking time:** 20 mins

**Total time:** 30 mins

**Servings:** 10

### INGREDIENTS:

1. 7 cups old-fashioned rolled oats
2. 2 tbsp. sunflower seeds
3. 2 cups wheat flakes
4. 1 tsp. cinnamon
5. 1 tbsp. chopped pecans
6. ¼ tsp. ginger
7. ¼ cup oat bran
8. 1/3 cup honey
9. 1 cup molasses
10. ¼ cup dried apples
11. ¼ cup raisins

### DIRECTIONS:

1. Turn oven temperature up to 350°F-180°C.
2. On a sheet pan, combine everything but the raisins and apples, and then bake at 350 degrees until golden, stirring occasionally.
3. Wait for it to cool down a bit, and then add in some fruit. Enjoy.

### NUTRITIONAL VALUE PER SERVING:
Calories: 120 /kcal; Carbs: 25 g; Protein: 3 g; Fat: 1 g.

## CHOCOLATE PROTEIN PUDDING POPS

**Prep time:** 5 mins + chilling time

**Cooking time:** 0 mins

**Total time:** 5 mins + chilling time

**Servings:** 4

### INGREDIENTS:

- 4 oz. chocolate-flavored instant pudding
- 2 scoops chocolate protein powder
- 2 cups cold low-fat milk

### DIRECTIONS:

1. Add the milk, pudding mix, and protein powder to a medium bowl and whisk vigorously for 2 minutes, or until the ingredients are well combined.
2. Put in paper cups or ice pop molds. Put a stick right in the middle of each ice pop mold or cup.
3. Put in the freezer for at least four hours, or until you reach the desired consistency. Before serving, take the molds or cups off.

### NUTRITIONAL VALUE PER SERVING:
Calories: 215 /kcal; Carbs: 36 12 g; Protein: g; Fat: 2 g.

## PEACH PINEAPPLE SORBET

**Prep time:** 5 mins + chilling time

**Cooking time:** 0 mins

**Total time:** 5 mins + chilling time

**Servings:** 4

### INGREDIENTS:

- ½ cup frozen peaches
- ½ cup frozen pineapple chunks
- ¼ cup sugar-free lemonade

### DIRECTIONS:

1. In a blender, combine peaches, pineapple, lemonade and mix until smooth.
2. Freeze the sorbet in Popsicle molds or a container for 4 hours or overnight.
3. Serve and enjoy.

### NUTRITIONAL VALUE PER SERVING:
Calories: 40 /kcal; Carbs: 10 g; Protein: 2 g; Fat: 0 g.

## PUMPKIN-VANILLA PUDDING

**Prep time:** 10 mins

**Cooking time:** 8 mins

**Total time:** 18 mins

**Servings:** 8

### INGREDIENTS:

- 1 whipped topping
- 1 tsp. ground cinnamon
- 2 eggs
- 2 tbsp. corn starch
- 1 vanilla bean
- ¼ cup pecans
- ¼ tsp. ground ginger
- 1/8 tsp. ground nutmeg
- ¼ tsp. ground cloves
- 8 oz. canned pumpkin
- 1¾ cup 1% milk
- ¼ cup Splenda sugar blend

### DIRECTIONS:

1. Whisk together the corn starch and sweetener in pot.
2. Whisk together the egg yolks and milk in a small bowl.
3. Gradually add the sweetener mixture into the egg mixture and put the pot over medium heat.
4. Cook the mixture for 3 to 5 minutes and then add cinnamon, pumpkin, cloves, nutmeg and ginger in a mixing bowl.
5. Now add vanilla bean seeds after five minutes of cooking and take the pot off the heat.
6. Place it in a bowl and wrap it with plastic wrap.
7. Chill for 1 hour and serve with whipping cream.

### NUTRITIONAL VALUE PER SERVING:
Calories: 85 /kcal; Carbs: 9 g; Protein: 3 g; Fat: 4 g.

## FIG AND WALNUT YOGURT

**Prep time:** 15 mins

**Cooking time:** 0 mins

**Total time:** 15 mins

**Servings:** 6

**INGREDIENTS:**

- 1 oz. crumbled goat cheese
- 4 large fresh figs, chopped
- ¼ cup nonfat, plain Greek yogurt
- 2 tbsp. freshly squeezed orange juice
- 12 mini phyllo dough shells
- 12 leaves fresh mint, chopped
- 12 walnut halves

**DIRECTIONS:**

1. Combine goat cheese, yogurt and orange juice in a small mixing bowl.
2. Fill 1 tbsp. of the cheese mixture into each phyllo shell.
3. Place a walnut half, a fig slice and 1 mint leaf on top of each. Keep it refrigerated before serving and enjoy.

**NUTRITIONAL VALUE PER SERVING:**

Calories: 130 /kcal; Carbs: 14 g; Protein: 4 g; Fat: 7 g.

## CHOCO BERRY PUDDING

**Prep time:** 5 mins + chilling time

**Cooking time:** 0 mins

**Total time:** 5 mins + chilling time

**Servings:** 8

**INGREDIENTS:**

- 2 packages instant white chocolate pudding mix, sugar-free
- 8 oz. fat-free whipped topping
- 4 cups sliced fresh strawberries
- 4 cups fat-free milk

**DIRECTIONS:**

1. Combine milk and pudding mix in a dish and stir well.
2. Spread half of the pudding and half of the strawberry slices in a big glass bowl.
3. Layers should be repeated.
4. Chill it in fridge before serving.
5. Serve with whipped topping on top.

**NUTRITIONAL VALUE PER SERVING:**

Calories: 112 /kcal; Carbs: 21 g; Protein: 5 g; Fat: 2 g.

## CHOCOLATE ALMOND PUDDING

**Prep time:** 5 mins + chilling time

**Cooking time:** 15 mins

**Total time:** 20 mins + chilling time

**Servings:** 4

**INGREDIENTS:**

- 1/3 cup Splenda sugar blend
- 1 tsp. almond extract
- 1 tsp. sliced almonds
- 2 tbsp. cornstarch
- ¼ cup unsweetened cocoa
- 2¼ cups reduced fat milk
- 1/8 tsp. salt
- ½ cup fat-free whipped topping

**DIRECTIONS:**

1. Combine cocoa, salt, Splenda sugar blend and cornstarch in a medium saucepan.
2. Stir in the milk gradually and cook over medium heat until the mixture boils.
3. Remove the pan from the heat and add the almond extract.
4. Refrigerate the pudding for 2 to 3 hours.
5. Add a dollop of whipped topping and a sprinkling of almonds on top and enjoy.

**NUTRITIONAL VALUE PER SERVING:**

Calories: 108 /kcal; Carbs: 19 g; Protein: 4 g; Fat: 1 g.

MAINTENANCE DIET

# MEAL PLANS

# Stage 1: CLEAR LIQUID

## MEAL PLAN

| DAYS | Breakfast | Lunch | Dinner |
|---|---|---|---|
| 1 | Peppermint Tea | Lemon, Mint And Cucumber Infused Water<br>Chicken Bone Broth<br>Mint Mojito | Clear Vegetable Stock<br>Lemon Balm Tea |
| 2 | Almond Tea | Infused Chicken Broth<br>Kiwi And Kale Detox Water<br>Strawberry Juice | Savory Beef Broth<br>Peanut Tea |
| 3 | Orange Vanilla Tea | Watermelon And Strawberry Mint Water<br>Strawberry, Mint, And Lemon Drink<br>Pork Bone Broth | Red Apple And Carrot Tea<br>Fishy Tomato Broth |
| 4 | Apricot And Orange Juice | Vegetable Beef Stock<br>Lime Cucumber Mint Water | Bok Choy Stock<br>Citrus Cucumber Water |
| 5 | Ginger Tea | Raspberry Orange Water<br>Pork And Fuzzy Gourd Broth | Savory Beef Broth<br>Strawberry Lemonade Water |
| 6 | Apple And Kale Juice | Southwest Style Chicken Broth<br>Blueberry Lavender Water | Beef And Seaweed Stock<br>Lemon Berry Water |
| 7 | Watermelon Juice | Pork Rib And Bean Stock<br>Spicy Infused Cucumber Water | Vegetable Fish Stock<br>Rosemary Grapefruit Infused Water |
| 8 | Mango Juice | Pork And Fuzzy Gourd Broth<br>Kiwi Passion Fruit And Mint Water | Vegetable Beef Stock<br>Ginger Tea |
| 9 | Orange Carrot Tea | Infused Chicken Broth<br>Apple Cinnamon Water | Clear Vegetable Stock<br>Blueberry And Orange Water |
| 10 | Apple And Kale Juice | Fishy Tomato Broth<br>Watermelon And Strawberry Mint Water | Bok Choy Stock<br>Watermelon Sorbet |

# Stage 2: FULL LIQUID

## MEAL PLAN

| DAYS | Breakfast | Lunch | Dinner |
|---|---|---|---|
| 1 | Apricot And Orange Juice<br>Banana Mixed Berry Smoothie | Beef And Seaweed Stock<br>Lemon Berry Water<br>Neapolitan Smoothie | Chocolate Cherry Shake<br>Pork And Fuzzy Gourd Broth<br>Kiwi Passion Fruit And Mint Water |
| 2 | Ginger Tea<br>Banana Cream Protein Shake | Caramel Almond Protein Shake<br>Vegetable Fish Stock<br>Rosemary Grapefruit Infused Water | Pineapple Coconut Cooler<br>Red Apple And Carrot Tea<br>Fishy Tomato Broth |
| 3 | Raspberry Plum Smoothie<br>Peppermint Tea | Banana Apple Flax Smoothie<br>Lemon, Mint And Cucumber Infused Water<br>Chicken Bone Broth | Clear Vegetable Stock<br>Green Kiwi Spinach Smoothie |
| 4 | Almond Tea<br>High Protein Milk | Watermelon And Strawberry Mint Water<br>Green Machine Protein Shake<br>Pork Bone Broth | Savory Beef Broth<br>Peanut Tea<br>Vanilla Bean Protein Shake |
| 5 | Apple And Kale Juice<br>Café Mocha Protein Blend | Vegetable Beef Stock<br>Ginger Tea<br>Mango Peach Pineapple Smoothie | Coconut Lime And Mint Cooler<br>Southwest Style Chicken Broth<br>Blueberry Lavender Water |
| 6 | Matcha Mango Smoothie<br>Watermelon Juice | Infused Chicken Broth<br>Apple Cinnamon Water<br>Pumpkin Spice Smoothie | Strawberry Kiwi Cooler<br>Pork Rib And Bean Stock<br>Spicy Infused Cucumber Water |
| 7 | Chocolate Raspberry Truffle Protein Shake<br>Mango Juice | Fishy Tomato Broth<br>Watermelon And Strawberry Mint Water | Double Chocolate Smoothie<br>Bok Choy Stock<br>Watermelon Sorbet |

# Stage 3: PUREES AND SOFT FOODS

## 2 Weeks - MEAL PLAN

| DAYS | Breakfast | Lunch | Dinner |
|---|---|---|---|
| 1 | Egg White Scramble | Italian Chicken Puree | Coconut Milk Flan |
| 2 | Matcha Mango Smoothie | Enchilada Bean Puree | Herby Tempeh Puree |
| 3 | Café Mocha Protein Blend | Rosemary Chicken And Blue Cheese Puree | Spicy Cauliflower Puree |
| 4 | Chocolate Chia Pudding | Mediterranean Chicken Puree | Cauliflower And Beef Puree |
| 5 | Strawberries With Whipped Yogurt | Ginger Garlic Tofu Puree | Pepper Pumpkin Puree |
| 6 | Mango Peach Pineapple Smoothie | Chimichurri Chicken Puree | Chicken Ricotta Puree |
| 7 | Blueberry Vanilla Smoothie | Turkey Tacos with Beans Puree | Eggs Puree Delight |
| 8 | Chocolate Protein Pudding | Curry Chicken Lentil Soup Spinach And Mushroom Muffins | Taco Soup Shrimp Salad |
| 9 | Quinoa Breakfast Bowl | Roasted Vegetable Quinoa And Chickpea Salad | Italian Herb Muffins Cheesy Chicken And Broccoli Casserole |
| 10 | Peanut Butter Pancakes | Cheesecake Cottage Cheese Mixed Berry Shortcake Yogurt Crumble | Salmon And Fennel En Papillote Egg White Omelet |
| 11 | Yogurt Parfait With Raspberries And Chia Seeds | Carrot Pudding Meat Loaf | Cranberry Chicken Salad Fresh Hummus |
| 12 | Farmer's Market Scramble | Seafood Cakes Creamy Tuscan Shrimp | Pork Taco Soup Cucumber, Avocado, Black Bean, Corn And Tomato Salad |
| 13 | Vanilla Chia Pudding | Lentil And Vegetable Soup Classic Tuna Salad | Creamy Tomato Soup Braised Collards With Pork And Beans |
| 14 | Buttermilk Pancakes | Bacon And Avocado Salad Spinach And Mushroom Egg Cups | Mediterranean Tomato Fish Sweet Potato Tuna Sala |

# Stage 4: MAINTENANCE DIET

## Week 1-2 - MEAL PLAN

| DAYS | Breakfast | Lunch | Dinner |
|---|---|---|---|
| 1 | Veggie Quiche Muffins | Classic Turkey And Swiss Wrap | Garlic Shrimp Stir Fry |
| 2 | Steel Cut Oat Blueberry Pancakes | Cumin Mushroom Quesadillas | Buffalo Lettuce Wraps |
| 3 | Very Berry Muesli | Ultimate Veggie Sandwich | Lemon Caper Chicken |
| 4 | Strawberry And Mushroom Sandwich | Turkey Sandwich | Tomato And Coconut Chicken Curry |
| 5 | Strawberries With Whipped Yogurt | Pita Pizza | Curry Shrimp And Vegetables |
| 6 | Cake Batter Protein Balls | Mexican Style Stuffed Summer Squash | Chipotle Lime Salmon |
| 7 | Chocolate Chia Pudding | Spinach Turkey Wraps | Italian Chicken |
| 8 | Sweet Millet Congee | Barley And Mushroom Risotto | Chili Lime Burgers<br>Shrimp Salad |
| 9 | Smoothie Bowl With Greek Yogurt | Coconut And Tofu Curry | Italian Herb Muffins<br>Squid And Prawn Skewers |
| 10 | Breakfast Quinoa Bowls | Barley And Mushroom Risotto<br>Mixed Berry Shortcake Yogurt Crumble | Scallops With Chilli And Lime Butter |
| 11 | Perfect Granola | Bacon, Lettuce, Tomato, And Cream Cheese Sandwich | Caprese Steak<br>Fresh Hummus |
| 12 | American Scramble | Seafood Cakes<br>Simple Sloppy Joe | Asian Salmon<br>Cucumber, Avocado, Black Bean, Corn And Tomato Salad |
| 13 | Cheese-Filled Acorn Squash | Lentil And Vegetable Soup<br>Classic Tuna Salad | Creamy Tomato Soup<br>Crispy Chicken Tenders |
| 14 | Cheesy Spinach Bake | Coconut And Tofu Curry<br>Spinach And Mushroom Egg Cups | Mediterranean Tomato Fish<br>Crispy Chicken Tenders |

# Stage 4: MAINTENANCE DIET

## Week 3-4 - MEAL PLAN

| DAYS | Breakfast | Lunch | Dinner |
|---|---|---|---|
| 1 | Greek Yogurt, Granola, And Berry Parfait | Eggplant Rollatini<br>Chicken Ricotta | Chicken Nachos And Sweet Bell Peppers |
| 2 | Eggs Florentine | Cauliflower And Cheese Casserole<br>Roasted Chicken With Vegetables | Creamy Beef Stroganoff And Mushrooms |
| 3 | Mexican Scrambled Eggs | Basil And Garlic Grilled Chicken | Italian Beef Sandwiches |
| 4 | Chocolate Chia Pudding | Greek Yogurt Chicken | Beef And Bean Casserole |
| 5 | Breakfast Parfaits | Herb Roasted Salmon | Baked Chicken With Mix Vegetables |
| 6 | Oat Waffles | Mediterranean Meatballs | Chicken And Mushroom Risotto |
| 7 | Yogurt Parfait With Raspberries And Chia Seeds | Mustard Roast Beef | Italian Chicken Sandwiches |
| 8 | Chocolate Protein Pudding | Chipotle Lime Grilled Chicken | Taco Soup<br>Cinnamon Chicken |
| 9 | Grain Breakfast Bowls | Mediterranean Pork | Italian Herb Muffins<br>Lemon Caper Tilapia |
| 10 | Quinoa Chia Porridge | Spicy Chicken Breasts | Lemon Pepper Grilled Salmon<br>Egg White Omelet |
| 11 | Protein Pancakes | Asian Beef Kababs | Yogurt Chicken Breast<br>Fresh Hummus |
| 12 | Shakshuka Egg Bake | Seafood Cakes<br>Beef Pepper Steak | Pork Taco Soup<br>Cucumber, Avocado, Black Bean, Corn And Tomato Salad |
| 13 | Vanilla Chia Pudding | Lentil And Vegetable Soup<br>Peanut Butter Salmon | Creamy Tomato Soup<br>California Grilled Chicken |
| 14 | Breakfast Pizza | Bacon And Avocado Salad<br>Chipotle Lime Grilled Chicken | Coconut Baked Chicken<br>Sweet Potato Tuna Salad |

# Appendix 1

## RECIPE INDEX

| | | |
|---|---|---|
| Peppermint Tea | 10 | |
| Almond Tea | 10 | |
| Orange Vanilla Tea | 10 | |
| Apricot And Orange Juice | 11 | |
| Chicken Bone Broth | 11 | |
| Lemon, Mint And Cucumber Infused Water | 11 | |
| Citrus And Mint Infused Water | 11 | |
| Mango And Pineapple Water | 12 | |
| Honeydew And Kiwi Infused Water | 12 | |
| Mint Mojito | 12 | |
| Infused Chicken Broth | 12 | |
| Sweet And Sour Lychee Infused Water | 12 | |
| Kiwi And Kale Detox Water | 13 | |
| Watermelon and Lemon Water | 13 | |
| Mango And Ginger Infused Water | 13 | |
| Lavender And Blueberry Infused Water | 13 | |
| Pina Colada Infused Water | 13 | |
| Strawberry, Orange And Mint Infused Water | 14 | |
| Watermelon Juice | 14 | |
| Ginger Tea | 14 | |
| Orange Juice | 14 | |
| Key Lime Tea | 14 | |
| Strawberry Juice | 15 | |
| Grape Juice | 15 | |
| Mango Juice | 15 | |
| Apple And Kale Juice | 15 | |
| Clear Vegetable Stock | 16 | |
| Watermelon Sorbet | 16 | |
| Lemon Balm Tea | 16 | |
| Orange Carrot Tea | 16 | |
| Red Apple And Carrot Tea | 17 | |
| Pork Bone Broth | 17 | |
| Peanut Tea | 17 | |
| Savory Beef Broth | 17 | |
| Vegetable Chicken Broth | 18 | |
| Southwest Style Chicken Broth | 18 | |
| Lemon And Cucumber Water | 18 | |
| Strawberry Lemonade Water | 19 | |
| Apple Cinnamon Water | 19 | |
| Blueberry And Orange Water | 19 | |
| Watermelon And Strawberry Mint Water | 19 | |
| Mango Ginger Water | 20 | |
| Raspberry Orange Water | 20 | |
| Classic Cucumber Water | 20 | |
| Lemon Berry Water | 20 | |
| Strawberry, Mint, And Lemon Drink | 20 | |
| Blueberry Lavender Water | 21 | |
| Lemon Lime Water | 21 | |
| Pineapple And Orange Water | 21 | |
| Lime Cucumber Mint Water | 21 | |
| Citrus Cucumber Water | 21 | |
| Peach Mint Water | 22 | |
| Beef And Seaweed Stock | 22 | |
| Pork Rib And Bean Stock | 22 | |
| Vegetable Fish Stock | 22 | |
| Bok Choy Stock | 23 | |
| Vegetable Beef Stock | 23 | |
| Fishy Tomato Broth | 23 | |
| Pork And Fuzzy Gourd Broth | 24 | |
| Rosemary Grapefruit Infused Water | 24 | |
| Citrus Infused Green Tea | 24 | |
| Spicy Infused Cucumber Water | 24 | |
| Strawberry Lemon And Basil Water | 25 | |
| Watermelon, Jalapeno And Mint Water | 25 | |
| Mango Coconut And Lime Water | 25 | |
| Orange Grape And Rosemary Water | 25 | |
| Kiwi Passion Fruit And Mint Water | 26 | |
| Cucumber Lime And Thyme Water | 26 | |
| Apple Ginger And Cinnamon Water | 26 | |
| Strawberry Lime And Rosemary Water | 26 | |
| Banana and Chocolate Smoothie | 28 | |
| Superfood Smoothie | 28 | |
| Strawberry And Banana | | |

| | | |
|---|---|---|
| Smoothie 28 | Ultimate Berry Blend Smoothie 34 | Italian Chicken Puree 43 |
| Greek yogurt And Berry Smoothie 28 | Green Kiwi Spinach Smoothie 35 | Enchilada Bean Puree 43 |
| Caramel Almond Protein Shake 28 | Coconut Lime And Mint Cooler 35 | Rosemary Chicken And Blue Cheese Puree 43 |
| Peanut Butter Cup Smoothie 29 | Pineapple Coconut Cooler 35 | Mediterranean Chicken Puree 44 |
| Pumpkin Spice Smoothie 29 | Blueberry Vanilla Smoothie 35 | Ginger Garlic Tofu Puree 44 |
| Double Chocolate Smoothie 29 | Peaches And Creamy Coconut Smoothie 36 | Mexican Egg Puree 44 |
| Mango And Pineapple Smoothie 29 | Strawberry Kiwi Cooler 36 | Chimichurri Chicken Puree 45 |
| Pina Colada Smoothie 30 | Peanut Butter And Banana Power Smoothie 36 | Chicken And Black Bean Mole Puree 45 |
| Avocado Smoothie 30 | Lemon Meringue Pie Smoothie 36 | Caribbean Pork Puree 45 |
| Green Mango Smoothie 30 | | Moroccan Fish Puree 46 |
| Banana Cream Protein Shake 30 | Refreshing Strawberry Smoothie 36 | Creamy Shrimp Scampi Puree 46 |
| Guava Smoothie 30 | Creamy Pumpkin Pie Smoothie 37 | Ricotta And White Bean Puree 46 |
| Watermelon, Cantaloupe and Mango Smoothie 31 | Blue Raspberry Cooler 37 | Turkey Tacos with Beans Puree 46 |
| BlackBerry And Banana Smoothie 31 | Neapolitan Smoothie 37 | Sesame Tuna Salad Puree 47 |
| Green Smoothie with Raspberries 31 | High Protein Milk 38 | Turkey Chili Puree 47 |
| Chocolate Cherry Shake 31 | Cool Cucumber-Lime Smoothie 38 | Coconut Milk Flan 47 |
| Veggie-Full Smoothie 32 | Raspberry Refresher 38 | Herby Tempeh Puree 48 |
| Mango Peach Pineapple Smoothie 32 | Vanilla Bean Protein Shake 38 | Spicy Tofu Puree 48 |
| Green Kiwi Spinach Smoothie 32 | Banana Cream Protein Shake 38 | Spicy Cauliflower Puree 48 |
| Simple Cantaloupe Smoothie 32 | Lemon Pie Protein Shake 39 | Cauliflower And Beef Puree 48 |
| Cherry Berry Lime Smoothie 32 | ABC Smoothie 39 | Italian Style Chicken Puree 49 |
| Strawberry Banana And Orange Smoothie 33 | Café Mocha Protein Blend 39 | Hearty Beef And Potato Puree 49 |
| Raspberry Plum Smoothie 33 | Green Machine Protein Shake 39 | Chicken And Pumpkin Puree 49 |
| Banana Apple Flax Smoothie 33 | Chocolate Raspberry Truffle Protein Shake 40 | Italian Tomato And Beef Puree 50 |
| Power C Smoothie 34 | Berry Bliss Protein Shake 40 | Thai Style Chicken Blended Puree 50 |
| Blackberry Peach Smoothie 34 | Pina Colada Protein Shake 40 | Lemon Salmon Puree 50 |
| Strawberry Pineapple Smoothie 34 | Pumpkin Nut Smoothie 40 | Pureed Salmon With Dill And Cream Cheese 50 |
| Berry Spinach Smoothie 34 | Very Berry Smoothie 41 | Lemony Mustard Puree 51 |
| | Matcha Mango Smoothie 41 | |

| Recipe | Page |
|---|---|
| Worcestershire And Cream Chicken Puree | 51 |
| Indian Curry Chicken Puree | 51 |
| Parmesan Tilapia Puree | 51 |
| Crab Shallot Puree | 52 |
| Cauliflower And Cheese Mash | 52 |
| Creamy Lemon Shrimp Puree | 52 |
| Jalapeno Bean Puree | 52 |
| Pear And Ricotta Puree | 53 |
| Chicken Puree | 53 |
| Black Bean And Red Pepper Puree | 53 |
| Scrambled Egg Puree | 53 |
| Pureed Egg Salad | 54 |
| Tangy Chicken Puree | 54 |
| Basic Fish Puree | 54 |
| Pureed Salmon | 54 |
| Leek And Broccoli Tofu Puree | 55 |
| Cauliflower Almond Puree | 55 |
| Strawberry Protein Parfait | 55 |
| Butternut Squash Puree | 55 |
| Cheesy Cauliflower Puree | 56 |
| Pepper Pumpkin Puree | 56 |
| Vegetable Puree | 56 |
| Corn Puree | 56 |
| Chicken Ricotta Puree | 57 |
| Eggs Puree Delight | 57 |
| Ginger Carrot Puree | 57 |
| White Bean Puree | 57 |
| Strawberry Puree | 58 |
| Carrot Puree | 58 |
| Blackberry Puree | 58 |
| Spinach Puree | 58 |
| Zucchini Puree | 58 |
| Mango Puree | 59 |
| Buffalo Shrimp Puree | 59 |
| Broccoli Puree | 59 |
| Sweet Potato Puree | 59 |
| Apple Pear Puree | 59 |
| CHICKEN Bean Puree | 60 |
| Avocado Puree | 60 |
| Spinach Almond Milk Puree | 60 |
| Chicken Chili Puree | 60 |
| Edamame Puree | 60 |
| Avocado Tomato Puree | 61 |
| Peach Puree | 61 |
| Mushy Pea Puree | 61 |
| Apple Puree | 61 |
| Cheesy Egg Puree | 62 |
| Curried Broccoli Puree | 62 |
| Best Chocolate Porridge | 64 |
| Chocolate Chia Pudding | 64 |
| Pumpkin Custard | 64 |
| Lemon-Blackberry Frozen Yogurt | 64 |
| Creamy Cauliflower Dish | 65 |
| Beetroot And Butterbean Hummus | 65 |
| Raisin And Oats Mug Cakes | 65 |
| Buffalo Chicken Dip | 65 |
| Peanut Butter Protein Bites | 66 |
| Egg White Scramble | 66 |
| Ham And Swiss Eggs | 66 |
| Greek Yogurt Bark | 66 |
| Tropical Porridge | 67 |
| Porridge With Berries | 67 |
| Meat Loaf | 67 |
| Curry Chicken Lentil Soup | 67 |
| Strawberries With Whipped Yogurt | 68 |
| Gazpacho | 68 |
| Carrot Pudding | 68 |
| Roasted Vegetable Quinoa And Chickpea Salad | 69 |
| Fancy Scrambled Eggs | 69 |
| Cheesecake Cottage Cheese | 69 |
| Loaded Baked Potato Soup | 69 |
| Mixed Berry Shortcake Yogurt Crumble | 70 |
| Banana Brule Yogurt Parfait | 70 |
| Yogurt Popsicles | 70 |
| No Oats Cereal | 70 |
| Cinnamon Flax And Almond Cakes | 71 |
| Coconut Almond Cakes | 71 |
| Shrimp Cauliflower Chowder | 72 |
| Seafood Cakes | 72 |
| Lentil And Vegetable Soup | 72 |
| Bacon And Avocado Salad | 73 |
| Butternut Squash Soup | 73 |
| Cauliflower Garlic Soup | 73 |
| Baby Arugula And Parmesan Salad | 74 |
| High Protein Tomato Soup | 74 |
| Chicken Salad | 74 |
| Greens soup | 74 |
| Classic Tuna Salad | 75 |
| Tomato, Cucumber And Basil Salad | 75 |
| Taco Soup | 75 |
| Shrimp Salad | 75 |

| | | |
|---|---|---|
| Cinnamon Spice Cereal 76 | Creamy Tomato Soup 84 | Steel Cut Oat Blueberry Pancakes 95 |
| Cucumber, Avocado, Black Bean, Corn And Tomato Salad 76 | Spinach And Mushroom Muffins 85 | Very Berry Muesli 95 |
| Italian Herb Muffins 76 | Mediterranean Tomato Fish 85 | Strawberry And Mushroom Sandwich 96 |
| Cauliflower Tots 77 | Sweet Potato Tuna Sala 85 | Cake Batter Protein Balls 96 |
| Almond Crusted Mozzarella Strips 77 | Almond Banana Greek Yogurt 86 | Turkey Sausage And Mushroom Strata 96 |
| Cheesy Chicken And Broccoli Casserole 77 | Peanut Butter Banana Ice Cream 86 | Sweet Millet Congee 96 |
| Salmon And Fennel En Papillote 78 | Balsamic Salmon 86 | Smoothie Bowl With Greek Yogurt 97 |
| Chicken Patties 78 | Savory Quinoa Muffins 86 | Breakfast Quinoa Bowls 97 |
| Italian Meatloaf 78 | Broccoli Cheese Soup 87 | Perfect Granola 97 |
| Cranberry Chicken Salad 79 | Chickpea Soup 87 | Cinnamon Sugar Oatmeal Casserole 98 |
| Spinach And Mushroom Egg Cups 79 | Tomato Soup 87 | American Scramble 98 |
| Creamy Tuscan Shrimp 79 | Spinach And Feta Cheese Omelet 88 | Cheese-Filled Acorn Squash 98 |
| Braised Collards With Pork And Beans 79 | Super Scramble 88 | Cheesy Spinach Bake 99 |
| Deviled Egg And Bacon 80 | Crab Cakes 88 | Greek Yogurt, Granola, And Berry Parfait 99 |
| Pork Taco Soup 80 | Apple Crumble 88 | Eggs Florentine 99 |
| Coconut Chicken Soup 80 | Strawberry Cheesecake Pudding Parfait 89 | Mexican Scrambled Eggs 99 |
| Baked Fish With Almond Chutney 81 | Avocado Egg Salad 89 | Denver Scramble 100 |
| Turkey Kale Meatballs 81 | Curried Chickpeas 89 | Ground Beef And Spinach Scramble 100 |
| Crockpot Chicken Curry 81 | Cinnamon Bun Protein Oatmeal 90 | Quinoa Breakfast Bowl 100 |
| Egg White Omelet 82 | Chicken and Rice Skillet 90 | Scrambled Eggs With Avocado On Toast 101 |
| Cherry Berry Frozen Greek Yogurt 82 | Italian Poached Eggs 90 | Quinoa-Pear Breakfast Bake 101 |
| Curried Cauliflower Soup 82 | Fried Eggs On Parmesan Cheese Crust 90 | Cauliflower Breakfast Casserole 101 |
| Curried Lentil Soup 83 | Chocolate Protein Pudding 91 | Oat Waffles 102 |
| Chicken And Bean Bake 83 | Soft Crab Salad 91 | Breakfast Parfaits 102 |
| White Veggie Scramble 83 | Soft Chicken Salad 91 | Herb-Baked Eggs 102 |
| Fresh Hummus 84 | Enchilada Eggs 91 | Yogurt Parfait With Raspberries And Chia Seeds 102 |
| Key Lime Pie 84 | Cream Of Mushroom Chicken 92 | Grain Breakfast Bowls 103 |
| Broccoli Soup 84 | Creamy Deviled Eggs 92 | Quinoa Chia Porridge 103 |
| | Veggie Quiche Muffins 95 | |

| Recipe | Page |
|---|---|
| Mango, Chia And Almond Breakfast Bowl | 103 |
| Blueberry Almond Oats | 103 |
| Protein Pancakes | 104 |
| Shakshuka Egg Bake | 104 |
| Denver Egg Muffins | 104 |
| Cheesy Egg Casserole | 105 |
| Breakfast Burritos | 105 |
| Chia Pudding | 105 |
| Breakfast Pizza | 106 |
| Farmer's Market Scramble | 106 |
| Raspberry Lemon Muffins | 106 |
| Protein Waffles | 107 |
| Pumpkin Spice Muffins | 107 |
| Egg White Pizza | 107 |
| Southwest Scramble | 108 |
| Italian Style Scramble | 108 |
| Cheeseburger Scramble | 108 |
| Turkey, Zucchini And Tomato Hash | 108 |
| Spinach And Cheddar Quiche | 109 |
| Tofu Scrambler | 109 |
| Vegan Breakfast Scramble | 109 |
| Oat And Berry Acai Bowl | 110 |
| Vanilla Chia Pudding | 110 |
| Egg Muffins | 110 |
| Turkey Burritos | 110 |
| Mini Frittatas | 111 |
| Peanut Butter Pancakes | 111 |
| Broccoli And Cheese Omelet | 111 |
| Mushroom Frittata | 112 |
| Buttermilk Pancakes | 112 |
| Veggie Eggs | 112 |
| Cumin Mushroom Quesadillas | 114 |
| Classic Turkey And Swiss Wrap | 114 |
| Spinach Turkey Wraps | 114 |
| Avocado, Cream Cheese And Bacon Sandwich | 115 |
| Chicken Salad Sandwich | 115 |
| Classic Turkey, Cranberry, And Cream Cheese Sandwich | 115 |
| Ultimate Veggie Sandwich | 115 |
| Fresh Mozzarella And Tomato Sandwich | 116 |
| Baked Ham And Cheese Sandwich | 116 |
| Salmon Sandwich | 116 |
| Turkey Sandwich | 116 |
| Egg Salad Sandwich | 116 |
| Bacon, Lettuce, Tomato, And Cream Cheese Sandwich | 117 |
| Pita Pizza | 117 |
| Simple Sloppy Joe | 117 |
| Mediterranean Chicken | 118 |
| Mexican Style Stuffed Summer Squash | 118 |
| Barley And Mushroom Risotto | 118 |
| Coconut And Tofu Curry | 118 |
| Eggplant Rollatini | 119 |
| Chicken Ricotta | 119 |
| Eggplant, Chickpea, And Quinoa Curry | 119 |
| Cauliflower And Cheese Casserole | 120 |
| Roasted Chicken With Vegetables | 120 |
| Basil And Garlic Grilled Chicken | 120 |
| Black Bean And Butternut Squash Enchiladas | 120 |
| Tuna Casserole | 121 |
| Greek Yogurt Chicken | 121 |
| Herb Roasted Salmon | 121 |
| Roasted Pesto Salmon | 122 |
| Baked Halibut | 122 |
| Fried Cod Fillets | 122 |
| Baked Salmon | 122 |
| Lemon And Parsley Crab Balls | 123 |
| Cabbage and Meat Curry | 123 |
| Grilled Chicken Wings | 123 |
| Stuffed Chicken Breast | 123 |
| Sweet and Sour Salmon | 124 |
| Tuna And Mango Kababs | 124 |
| Beef And Vegetable Chili Dry | 124 |
| Vegetable Curry | 125 |
| Spicy Chicken Breasts | 125 |
| Mediterranean Pork | 125 |
| Mediterranean Meatballs | 125 |
| Roasted Pork | 126 |
| Asian Beef Kababs | 126 |
| Beef Pepper Steak | 126 |
| Mustard Roast Beef | 127 |
| Peanut Butter Salmon | 127 |
| Chipotle Lime Grilled Chicken | 127 |
| Easy Chicken Curry | 127 |
| Chicken And Mushroom Gravy | 128 |
| Grilled Balsamic Chicken | 128 |
| Lasagna Stew | 128 |
| Chicken And Vegetable Stew | 129 |

| | | | | | |
|---|---|---|---|---|---|
| Taco Chicken | 129 | Chicken Nachos And Sweet Bell Peppers | 139 | Yogurt Chicken Breast | 147 |
| Queso Chicken Chili | 129 | Creamy Beef Stroganoff And Mushrooms | 139 | Beef Stew | 147 |
| Inside Out Egg Rolls | 129 | | | California Grilled Chicken | 147 |
| Spicy Thai Chicken Slaw | 130 | Sloppy Joes | 140 | Coconut Baked Chicken | 148 |
| Instant Pot Turkey Chili | 132 | Italian Beef Sandwiches | 140 | Salmon Cakes | 148 |
| Garlic Shrimp Stir Fry | 132 | Italian Chicken Sandwiches | 140 | Grilled Cajun Salmon | 148 |
| Buffalo Lettuce Wraps | 132 | Baked Beef With Fennel And Asparagus | 141 | Lemon Basil Halibut | 148 |
| Lemon Caper Chicken | 132 | Broccoli And Cheese Casserole | 141 | Rice Pudding | 151 |
| Shrimp And Broccoli | 133 | | | Strawberry Pudding | 151 |
| Tomato And Coconut Chicken Curry | 133 | Fried Chicken Fillets | 141 | Blueberry Muffins | 151 |
| | | Chicken Casserole | 141 | Choco Frosty | 151 |
| Beef Enchilada Casserole | 133 | Beef And Bean Casserole | 142 | Cheesecake Bombs | 151 |
| Curry Shrimp And Vegetables | 134 | Minced Beef Balls | 142 | Matcha Ice Cream | 152 |
| Lemon And Fennel Chicken Thighs | 134 | Baked Chicken With Mix Vegetables | 142 | Mix Berry Sorbet | 152 |
| Chipotle Lime Salmon | 134 | Chicken And Mushroom Risotto | 142 | Fat-Free Cheesecake | 152 |
| Shrimp Over Zucchini Noodles | 135 | Minced Beef And Spaghetti Squash Casserole | 143 | Fat-Free Granola | 152 |
| | | | | Chocolate Protein Pudding Pops | 153 |
| Chili Lime Burgers | 135 | Coconut And Chicken Curry | 143 | Peach Pineapple Sorbet | 153 |
| Lemon Butter Shrimp | 135 | Garlic And Herb Grilled Beef | 143 | Pumpkin-Vanilla Pudding | 153 |
| Italian Chicken | 136 | Cinnamon Chicken | 144 | Fig And Walnut Yogurt | 153 |
| Honey Mustard Salmon | 136 | Chicken Tenders | 144 | Choco Berry Pudding | 154 |
| Seafood Parcels | 136 | Basil-Lime Scallops | 144 | Chocolate Almond Pudding | 154 |
| Squid And Prawn Skewers | 137 | Shrimp and Pineapple Kabobs | 144 | | |
| Scallops With Chilli And Lime Butter | 137 | Sautéed Shrimp | 145 | | |
| Chicken And Broccoli Rice Bowl | 137 | Orange Chicken | 145 | | |
| Steamed Trout | 137 | Lemon Caper Tilapia | 145 | | |
| Trout With Citrus And Basil Sauce | 138 | Herb Marinated Chicken | 145 | | |
| | | Tomato Salmon | 146 | | |
| Caprese Steak | 138 | Lemon Pepper Grilled Salmon | 146 | | |
| Green Fish Curry | 138 | | | | |
| Asian Salmon | 138 | Pepper Steak with Mustard Sauce | 146 | | |
| Crispy Chicken Tenders | 139 | Chicken Meatballs | 146 | | |

# Appendix 2

## MEASUREMENT CONVERSION CHART

### Volume Equivalents (Dry)

| US Standard | Metric (Approximate) |
|---|---|
| ⅛ teaspoon | 0.5 mL |
| ¼ teaspoon | 1 mL |
| ½ teaspoon | 2 mL |
| ¾ teaspoon | 4 mL |
| 1 teaspoon | 5 mL |
| 1 tablespoon | 15 mL |
| ¼ cup | 59 mL |
| ⅓ cup | 79 mL |
| ½ cup | 118 mL |
| ⅔ cup | 156 mL |
| ¾ cup | 177 mL |
| 1 cup | 235 mL |
| 2 cups or 1 pint | 475 mL |
| 3 cups | 700 mL |
| 4 cups | 1 L |

### Volume Equivalents (Liquid)

| US Standard | US Standard (Ounces) | Metric (Approximate) |
|---|---|---|
| 2 tablespoons | 1 fl. oz. | 30 ml |
| ¼ cup | 2 fl. oz. | 60 ml |
| ½ cup | 4 fl. oz. | 120 ml |
| 1 cup | 8 fl. oz. | 240 ml |
| 1½ cups | 12 fl. oz. | 355 ml |
| 2 cups or 1 pint | 16 fl. oz. | 475 ml |
| 4 cups or 1 quart | 32 fl. oz. | 1 L |
| 1 gallon | 128 fl. oz. | 4 L |

### Weight Equivalents

| US Standard | Metric (Approximate) |
|---|---|
| 1 ounce | 28 g |
| 2 ounces | 57 g |
| 5 ounces | 142 g |
| 10 ounces | 284 g |
| 15 ounces | 425 g |
| 16 ounces or 1 pound | 455 g |
| 1.5 pounds | 680 g |
| 2 pounds | 907 g |

### Temperature Equivalents

| Fahrenheit (F) | Celsius (C) (Approximate) |
|---|---|
| 225°F | 107°C |
| 250°F | 120°C |
| 300°F | 150°C |
| 325°F | 165°C |
| 350°F | 180°C |
| 375°F | 190°C |
| 400°F | 200°C |
| 425°F | 220°C |
| 450°F | 230°C |
| 475°F | 245°C |
| 500°F | 260°C |

# CONCLUSION

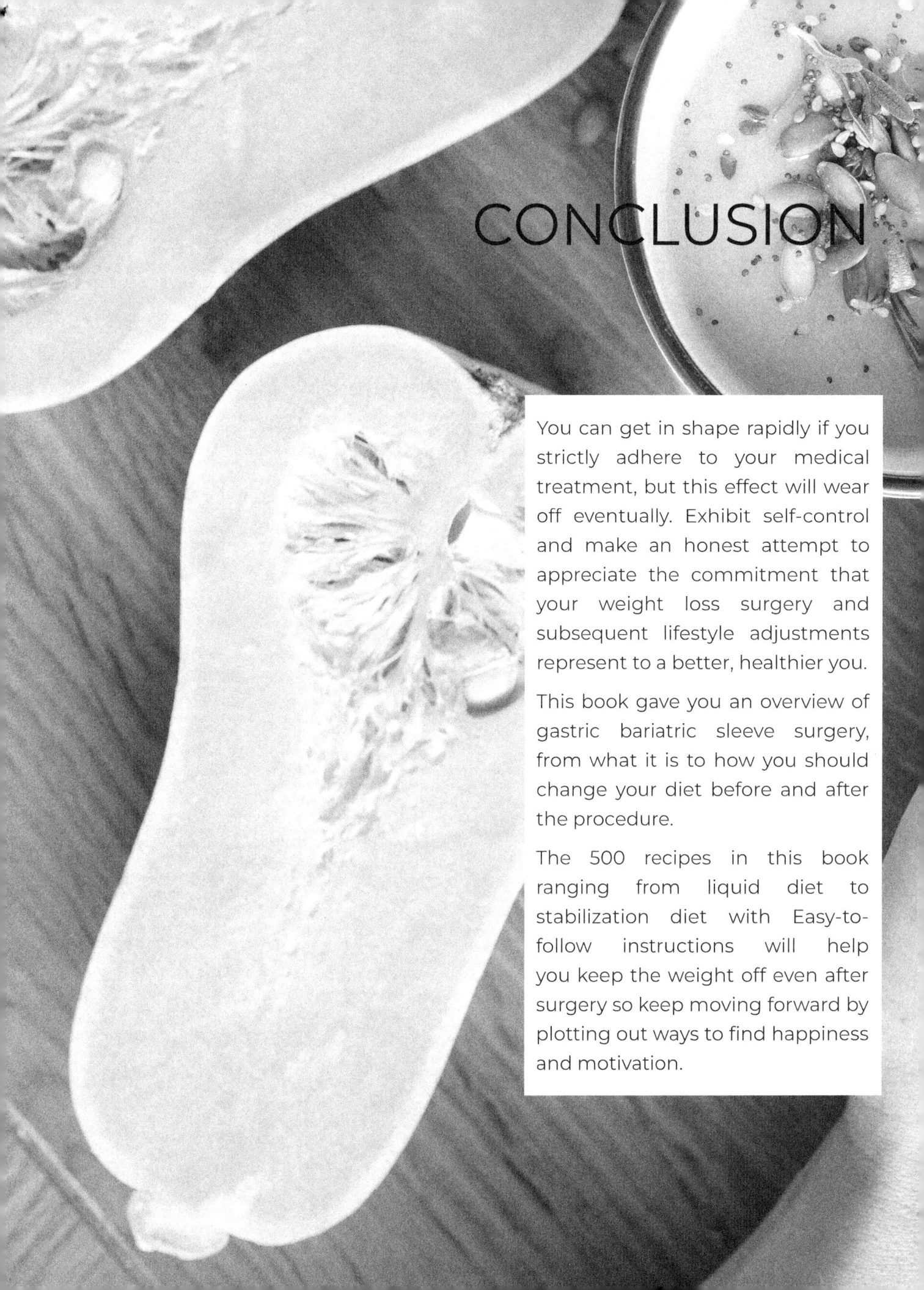

You can get in shape rapidly if you strictly adhere to your medical treatment, but this effect will wear off eventually. Exhibit self-control and make an honest attempt to appreciate the commitment that your weight loss surgery and subsequent lifestyle adjustments represent to a better, healthier you.

This book gave you an overview of gastric bariatric sleeve surgery, from what it is to how you should change your diet before and after the procedure.

The 500 recipes in this book ranging from liquid diet to stabilization diet with Easy-to-follow instructions will help you keep the weight off even after surgery so keep moving forward by plotting out ways to find happiness and motivation.

# WEIGHT LOSS JOURNAL

# SETTING MY GOAL

## GOAL #1

....................................................................................................................................

....................................................................................................................................

## GOAL #2

....................................................................................................................................

....................................................................................................................................

## GOAL #3

....................................................................................................................................

....................................................................................................................................

# WEIGHT TIMELINE

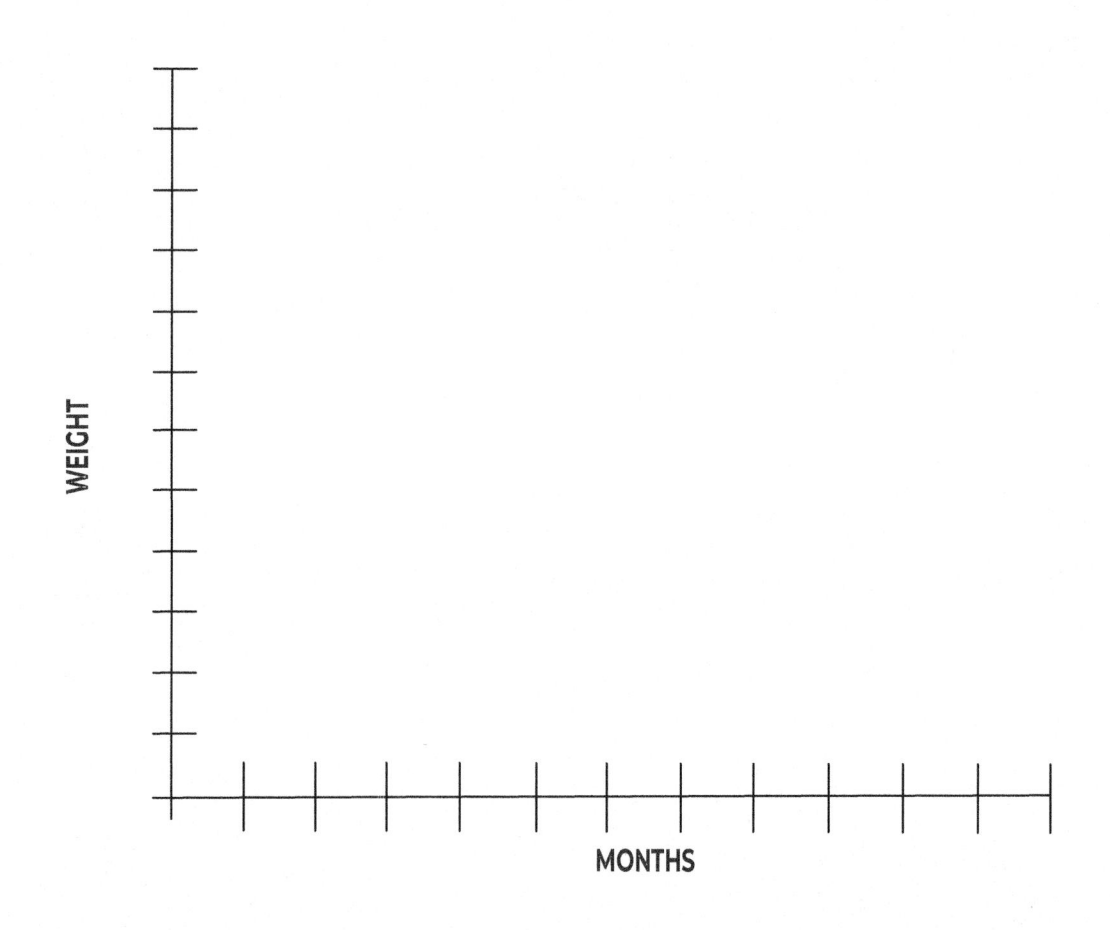

WEIGHT

MONTHS

**MILESTONES**

............................................

............................................

............................................

............................................

**REWARDS**

............................................

............................................

............................................

............................................

# MONTH N. 1

Date: ..................

> Glue in a foto of yourself, not the perfect one!
> So you can look back at it at the end of your journey to be amazed!

| MEASUREMENTS | |
|---|---|
| CHEST | |
| WAIST | |
| HIPS | |
| THIGH | |
| CALF | |
| WEIGHT | |

**Good Habits to Build**
..................................................
..................................................
..................................................
..................................................

**Good Habits to Cut**
..................................................
..................................................
..................................................
..................................................

**How I'm Feeling**
..................................................
..................................................
..................................................
..................................................

**Reasons to Keep Going**
..................................................
..................................................
..................................................
..................................................

# MONTH N. 2

Date: ..................

*Glue in a foto of yourself, not the perfect one! So you can look back at it at the end of your journey to be amazed!*

| MEASUREMENTS | |
|---|---|
| CHEST | |
| WAIST | |
| HIPS | |
| THIGH | |
| CALF | |
| WEIGHT | |

**Good Habits to Build**

..................................................
..................................................
..................................................
..................................................

**Good Habits to Cut**

..................................................
..................................................
..................................................
..................................................

**How I'm Feeling**

..................................................
..................................................
..................................................
..................................................

**Reasons to Keep Going**

..................................................
..................................................
..................................................
..................................................

# MONTH N. 3

Date: ..................

> Glue in a foto of yourself, not the perfect one!
> So you can look back at it at the end of your journey to be amazed!

| MEASUREMENTS | |
|---|---|
| CHEST | |
| WAIST | |
| HIPS | |
| THIGH | |
| CALF | |
| WEIGHT | |

**Good Habits to Build**
..................................................
..................................................
..................................................
..................................................

**Good Habits to Cut**
..................................................
..................................................
..................................................
..................................................

**How I'm Feeling**
..................................................
..................................................
..................................................
..................................................

**Reasons to Keep Going**
..................................................
..................................................
..................................................
..................................................

# MONTH N. 4

Date: ..................

*Glue in a foto of yourself, not the perfect one! So you can look back at it at the end of your journey to be amazed!*

| MEASUREMENTS | |
|---|---|
| CHEST | |
| WAIST | |
| HIPS | |
| THIGH | |
| CALF | |
| WEIGHT | |

**Good Habits to Build**
..................................................
..................................................
..................................................
..................................................

**Good Habits to Cut**
..................................................
..................................................
..................................................
..................................................

**How I'm Feeling**
..................................................
..................................................
..................................................
..................................................

**Reasons to Keep Going**
..................................................
..................................................
..................................................
..................................................

# MONTH N. 5

Date: ..................

> Glue in a foto of yourself, not the perfect one!
> So you can look back at it at the end of your journey to be amazed!

| MEASUREMENTS | |
|---|---|
| CHEST | |
| WAIST | |
| HIPS | |
| THIGH | |
| CALF | |
| WEIGHT | |

**Good Habits to Build**

..................................................
..................................................
..................................................
..................................................

**Good Habits to Cut**

..................................................
..................................................
..................................................
..................................................

**How I'm Feeling**

..................................................
..................................................
..................................................
..................................................

**Reasons to Keep Going**

..................................................
..................................................
..................................................
..................................................

# MONTH N. 6

Date: ..................

*Glue in a foto of yourself, not the perfect one!
So you can look back at it at the end of your journey to be amazed!*

| MEASUREMENTS | |
|---|---|
| CHEST | |
| WAIST | |
| HIPS | |
| THIGH | |
| CALF | |
| WEIGHT | |

**Good Habits to Build**
..................................................
..................................................
..................................................
..................................................

**Good Habits to Cut**
..................................................
..................................................
..................................................
..................................................

**How I'm Feeling**
..................................................
..................................................
..................................................
..................................................

**Reasons to Keep Going**
..................................................
..................................................
..................................................
..................................................

# MONTH N. 7

Date: ....................

> Glue in a foto of yourself, not the perfect one!
> So you can look back at it at the end of your journey to be amazed!

| MEASUREMENTS | |
|---|---|
| CHEST | |
| WAIST | |
| HIPS | |
| THIGH | |
| CALF | |
| WEIGHT | |

**Good Habits to Build**
....................................................................
....................................................................
....................................................................
....................................................................

**Good Habits to Cut**
....................................................................
....................................................................
....................................................................
....................................................................

**How I'm Feeling**
....................................................................
....................................................................
....................................................................
....................................................................

**Reasons to Keep Going**
....................................................................
....................................................................
....................................................................
....................................................................

# MONTH N. 8

Date: ..................

*Glue in a foto of yourself, not the perfect one! So you can look back at it at the end of your journey to be amazed!*

| MEASUREMENTS | |
|---|---|
| CHEST | |
| WAIST | |
| HIPS | |
| THIGH | |
| CALF | |
| WEIGHT | |

**Good Habits to Build**
..................................................
..................................................
..................................................
..................................................

**Good Habits to Cut**
..................................................
..................................................
..................................................
..................................................

**How I'm Feeling**
..................................................
..................................................
..................................................
..................................................

**Reasons to Keep Going**
..................................................
..................................................
..................................................
..................................................

# MONTH N. 9

Date: ..................

*Glue in a foto of yourself, not the perfect one! So you can look back at it at the end of your journey to be amazed!*

| MEASUREMENTS | |
|---|---|
| CHEST | |
| WAIST | |
| HIPS | |
| THIGH | |
| CALF | |
| WEIGHT | |

**Good Habits to Build**

..................................................
..................................................
..................................................
..................................................

**Good Habits to Cut**

..................................................
..................................................
..................................................
..................................................

**How I'm Feeling**

..................................................
..................................................
..................................................
..................................................

**Reasons to Keep Going**

..................................................
..................................................
..................................................
..................................................

# MONTH N. 10

Date: ..................

*Glue in a foto of yourself, not the perfect one! So you can look back at it at the end of your journey to be amazed!*

| MEASUREMENTS | |
|---|---|
| CHEST | |
| WAIST | |
| HIPS | |
| THIGH | |
| CALF | |
| WEIGHT | |

**Good Habits to Build**

..............................................................
..............................................................
..............................................................
..............................................................

**Good Habits to Cut**

..............................................................
..............................................................
..............................................................
..............................................................

**How I'm Feeling**

..............................................................
..............................................................
..............................................................
..............................................................

**Reasons to Keep Going**

..............................................................
..............................................................
..............................................................
..............................................................

# MONTH N. 11

Date: ..................

*Glue in a foto of yourself, not the perfect one! So you can look back at it at the end of your journey to be amazed!*

| MEASUREMENTS ||
|---|---|
| CHEST | |
| WAIST | |
| HIPS | |
| THIGH | |
| CALF | |
| WEIGHT | |

**Good Habits to Build**

..............................................
..............................................
..............................................
..............................................

**Good Habits to Cut**

..............................................
..............................................
..............................................
..............................................

**How I'm Feeling**

..............................................
..............................................
..............................................
..............................................

**Reasons to Keep Going**

..............................................
..............................................
..............................................
..............................................

# MONTH N. 12

Date: ..................

*Glue in a foto of yourself, not the perfect one! So you can look back at it at the end of your journey to be amazed!*

| MEASUREMENTS | |
|---|---|
| CHEST | |
| WAIST | |
| HIPS | |
| THIGH | |
| CALF | |
| WEIGHT | |

**Good Habits to Build**

..................................................
..................................................
..................................................
..................................................

**Good Habits to Cut**

..................................................
..................................................
..................................................
..................................................

**How I'm Feeling**

..................................................
..................................................
..................................................
..................................................

**Reasons to Keep Going**

..................................................
..................................................
..................................................
..................................................

# GET YOUR BONUS

# HERE!!

Printed in Dunstable, United Kingdom